COND... OF

ILLUSION

*The call to abandon their illusions about their conditions
is a call to abandon a condition which requires illusions.*

Karl Marx

£1.85

childrens rights

73 BALFOUR STREET
LONDON, S.E. 17
01-703 7217

workshop

CONDITIONS OF ILLUSION:

Papers from the Women's Movement

Edited by Sandra Allen, Lee Sanders and Jan Wallis

Published by   Feminist Books Ltd.
P.O. Box HP5
Leeds LS6 1LN
England

Jacket drawing by Liz Mackie

ISBN   0 904426 02 5   hardback

ISBN   0 904426 03 3   paper

Made and printed in England by Simba Print Leeds.

The articles in this book have all been written since the publication in 1972 of *The Body Politic*, the first collection of writings from the women's movement. While we have tried to include articles on many of the important issues affecting women's lives, we make no claim that this book represents all the viewpoints held by the different groups that make up the women's movement and the debate going on within it. We hope that the Documents and Guide to groups give some idea of the breadth and variety of activities and struggles which have developed out of women's changing consciousness.

Feminist Books

We are a collective of four women, three of whom have worked for over two years on the compilation of this book. This is our second publication, the first being *Wedlocked Women* by Lee Comer (September 1974). We act not only as a publishing house but also as a distribution centre for feminist literature.

About this book

Women working in and with the Feminist Books Collective did the editing, typesetting, lay-out and design of *Conditions of Illusion* and are distributing it. We regret that the high price of paper has made this book more expensive than we would have liked. Any profits will go directly to the financing of further publications from the women's movement.

**Sandra Allen, Lee Sanders and Jan Wallis
Leeds, December 1974**

CONTENTS

BODY POLITICS

SEXUALITY & IDEOLOGY

THE PATTER OF TINY CONTRADICTIONS

And the struggle goes on

DOCUMENTS

GUIDE TO GROUPS

Body Politics

Crisis in Childbirth

The whole process of childbirth today has been taken away from the women who actually bear the children into the clinical world of male obstetricians, and it is getting progressively harder for a normal healthy woman to experience normal healthy childbirth (though potentially 97% of us could). The medical profession takes over and dominates our bodies and feelings for nine months plus; controlling and putting us down while we're in their hospitals; while at home, the magazines we may read eulogise the beauty and dignity of our impending motherhood. In the same magazines, we also read emotive articles extolling every woman's right to sensationless childbirth, with scarcely ever a reference to any accompanying dangers or discomforts.

Within our smaller personal world, once pregnant, there can also be another subtler kind of pressure - to give birth 'naturally', to be a success without drugs, to be the only one on the ward without stitches.

The midwife suggested that I have a shot of pethedine...
I felt defeated and confused. I remembered C., my pregn-
ancy teacher, saying that pethedine was bad and that she
hadn't used it. I remembered other women saying how
confused they felt with pethedine - I felt a failure, I
shouldn't 'need' it.

I hope to outline here the major areas of pregnancy and birth that seem to cause us most anxiety. They cause anxiety to some doctors as well as to many women but the medical profession is so absolute and all powerful that radical change seems remote at present. But it helps if you at least know what you're up against and what alternatives there are.

In a typical pregnancy, a booking for home or hospital confinement must be made at about three months. Unfortunately, this has become much less of a choice in recent years. In Holland, 50% of all births take place at home and they have the lowest infant mortality rate in the world. America, where there are no domiciliary confinements at all and a very high level of obstetric interference, comes fourteenth down the list! The BMA has a declared policy of working towards 100% hospital births (*Peel Report 1970*) though there is no evidence that the increased number of hospital births is responsible for the reduction in infant mortality. In fact, the Committee, which saw one as the logical outcome of the other and decided that from then on all women should be confined in hospitals, actually based their recommendations on a statistical fallacy. (*Effectiveness and Efficiency: Random Reflections on Health Services. Prof. A. L. Cochrane.*

The Association for Improvements in the Maternity Services (AIMS), in a survey of over 2,000 women who had experienced both home and hospital delivery, found that 84% preferred their home confinement. As far as I can tell, the BMA has not done any consumer research on this subject. However, if you're under thirty, preferably under twenty five, healthy and with adequate home surroundings, there should be no valid reasons for being hospitilised if you don't want to be, though if your GP only believes in hospitals you may have difficulty. For instance, a friend of mine, really anxious to be at home for her second birth, was told by her GP that she couldn't, as she'd run a high temperature after her first delivery. When she was eight months pregnant and still anxious, though resigned, he told her casually that the temperature wouldn't have made the slightest difference, it was just that he 'didn't believe in home confinements'. By then, of course, it was too late for her to change her booking. Most women, though, do want the extra clinical security of hospital for a first birth at least; but only for the birth and not for too long afterwards. A woman (who later changed to a home confinement) relates this conversation with a male doctor on her first hospital visit.

He: How long do you want to stay for?
She: 48 hours at the most.

He: *Well, I'll book you in for ten days.*
She: But you just asked me and I said 48 hours.
He: *Well, no, I think we'll make it ten days like we
   always do.*
She: But......

You may feel that you'll just discharge yourself anyway
if you feel fine, but a hospital would be most reluctant
to let you go as there would be no midwife booked to
attend you at home unless you were officially due to come
home after 48 hours or five days or whatever.

To continue with pregnancy.....at about four months you
start regularly attending hospital or clinic for checks on
blood pressure, urine, the baby's position etc. and this can
be quite a humiliating and anxiety-making process. There
is a mass appointment system, mass queuing, sometimes
in twice-used gowns, no creche provisions (in fact, often
signs warning you not to bring children) and, finally, no
chance to ask your carefully saved up questions, as the
doctor talks over your belly to his students for the two
minutes you actually spend up on the couch. One woman
said, 'For five months, all they ever said to me was 'spend
a penny along here, trot down the passage there, pop
your clothes in here, hop up on there, jump down from
here and run along home now

Of course, our National Health Service has created for
itself terrible space and staffing difficulties, but pregnant
women are not the cattle they are so often likened to;
in fact, they are particularly vulnerable and prone to fears
and anxieties. In few hospital clinics would it be possible
for a man to actually get through to the doctor either
out of interest or because he had his own questions to
ask, nor do I know of any hospital relaxation classes that
men can join. The National Childbirth Trust does run
classes that are either specifically for couples, or which include fathers for some sessions, but of course, they are
outside the state system. I've also found domiciliary clinics,
never hospitals, where children could climb up on the
couch, listen through the foetal stethoscope etc. Creche
facilities seem an urgent requirement if, in future, women

are going to be hospitalised for second or subsequent births.

However, almost all hospitals will now allow husbands to be present at the birth of their child. Husbands, yes, fathers not automatically and anyone else, like a woman friend you might particularly want, not likely. A husband must sign a consent form to say that he'll do as asked when the time comes and he will not be encouraged to stay if you are admitted to hospital while still in the early stage of labour. Instead, he'll get a 'go home to bed, there's nothing you can do, ring in nearer the time' type of brushoff. This is sad as, probably, the idea that you both had was that those long dragging hours were just the time when you could give each other comfort and support. Women do need company tremendously and should never ever be left alone in labour. It goes without saying that the person with them should be a companion of their choice! Dependence on the companion becomes very great and should not be denied by staff.

Sister asked John if he'd leave as another patient had to be admitted. John said he'd prefer to stay but Sister then said he looked white and must go. Without John, I just became a load of old rubbish and didn't manage my breathing at all, resorted to gas and air, and went quite dopey.

Your companion will have to leave if you need a Caesarian, which is fair enough as it is usually an emergency operation, but also if you need a forceps delivery. These are becoming so routine that it might be time to ask whether fathers shouldn't be permitted to stay, but more about forceps delivery later.

At nine months, or thereabouts, you reach the end of pregnancy and the baby is due. Unwarranted medical interference with the natural course of labour, or 'active management' as doctors prefer to call it, may start here and this is a very delicate area. It's extremely hard for women/parents to know whether something is medically urgent or necessary, or whether the doctor is merely following his own beliefs on intervention. In a truly clinical situation, most of us would probably not think of contradicting or flatly disagreeing (well, we might think of it but we wouldn't do it!) but childbirth is not, or at least has not been until recently, a truly clinical situation, but a natural normal, everyday function for which most women's bodies are already pretty well equipped.

In recent years, there has been a dramatic and worrying increase in the trend towards 'nine to five obstetrics' or 'daylight deliveries'. This process involves starting labour artificially (or hastening weak contractions) by stimulating the uterus with drip fed Syntocinon. A drip set up (attached to the arm) at nine in the morning will almost invariably produce a baby by late afternoon. The drip remains in position for the whole time and regulates conractions throughout labour. The woman must remain in bed the whole time. Most hospitals emphatically maintain that artificial induction is used only if medically necessary, i.e. high blood pressure, baby very overdue; but I know of at least one hospital (in Essex) where even women who manage to arrive in spontaneous labour are immediately put on the drip to ensure the babies are born before the day staff go off duty. Also, a distinguished obstetrician is quoted as saying 'for years we've been harrassed by women saying - please I'm fed up with this pregnancy - and we've resisted. Now we don't, we induce up to 50% of women, mainly at their own request ...I think the concept of a system that controls labour is fair and will be perfected'.

The medical argument for induction is that two of the greatest hazards in labour are its timing and its length and both of these can be manipulated, with near total safety in an induced birth. But against this, a *British Medical Journal* article (October 1973) showed that babies of induced mothers suffered significantly more from jaundice than those of spontaneously delivered mothers (as did also the infants of women given epidurals). Surely there must be some point to the natural timing of labour - for most of us at least? To many women, I'm sure, controlled labour seems a good idea, but if there is no choice, merely a 'come in at 9 a.m. on Monday if you haven't started' then it just seems another way of narrowing choice.

Many women feel a sense of loss and failure at not starting their own labours and, also, with Syntocinon, there tends to be no gradual build-up in the strength of contractions, so that they can be understood and come to terms with. Labour starts as it continues - at full speed and top strength. I think that a consent form of some kind is needed now, on which a woman indicates whether she is willing to have her labour induced for other than obvious reasons such as high blood pressure.

Women should be fully informed about all aspects of modern labour as a matter of course, fairly early on in pregnancy, and this should include the disadvantages, as well as the advantages of analgesia in labour. The media place great emphasis on every woman's right to an epidural. drugs etc. but they seldom mention the drawbacks, nor do they seem to give an equal amount of publicity to psychoprophylaxsic techniques or other ways of 'natural' child bearing. (It's unlikely that your GP or clinic will have given you information on these available alternatives either.)

Regional anaesthesia, like an epidural (an injection into the base of the spine that makes the lower part of the body numb), is offered more and more frequently to women nowadays, though it is still far from routine, mainly because it requires the attendance of an anaesthetist throughout. It always sounds marvellous - the woman sits up in bed reading etc., feeling nothing at all, while her uterus is actually contracting in full labour. However, the infant can suffer from the effects of this inhibited labour, as the mother has a greatly restricted pushing urge; this means that the baby will almost certainly have to be delivered by forceps, the woman will need an episiotomy, and the baby will probably be cot nursed for up to 48 hours, while it recovers from its birth shock. (Cot nursing means that it will not be fed, handled, sometimes even not seen by its parents.)

The administering of drugs like Pethedine or Pethilorfan,

13

and inhalation analgesia (gas and oxygen), is seen by most medical staff as routine and a part of even the most normal labour and drugs are sometimes literally forced on women who do not want or need them. (Pethedine is not actually a completely convincing pain killer, a research project showed that 50% - 60% of mothers found their pain relieved, but 30% given a placebo found their pain relieved too!) Drug refusal, no matter how tactfully done, seems to provoke an unpleasant reaction from the attendants - they seem to take a rejection of their goodies as a personal insult! Of course, they also think you're going to be more troublesome and noisy.

A nurse told her she was stupid not to have taken Pethedine - that was not particularly helpful, nor was it helpful when Sister wandered into our room and told her not to make such a noise and deliberately left the door open wide so that everyone could hear ....

Probably the majority of women do want some relief in labour; all of us have our levels of pain tolerance and thank God the days of Victorian melodrama are gone - women screaming for days on end, clinging on to knotted sheets, but even so, there must be an informed choice and then the woman must have the positive right to accept or refuse. (An aspect I haven't room to cover here is why, sadly, most women are afraid of their bodies and its sensations and are most willing to be very heavily drugged and passively managed during birth; our cultural attitudes towards childbirth differ sharply in practise from the romanicised life-giving female stereotype - perhaps, though, the old male custom of 'churching' women after they've given birth has technically died out, many of the ideas of shame, guilt and deserved pain remain.)

Drugs administered against the will of the patient would seem to be a gross violation of liberty, but the woman, once trapped on the delivery table, is not the best able to protest!

...next thing was Night Sister saying I had to have sleep and giving me an injection straight off before I even opened my mouth. I felt most disappointed as I in no way

*needed it. I really only wanted company and to know how
I was doing....About 6 a.m. Night Sister came back and
was most aggravated by me, as she said I had not been
resting but fighting the drugs (quite right, I had!) She had
another injection which I asked not to be given and said
I wanted to sit up. I was told to lie down and rest - she
was extremely angry with me and said to stop this breathing and rest. She gave me the injection saying have what
you can on the NHS. I am afraid I was rather upset and
just wanted her to go away and leave me alone. I felt
totally helpless and frustrated.....*

Research shows now that Pethedine, Pethilorfan and, particularly, epidurals all inhibit the baby's sucking ability.
This inhibition may last up to two months. Obviously, a
sleepy baby not feeding well has an effect, which may be
considerable, on the parent/child interaction. Visual response
and also muscular co-ordination can be affected, as is the
rate at which the baby becomes accustomed to loud noises, bright lights etc. A current study at Cambridge seems
to show that differences in infant handling and interaction
were still apparent, after one year, between women who'd
received heavy doses of Pethilorfan and those who hadn't.
It seems unlikely that any drug will be found, in the near
future at least, which while sedating the woman, isn't
going to affect the highly vulnerable nervous system of.
the newborn. Pethedine should certainly not be taken too
near the end of the first stage , otherwise you'll be dopey
just when you want to be wide-awake and alert to push
out the baby. 'It is more difficult to control the impulse
towards flight and to create conscious and positive entering
into labour if Pethedine is given' *(Sheila Kitzinger).* It's
even more important not to continue with gas and oxygen into the second stage, especially if it's your first time
and you don't know how it will affect you, otherwise
this might happen.

*I took a few lungfuls of gas. My body became a mass of
tingling sensations - everything got blurred and the contra-
ction passed with me totally out of control and unaware
of what was happening.*

Or - even worse -

When a nurse said to me 'I'll show you how to use the gas', I made the worst mistake possible and breathed hard into the machine so that I completely went out. I had hallucinations and was conscious of screaming and screaming.

At the end of the second stage, as the baby's head is about to crown, a cut is made, almost routinely, in most hospitals, in the woman's perineum.

I asked if I could give birth naturally, but was told that the hospital's policy was to make an incision and there could be no variation from this for an individual woman's whims.

This routine cut may well not be necessary. It is done for speed (theirs, not yours), and convenience (theirs, not yours), and once again, the patient is not consulted - although it's your body that is being hacked about. This episiotomy has to be stitched - sometimes not for an hour or more after delivery, and the stitching is often done by a handy student learning to suture, not necessarily an obstetric student. One midwife I know insists that, on the rare occasions when she has found an episiotomy necessary, it be stitched only by an obstetric student. This process - accepted and taken absolutely for granted by many women nowadays - can be the most painful part of the entire labour and the effects of the cut felt by the woman for many months. A survey on this subject by the National Childbirth Trust found that one third of their sample complained of pain at the time of stitching, one third had been sutured without local anaesthetic and 15% of those who'd had an anaesthetic said the doctor didn't wait until it took effect. A typical comment was 'The stitching was far worse than the whole of labour'. There is,still, despite a very good booklet by Sheila Kitzinger and the National Childbirth Trust, very little understanding of or interest in, on the part of male doctors, the importance and sensitivity of the vagina and perineum to women; not only in their immediate comfort after birth, but in their sexual lives which may be badly affected for some time, mainly because of physical discomfort, but also because of the psychological feelings about the damaged vagina, which they'd obviously feel unable to talk to their doctor about. Midwives, who would, on the whole, be much more sympathetic, are not allowed to do suturing. In domiciliary confinements, episiotomy is very rare. In a gentle, tranquil atmosphere, a midwife, with only one patient to attend to, and a relaxed woman can work together to bring out the baby's head naturally and slowly. Peace and an unhurried atmosphere are rarely present in hospital, which I think is a major reason for forceps deliveries becoming so much more common. In some hospitals, particularly in the London area, they account for as many as 60% of all births. Forceps (like sugar tongs clamped either side of the baby's head) should be used when the mother is very tired or not making progress or if the baby is becoming tired.But forceps often seemed to be used as just another routine way of hurrying things along. Perhaps the woman is so overwrought, either through lack of sympathetic help, or through being moved from place to place as if she's part of a conveyer belt system, that she can no longer find energy and resources sufficient to push her baby out unaided. Needless to say, forceps are very seldom needed when a baby is born at home. It's interesting to note that here in Yorkshire, at least one modern maternity unit isn't equipped for even the routine of a forceps delivery, and a friend of mine, needing one, had a half hour ambulance ride in the middle of the night to the nearest 'proper' hospital. She had most particularly wanted a home confinement and had been refused but I cannot see at all the advantage that a maternity unit, as opposed to a hospital, has over your own bedroom. In fact, the irony of that situation was that undoubtedly in her own home, she'd not have needed a forceps delivery anyway!

It would really take another article to continue with the problems encountered after birth, breastfeeding, hospital procedures that seem to ignore the desire of most parents to establish a relationship with their child right from its birth. There are still hospitals where fathers cannot handle their child at all and mothers only at feeding time. All I can suggest, as a way of combating any process that you don't want to be involved in, is just to get yourself really well informed and certain of your wishes and rights. This only works for those of us with massive self confidence, access to the right kind of books etc. But maybe there will be some changes. I've just read an article while I've been finishing this, in *The Practitioner* (June 1974), which puts out a feeler in the right direction. The article is a survey of women forced into home confinements by the ancillary workers strike in 1973. The authors found that 80% of the mothers would want their next child to be born at home. They 'are led to suggest that 100% hospital delivery may not be in the best interests of some mothers'; also, that '..more research into client preferences of maternity services is needed and the social and psychological rewards to the mother of childbirth should be weighed more critically with medical criteria'. They also noted, 'It is often pointed out by supporters of women's rights that gynaecologists are overwhelmingly male and that male values tend to be the dominant ones projected'. Which made it seem to me a thoughtful and hopeful article, and it has certainly provided a more hopeful (well, slightly more hopeful) conclusion, than the one I had previously written!

Christine Beels
1974

Amended version of a paper first given at the Sexual Politics Conference, held in Leeds in March 1974.

Why I laughed when Anna was born

When Anna was born, when her blue head pushed out, face downwards between my thighs, before she even turned her head round towards my left thigh ready to push her shoulders out, she opened her mouth and cried, her head turned from blue to red and I laughed - I laughed the same laugh that I have since sometimes laughed after orgasm. It is not a pretty laugh, it frightens Anna ('Don't make love. Please don't make that noise. I can't stand it) and also my lover. It is a laugh of power, the strength of life flowing throughout my body. The words I want to use to describe this laugh look ridiculous written down and explain nothing. Which was why I thought I would write the story of Anna's birth; only now I find that I have to start even further back and talk about the birth of my first baby, a breach baby who died a few hours after birth. I cry now when I think of that birth, ten years ago, so why it must be told to explain a laugh eighteen months later I do not really know.

But though it is a sad story, it is not at all like all the accounts of pain and screaming that I'd read in so many stories and, perhaps, this is because I never identified with those stories, never felt that they had anything to do with the way I would have a baby, even when I was fifteen and knew nothing about the stages and processes of labour.

Five years later when I was twenty and seven months pregant, I still knew hardly anything about the process of labour and learnt nothing from the hospital. At seven months I started going to relaxation classes a la Dick Read with a lady who lived nearby, but as the baby was born when I was eight months and one week pregnant I never finish-

19

ed those classes.

I started labour the night after I'd been to the ante-natal clinic and been shown an X-ray picture that showed conclusively that the baby's feet were stuck up near its head and that there was no possibility of it turning round now - it would be born bottom first.

It was between one and two o'clock in the morning when Andrew and I arrived at the hospital. I had very slight contractions but they were every minute - that was the way they started; I'd been told to call the ambulance when contractions were about every two minutes. I was admitted into the hospital; a nurse put her hand on my stomach and said I was in false labour but it was too late to send me home now; I might as well stay the night and go home in the morning. They sent Andrew home. I had been going to insist he stay with me right the way through the birth but if I were not going to give birth that night and was going home tomorrow undelievered, what was the good of his hanging about all night?

I was given a bath and my pubic hair shaved (why if I was going home in the morning?) but they didn't bother with the enema, thank God. Then I was put on a hard, narrow bed in the delivery room as they were full up everywhere else; I was given two sleeping pills and told to go to sleep. But I couldn't sleep because, although I was not in any pain, I felt uncomfortable, partly because of the strange surroundings and the hard bed, but also because I had the same sensations I sometimes get at the beginning of a period.

Some hours later another woman was brought into the delivery room and gave birth to a daughter after what seemed hours of screaming. By this time I was feeling very uncomfortable and had hardly slept at all. I kept tossing and turning on the hard bed - if it had been a period and I had been at home, by this time I would have been walking up and down the room as it's the only thing that makes me feel better, but there is hospital I didn't dare.

Soon, another nurse came and examined me and gave me an injection of (I think) Pethedine. She said it was to help me to sleep. I was not told at any time that I was now in true labour and the baby would be born that night, but somehow, very hazily because I was sleepy and bewildered, I knew. Anyway, the injection certainly sent me to sleep - I must have slept for about two hours and when I awoke (about seven or eight in the morning), I was still in a drugged condition. I felt very pleasant, I was almost floating; gone was the discomfort of earlier and in its place was a great rolling and heaving motion that seemed to me like a wave rolling into shore, rising high, holding itself, then breaking on the beach, its water rolling backwards into the sea to be overtaken by another breaker poised above it. The whole sensation was effortless, I was almost like a spectator, relaxed and drowsy. It was only after about three of these heaves that I realised something that woke me up instantly - the baby was being born, its bottom was pushing itself out, it was so soft that it was meeting with no resistance. I called for attention (in my panic I forgot about the bedside bell) and soon I was surrounded by people. I was no longer in charge of my labour, there were no longer any pleasant sensations; I was dragged down the bed and my legs were draped over something hard; I could see surgical instruments, they were obviously going to cut me. My reaction was irrational, obviously in these circumstances an episiotomy was necessary but I'd been so determined that I wasn't going to be cut that I began to object. Gas and air was pushed onto my face; whether they thought I was in pain and needed anaesthetics or whether they thought it was the easiest way to keep me quiet I don't know; but I felt I was suffocating, I tried to push the mask away but it was held firmly and by the time I was free it was all over. I had a glimpse of a blue, blood-stained baby and then there was silence. No, it was worse than silence; all the people who had been so insistently with me an instant before had all withdrawn to the other side of the room; I was left entirely alone, I've never been so alone in my life, alone and empty, still strapped up on the bed and I could hear them whispering over on the other side of the room. The baby made not a sound.

Then a young doctor appeared beside me; he said he was sorry, the baby was poorly - it was a boy, what name had I chosen? The question astonished me, I said I hadn't thought of a name yet; he was gently insistent, please choose one. I said I didn't think it was very important at the moment, I was more concerned about what was wrong with the baby and would he live? He didn't answer either of my questions but said the baby had to have a name so he could be christened as he was so poorly. I was very angry, I don't know how I had the strength but I was. I. told him not to christen the baby but tell me what was wrong. He was very vague, they didn't know, he wasn't breathing properly, he'd need an oxygen tent and he might not live. Then he disappeared.

In all the ten days I was in hospital I never got a satisfactory answer to my questions. After the baby died (about midnight that night) one nurse I asked said there had been something wrong with his lungs, but all the doctors I asked were very evasive. I only found out the true cause of death when I read the death certificate they gave me as I left the hospital - the baby died of brain haemorrhage and his death was obviously caused by his birth.

I have to pause there - I can't go straight into the story of Anna's birth. I had to pause in life too. But when I knew I was pregnant again there was one thing I was adamant about from the beginning. I wasn't going into hospital this time, the baby was going to be born at home and I should know what was happening at each stage and remain in control of the process (to this end I went to natural childbirth classes). And there was one thing I was afraid about - it was a tremendous relief when the baby turned in the womb (turned is the wrong word - she did acrobatics - I had two knots in the cord to prove it) and the head engaged.

Also I had one misconception. I thought that as the first baby was born three weeks early that this one would be too. The result was that about a week before it was due, I was expecting to go into labour at any minute and sat at home and waited, yes, just literally waited for about a week or so; and then I got bored and went out every night, at first almost fearfully, expecting to give birth in the middle of the theatre or pub, but later with the conviction that I was not after all going to have a baby after all, I was going to be hugely and monstrously pregnant for the rest of my life.

But after all, when I was about eight or nine days overdue, I woke up in the middle of the night, felt small regular contractions and thought with relief, 'Well, that's started' and went back to sleep again.

But I don't want to give the impression that this was a perfect birth and everything was beautiful from the beginning. For it certainly didn't seem like that when I woke up again. It was about nine o'clock in the morning and I couldn't feel any contractions at all but I could feel a frightening pain right across the tops of my thighs and my cunt. I lay rigid and woke Andrew up.

There's something terribly wrong with me. I've got this awful pain and I don't know what it is.
He got me to show him where the pain was and asked how much it hurt.

Well, sometimes it's worse than others - it comes and goes.
He asked me to tell him when it started, when it stopped, when it started again. It was regular, lasting about a minute every two minutes. He was going to phone the midwife. I begged him not to, I said I wasn't in labour, there were no contractions, she would think I was so silly if I called her for nothing, she would be angry. But he went all the same.

All this time I'd been lying rigid, denying with all my body that I was in labour. As soon as Andrew left, I relaxed, I suddenly knew I was in labour after all, the pains slackened. When the midwife's nurse came about half an hour later, she confirmed that labour had started, she could feel small contractions but there was no urgency.

She gave Andrew instructions on what to get ready and said she would ask the midwife to come round later in the day. She was ready to leave when she suddenly changed her mind and decided to give me an internal examination. I was nearly fully dilated.

She went to call the midwife immediately while Andrew got things ready. When the midwife came, Andrew made a pot of coffee and they all three sat on the bed and we drank coffee and chatted. The midwife said I was nearly dilated but not to push just yet. I didn't actually feel any urge to push but found the breathing pattern I'd been taught to distract the mind from the desire to push actually helped to distract my mind off the slight pain I still felt and anyway the deep breathing patterns normally used during the first stage of labour didn't make sense as I still couldn't feel any contractions.

Then the midwife said it would be alright for me to push now. I felt no urge at all to push and it felt like a terrible anti-climax, almost a failure but she just said to wait until I did feel like it. So we sat and waited and to me it seemed an eternity though it was probably only a few minutes. And then I felt a push coming but I was so eager I completely mismanaged it and it had little effect. But no-one said anything and the next push I felt was overwhelming. There was no question of me wasting this one. My whole body seemed concentrated in one big movement and I felt so powerful and then afterwards I felt so peaceful. Now a pattern established itself. While I was pushing I couldn't imagine I'd ever be doing anything else, everything, the whole world was concerned with this great effort, but also I felt so strong, a superwoman with superhuman strength. And afterwards, in between the pushes, I couldn't imagine any other state but complete languour, I felt completely incapable of expending any energy but when the time came to push again I would be ready and rested. While I was pushing my face must have gone red with effort and as I relaxed afterwards, my breath came out with a sigh and moan not of pain but of effort; my muscles shook with fatigue and then as the delicious languour crept up I actually slept for a few seconds before I awoke to concentrate the rising power and strength.

Weaving through these alternating states of consciousness, I was aware of Andrew and the midwife and the nurse continuing their conversation. I heard it in snatches and it was at the same time very close and interesting yet taking place in a different world. They were talking about the appalling pay and conditions of nurses and Andrew was saying they should go on strike.

Then the midwife saw the head coming; I pushed two or three more times and then it was ready to crown. I don't remember now if the midwife told me to push gently, no need for effort because that is what happened anyway quite naturally. My breath was coming shallowly now, instead of pushing it was more like putting the brakes on, the head slowly, slowly pushing out and then the moment of crowning.

I think I stopped breathing, I almost think my heart stopped. Anyway, the world seemed to stop. I felt I was being torn wide open. It was aweful, wonderful but terrible at the same time. That is the one moment in childbirth that I would find it difficult to live through again. I remember it with fear but it lasted no time at all and it was not pain I felt. And I was whole, I didn't tear, there was no damage. It was a perfect crowning and Anna pushed her blue head out and began to cry.

So when I laughed, perhaps it was just a laugh of hysteria and relief after that moment of crowning, but I don't think so. I laughed because I had felt so strong and wonderful pushing out this new life and here it was, still inside me apart from its head, already making its own voice heard. This wasn't a one-woman show but a woman and baby combination. The baby had contributed as much to her birth as I had. It was already an independent individual making its own demands. In some awesome way, I was a bridge, a gateway between living and not-living. And here was this person halfway through the gate, bawling its head off and yet I could still feel the rest of its body inside me, unborn yet.

But all that happened more than eight years ago and I', probably exaggerating, certainly romanticising. Moreover, I'm sure I'm attributing to that occasion emotions I've had in other circumstances - emotions not so easy to state because whereas in childbirth the result is easy to see, the new life is palpably present, the surging strength pushes something concrete into being, in orgasms the power is felt, the striving is there, the joy, the strength of life - but what has been created, what is the result? Perhaps when I laugh in orgasm there is a note of bitterness (is this why Anna hates it so much?) - I will repeat this moment again and again, I will feel the wonder, the communication and closeness with the other person but it is ephemeral. That is why it must be repeated, clutched at again and again.

But Anna's birth is an experience complete, whole in itself. I have no need to repeat it. It had its issue and there is Anna, a lively, noisy, demanding eight year old to show for it. We worked together that morning to push a new life into the world and now it is hers, all hers to shape herself.

Jan Wallis
1974

Punitive Attitudes to Contraception & Abortion

Social acceptance of abortion has been growing during recent years; but precisely because of this, the spectrum of opinion has never been so wide. As more people come to accept the justice and humanity of our appeal for the right to freely available abortions, so at the same time, the groups which object to abortion, on various principles, react by hardening their attitudes and toughening their propaganda campaigns. Only a few years ago 'abortion' was a taboo subject in this country: now most people will have come across at least a superficial outline of some of the different arguments in the debate - campaigning on both sides has become increasingly vigorous, and it's no longer easy for anyone to keep a detached, open-minded attitude. So people polarise; and this ambivalence and conflict in society in general tends to be mirrored in the conflicts in the minds of women needing abortions.

The anti-abortion campaigns rely largely on dramatic - indeed traumatic - emotional appeals rather than on reasone argument. So on a theoretical and objective level they are comparatively easy to reject or ignore. But knowing a statement is untrue does not necessarily prevent it having an emotional effect. I believe that when a woman is herself faced with the need for an abortion, all the propaganda about 'murdered foetuses' and so on - the propaganda which she's supposedly dismissed - in fact contributes to a recoil from the process of abortion (which she may n not be prepared to admit) and a reluctance to try to cope with it. In other words, at this very vulnerable point, a woman is the victim not only of the moralistic and punitive attitudes of people around her, but also of often un-recognised (so more damaging) punitive reactions within herself.

This means she may be watching like a hawk for any hint of disapproval from her family or from the medical profession, because, quite without realising it, a small part of her *wants* this reaction and welcomes it as appropriate. (publicity has made us all increasingly aware of the attit-udes of doctors, psychiatrists, social workers, families, friends and neighbours towards someone who is seeking an abortion, and just how unsupportive some of them can be. Many examples are detailed in the pamphlet *Women and Abortion).* But at the same time she is all the more *afraid* of disapproval because it would serve to reinforce her own disapproval of her chosen course of action. If a doctor or an agency seems to be reluctant to tell her very much about the technicalities of the operation, she will read into this all the rumours she half remembers about what a terrible physical experience it is, together with mental pictures of blood and pain and medieval torture *instruments*. Then, on top of all this, she can feel depress-ed and guilty about her apparent inability to be rational about it, and to dismiss what she knows quite well to be untruths and morbid fantasies. Unfortunately, even any questioning, by counsellor or doctor, about whether she believes she is doing the right thing, however necessary it may be (to ensure that no-one is pressuring her to have an abortion against her own wish) and however sympathetic the questioner, also reinforces her own doubts.

Similar pressures apply to contraception. Internal moral-istic attitudes to sex may colour a woman's attitude to contraception; the foundations of these are laid at an early age. The vast majority of children grow up subjected to very contradictory moral conditioning about sex. The earliest anti-sex propaganda comes probably, when they are told 'not to play with themselves' at the age of two or three. Throughout their formative years, children take in quite different sets of values, all opposed to one another. As the values remain entirely theoretical until the first sexual experience reinforce one or the other, they are all, for the time being, accepted.

Without going into all the contributory factors, I've grouped these attitudes under four headings:

1. Sex is wrong. This is the first attitude for many children and it starts when the child is taught that anything associated with the genitals is 'rude', 'dirty' etc.

2. Sex is wrong-but-fun; the salacious enjoyment of the forbidden.

3. Sex is romantic; when and only when it's connected with Love and Marriage and the Right Man.

4. Sex is natural and enjoyable. Some children never get offered this alternative at all.

In most adults, some or all of these quite contradictory sets of values still exist at different levels, unreconciled. It's quite easy for a mother who believes that she enjoys sex and that she is 'sexually emancipated' to pass on, nevertheless, to her children the idea that sex is dirty, thus perpetuating the existing conflicts.

The relevant point for us is that, of those conflicting moral standpoints in the mind of an adolescent girl reaching her first sexual experiences, only the last (that sex is simply enjoyable) is at all conducive to the idea of taking contraceptive measures before heterosexual sex. If you think of sex as romantic, then coupled with the Right Man and After the Wedding Bells, you get Radiant Maternity and Feminine Fulfilment. And if you think of sex as wrong, in any context, whether it's dirty or wicked, 'forbidden fruit', or wrong outside marriage, you aren't inclined to use contraception because you don't want to admit (to yourself) that you actually intend to have sex. And I think, here, that we tend to forget how widespread is the belief, in adolescence, that sex *is* wrong; as one grows older, the fact that sex is enjoyable reinforces the view that it's right and natural.

Even after the belief that sex is wrong has been rejected from a woman's personal, moral structure, it may still deter her from seeking contraceptive advice, for two reasons. First, especially in adolescence, she may identify doctors and social workers with the authoritarian, moral views that she is rejecting. If the doctor symbolises something you're rebelling against, you don't go to him for help with that rebellion.

Secondly, she may be afraid of getting moral lectures from doctors or clinic staff. This is despite (indeed, because of) any amount of reassuring propaganda which states just the opposite. I'll illustrate this by analogy. In my teens, I kept meeting statements like 'masturbation isn't harmful'; 'Don't believe anyone who tells you masturbation is bad' etc. I never actually came across any book or person who said it *was* harmful. Nevertheless, it took me fifteen years to throw off the suspicions engendered by all that reassurance. In the same way, a leaflet that tells you that a clinic won't disapprove if you're unmarried, or that you have no need for embarrassment, often encourages precisely the atmosphere of disapproval and embarrassment which it is striving to avoid. Nobody bothers to say they won't disapprove of something unless they expect you to think they *will* disapprove; and this tells you that disapproval is the expected reaction.

In any case, changes in one's attitude or beliefs do not necessarily bring about changes in one's practice. If a habit of passive acceptance has grown from a romantic fantasy of impromptu ravishing, a decision to take more sexual initiative will not automatically break this habit at once. And a woman with three children who decides she doesn't want any more may nevertheless delay in seeking contraceptive advice because she is simply not used to the need for it.

Unfortunately, an unwanted pregnancy, and maybe an abortion, will tend to reinforce or re-introduce, for a while, the feeling that sex is bad or wrong; 'look at the awful consequences'. Thus a woman may shy away from any sexual contact for a period, sometimes for several months, after having an abortion. She is very likely to be feeling guilty about the need to have an abortion, and attaches this guilt either simply to having had sex, or to not having used contraception, or not having used it successfully. She may have believed that 'it won't happen to me'; and this, I believe is often connected with a fifth attitude to sex, which I hesitate to group with the former four, because it's not really about the sex act (fucking or lovemaking) at all:

5. Sex is for producing babies.

This line is much favoured by many writers of so-called 'sex education' pamphlets, who apparently hope that with the addition of a chapter on contraception, all will be made clear and no-one need any longer get pregnant through ignorance of 'the facts' Actually, of course, the descriptions in most of these pamphlets are so unlike the real experiences that anyone is likely to have, that sex as she knows it, and 'baby production' can easily occupy separate, water-tight compartments in a woman's mind. Objectively, she knows about it, subjectively, it doesn't impinge upon her experience, But it contributes to her sense of guilt if she gets pregnant accidentally; she can't believe she 'didn't know' about sex and pregnancy.

If, on the other hand, she is aware of contraceptive techniques and the need for them, and has been using contraception, she has probably believed that her method worked and that its failure must be due to her own inefficiency. Contraceptive information and advertising, where they exist, usually give the impression that it's pretty infallible. So whatever the circumstances a woman is likely to think of an accidental pregnancy as *her fault*. This makes for a very tricky situation in which to talk about future contraception, because any such approach, whether by a doctor or even by a close friend, is likely to confirm her own self-punitive attitude towards her failure to use effective contraception in the past. And, simultaneously, the impulse to avoid sex may make her disinclined to consider contraception at all.

What can one conclude from these examples of the effects of people's moral attitudes? One fairly obvious conclusion is to re-emphasise the vital importance of a sensitive approach to women who are being subjected to these pressures. We are sympathetic to women under external pressures, from hostile doctors, shocked family, and so on, because we can see the pressures and their effects. We need to recognise, too, the pressures we don't see, which may be affecting most the apparently organised and determined women; pressures which are perhaps responsible for some of the 'reaction' some doctors claim to have found, and which they use as an argument against abortion, but which in fact, is a *result* of these very arguments.

But sensitivity to the symptoms of pressure is not enough. This sort of analysis makes us aware that freely available contraception and abortion, when we achieve them, will not, on their own, solve the problem. The extent of the purely practical, technical difficulties is such that we would become pre-occupied with the means rather than the end - with the number of clinics rather than the women who need them - which is, in fact, the very charge we make against the NHS. Any pressure group is vulnerable in this way; so it is important for us to remember the need for a total re-orientation of values in the whole of our society, as well as for the practical provision of much-needed facilities.

Because of this, there is a need for greater emphasis to be put on our aim of establishing community self-help projects; pregnancy testing, counselling, women's health centres and ultimately, if it becomes possible, abortion clinics. Services of this kind are drastically needed in any case, because of NHS inadequacy; but one objective in offering women an alternative to the subjugating atmosphere of the NHS is to encourage them to take the initiative in the control of their own lives, and to assist them when they come up against the red tape and blank walls of the present system. A campaign aimed at self-help can raise everyone's awareness of our (very much under-estimated) ability to come together and to initiate for ourselves many of the changes we need, thereby freeing ourselves from all the pressures of other people's values; first in the limited area of contraception, abortion, health and welfare, but, growing from this, in the basis and structure of the whole of society. A concentration purely on the demand that existing authorities *provide facilities for us* does nothing about the psychological pressures which are inherent in the present structure; and only perpetuates the division of the society into those with power and the rest of us who are dependent on their decisions rather than on our own choices.

Living as we do in such a society, we need too to be aware of the danger that some of its assumptions may find their way unnoticed into our own thinking. We know how pressures combine to make women feel guilt where none is needed: concomitant pressures are on all of us to judge and be critical. Most of us grow up with judgment and criticism and we are surrounded by it all our lives. Involvement in any campaign can lead one to think one has al (or most) of the answers; we must not be tempted into saying (or even thinking) things like 'If I can contracept successfully, why can't she?' We are, ourselves, subject to the same constraints as other women; sex is not a mechanical act and we do not all have the same physical, psychological and environmental needs and experiences. Present forms of contraception are far from adequate, so that the effort involved in trying to prevent an unwanted pregnancy can result in a woman giving up altogether. (I have actually heard it said that a woman wouldn't be seeking an abortion if she were efficient and sensible - personally I feel that anyone successful in obtaining an abortion at this point in time, where the odds are still stacked against her, deserves warm congratularions of the sort more often offered to women continuing unwanted pregnancies to term.)

33

We must avoid the temptation of becoming a moral pressure group instead of a political force for freedom of choice. It is all too easy to play the role of expert. What we must aim to achieve instead is real communication and support. As women, we have the chance to support each other as we begin to choose to refer our lives to values beyond the simple level of automatic response to approval and disapproval. This is the real challenge.

Katy Jennison and Hilda Bartle

Amended version of a paper given at the Women's Abortion and Contraception Campaign Conference in Liverpool in 1973.

Abortion Accounts

How can compulsory child-bearing be justified by a society which calls itself 'democratic'?

Women cannot even begin to fight for freedom until at the very least we can control our bodies. Here are the stories of one woman who had an abortion before the Abortion Act of 1967 and of two-women's experiences after the Act - we all three belong to the Bristol Women's Liberation Group, but we are sure that almost every woman in our society has had experiences of unwanted pregnancies, back-street abortions or has been refused applications for abortions on the NHS.

The situations we are describing are not going to change until contraception is freely available to ALL women and new forms of absolutely safe contraceptives have been developed (Prostaglandins, the once a month Pill, could soon be available to women but are seen as a threat to the medical companies who now make millions out of the conventional Pill that has to be taken every day and changes the hormonal balance of the woman's body). Women must also have access to safe, free abortions - using the Karman Vacuum suction abortion in the first 11 weeks of pregnancy - on an out-patient basis.

Abortion - guilty or not guilty?

When I was 20 years old and living away from home in a bedsitter, I found to my dismay that I was pregnant. The father was a man with whom I had had a fairly continuing relationship for several years - a man who was by way of being a friend as well as 'boyfriend'. I knew I couldn't face marriage and a baby with a man who felt trapped by my pregnant state, and that any kind of firm commitment with this particular man would be doomed to failure in those circumstances. I didn't particularly want a baby; in fact I didn't want a baby. I had far too many interesting things still to do with my life and the role of housewife and mother didn't appeal to me.

At that time abortion was not legal in this country, except for those people who could afford a hundred to a hundred and fifty pounds for a Harley Street operation. We didn't come into that category! The only kind of abortion which was realistic in our case was an illegal, back-street job.

When we had finally decided that I was definitely pregnant and had made up our minds what we wanted to do about it, we made contact with someone who could help. I never knew the name of the woman who did it - with a syringe and carbolic soap in the middle of a bright October afternoon. That part wasn't horribly painful, only very uncomfortable and with one sharp pain. Within a couple of hours I had started losing a small amount of blood and by late evening the loss was well-established. At that stage I had only what amounted to a period pain with some backache. I dozed once or twice during the night but by 3 a.m. I was wide awake and losing a lot of blood. It was at least another four hours before the foetus came away - it looked more like a baby than I had expected. I remained in a good deal of pain, however, and after another couple of hours it became obvious that a doctor was needed. When I had been taken to hospital by ambulance, it was found that I must have been more than 12 weeks pregnant, and the placenta had to be removed by a doctor in Casualty, who left me in no doubt about his view of my 'immoral' behaviour.

In fact, I never felt guilty about the abortion. I took the decision after careful consideration of all the avenues open to me, and I felt then, as I do now, that it was the right thing for me to do. My only regret has always been that it was necessary for me to have a dangerous, illegal operation in order to retain freedom of choice over my own future.

Some years after this, and while it was still not possible to get an abortion legally except in rare cases, I was living near a friend who had several young children. She had become pregnant again and was very upset about it as she didn't see how she could possibly cope with another child, either on her husband's wage as a skilled worker, or in the flat in which they lived. In desperation she decided to have a back-street abortion, and, although I wasn't happy about it, I said I would help with the kids if necessary, and tried to be cheerful and encouraging.

The next morning the husband came and fetched me at 6 a.m. He had been up all night and had waited as long as possible but now he felt he must get medical help. His wife was haemorrhaging badly and I went to see what I could do. She was losing large clots of blood, and there was a sheet already soaking in the kitchen sink. I spent the next half hour or so mopping up blood and trying to be reassuring. I had myself given birth twice by then but I had never seen so much blood and we were both badly frightened. She was taken to hospital, where she was given blood transfusions, put on a drip, and given fifteen minute blood pressure and temperature checks. This terrible experience, together with that of the abortion I had myself undergone, persuaded me, more than anything, that all women should be able to chose to have properly performed abortions with no cost to themselves, physically, emotionally or financially.

No-one has been able to put a figure to the number of illegal operations performed before the 1967 Abortion Act, but a realistic assessment is considered to be one hundred thousand every year. This is largely based on the number of patients admitted to hospital in need of treatment. But there are, or were, many women who never receive medical attention at any time during or after a back-street abortion and I think any estimate made by the authorities is likely to be an underestimate.

There is a lot of pressure on women who have abortions, whether legal or illegal, to make them feel guilty about 'destroying a life'. Even though the birth of an unwanted baby may mean a poorer, harder life for other children in the family; although it may mean a mother's sanity, or worsened living conditions, one is still supposed to tear oneself to shreds regretting it. I believe that most of this guilt is the result of conditioning by this society. That sometimes it may be the expression of the person's conditioning that sex has to be paid for, if not with the prospect of hellfire, then at least with a lifetime of grinding poverty and service to the needs of the young.

Certainly, until contraception is 100% safe and trouble-free, abortion should be seen as an important last resort, provided free by the State on the decision of the woman and not according to the religious principles of her general practitioner. I think it has importance for Women's Liberation as a demand because if the State does provide it in this way, it becomes socially acceptable and it will all the sooner be guilt-free, and more particularly, women will begin to see their need for control over their own lives in other important areas also, such as employment and education.

Abortions are easy to get nowadays?

I was sitting in the hospital clinic, had just been told by the gynaecologist, an elderly man, silver-haired: 'Sorry, I cannot give you an abortion, we cannot help every woman who has become pregnant because of her own irresponsibility'. (What does he know about the pressures on women, sexual blackmail, fears felt by women, ignorance; he can quite smugly say that she, who all her life has been treated as an object without right of action or decision, should act 'responsibly' - what does he know about husbands throwing the woman's contraceptive on the fire after

38

scooping it out of her cunt with his finger, about men's assumptions that they are men only when they have the power to make their wives pregnant when they so wish, about women sleeping with men for a bit of human warmth and comfort, fleeing from loneliness?)

I was sitting there in the hospital crying my heart out in the little cubicle. Somehow I had been naive enough to think that I would naturally get an abortion. It had never occurred to me that some might see pregnancy as a fitting punishment for a woman's sexual escapade. And what of the child, should it also get punished? Well, you can have it adopted, they said coldly. Do they know what that means?' I was crying for what seemed like hours, I could have hanged myself for all the hospital staff knew or cared, nobody bothered to find out how I felt. It seems to me that at any other time, when a person is suffering from shock and crying hysterically, at least somebody would have shown some sympathy, but, because I was an 'immoral' woman who needed an abortion, I was treated as a pariah.

My own doctor had told me when I went to her for help: 'You have been a naughty girl!', although I am 32 years old and have borne two children already. (I had slept with another man than my husband and I thought that he had made me pregnant. In a real human community, it would not matter who was the father of a woman's child, because a child is a child is a child ..... but in our patriarchal society, the child must show the same colour and shape as its 'legal' father, because in our society, it is the fatherhood of the child that makes it 'legal'. How · can a child be 'illegitimate'? The child is always born out of a known mother, isn't that enough?

The Abortion Act of 1967 states that abortion is legal when the continuance of the pregnancy would involve more risk to the life of the pregnant woman or more injury to the physical or mental health of the pregnant woman, or any existing children of her family, than if the pregnancy were not terminated. Many, or perhaps most, so-called 'normal' men would have left a woman who was expecting another man's child. If this had happened in my case, I would have been left alone with a child of ten and a baby and no means of livelihood except for Social Security benefit. Would that not have caused my children great distress and very likely have led to neurosis for me?

I was sent off to see a psychiatrist to prove to him that I was under great mental stress. I was expected to break down and cry, begging for mercy - yet another woman humiliating herself in front of a man-representative of repressive male institutions. I just couldn't do it! I told him of my life, full of upheavals and a childhood with an unsupported mother full of fears ....But because I appeared in emotional control of myself, he judged that I could do without the abortion. (Had he never heard of women and men, who, because they do not show their emotions but bottle them up within themselves, are often far more dangerous than those who just let go and cry? A woman, deserted by her second husband when pregnant with her third child, was denied an abortion, went back home and killed her two small children. Perhaps she didn't cry either?)

It was also obvious from the psychiatrist's attitude that he considered that women do not have sexual needs. When I told him that I had left my first husband about four years before I met the second man I married, he seemed surprised that I had had any sexual relationships with men during those years! What business has he to call himself a psychiatrist if he knows so little of human needs and behaviour?

Also, the fact that I was married seemed to be against me, even though there was a real risk of my becoming an unsupported mother because of this pregnancy. Unmarried girls, particularly if they are students, appear to get abortions far more easily. Once a woman is married, she is seen as a man's responsibility and is left to his charge and whether she is beaten, destitute, continuously pregnant and ignorant of contraceptives is irrelevant. Unmarried mothers are an embarrassment to society while long-suffering wives are only part of our traditions.

I had wild fantasies of blowing up the clinic, murdering the gynaecologist or presenting him with the newborn baby: 'Here you are, you look after it!'. I thought of nurses, in revolt against male hierarchy at last, turning their attention to their sisters and setting up clinics, using their skills for giving women free contraceptives and abortions on demand. Almost all the work done in hospitals, from cleaning to nursing, is done by an army of women but, when women themselves need help in matters that upset their whole life, then there are no beds or help available. (What of the nurse who gave birth alone in her room and, when she found the child still-born, put it in a plastic bag and put it in the dustbin of the hospital incinerator room? She didn't want anybody to know!) What untold misery and loneliness of women!

I thought of parading outside the hospital, big-bellied, with a poster saying: 'I didn't want this child'. I wanted to find other women in my situation and together we would storm in demanding our rights as human beings to control our own bodies and lives..... but it all remained fantasies. I could have gone to a back-street abortionist but I had an experience in the first months of pregnancy that put fear into me of doing that; a friend brought a woman down from London to have a back-street abortion in Bristol. She stayed at my place, went to 'the woman', had contractions all night and bled so much that she was too weak to stand up. She haemorrhaged and was taken to hospital and almost didn't survive it. (What kind of society do we live in that women have to risk their lives for what should naturally be their right? How many women die this way every year? These women are sacrificed by capitalist society that will go to any lengths to keep women as unpaid and cheap labour in and outside the home and the family). In the local clinic I heard of a girl, 18 years old or younger, who had been forced to continue her pregnancy. When the child was born it was mongoloid! It is only a very sick society that will condemn human beings to such experiences.

In the end I had to bear the child.

Abortions are easy to get nowadays?

'Congratulations' he said to my question of whether the pregnancy test was positive or not. What a terrible cliche that is. I couldn't believe it; we hadn't been particularly stupid, or anything like that, but when the pill scare was on some while ago, I gladly came off the pill (I'd had quite a lot of trouble with it) and we'd taken to using those relatively harmless rubbers again, all but twice that is - and here I was, pregnant again. The thought of living through another unwanted pregnancy seemed too much to bear, and this time there'd be my other child's welfare to consider. The poor thing was a bit too young to cope with a mother turned madwoman, I explained to the doctor. He was very good about it all, a practising christian (I've since found out); he didn't try to influence me in any way, but just made sure that I was sure, which I was.

For a second opinion, which is needed, I had to go to a local clinic to see some specialist or other. This was the worst part of it; they kept me waiting for hours; other de-knickered and de-stockinged women came and went, and I sat on, getting more and more hung up and paranoid. Eventually I plucked up courage to go to the desk and demand in a hysterical squeak why I hadn't been seen yet, I was the first there etc. Checked my name, yes, go into one of those cubicles and take your pants and stockings off - at this I broke down crying and screaming...I went and sat there, tears rolling down my face. What the hell am I supposed to be doing in here? I'd rather be waiting outside than in this flowery box. A sort of mad rebellion got me, I picked up my bag and walked out, demanding to know what was going on. Two nurses looked at me, looked at each other, then looked ceilingwards; 'Go in there, take your pants and stockings off and wait till the doctor calls you.' I went back inside and practically tore the curtains down in my rage and hysteria. Eventually I saw the doctor, who agreed with my GP and myself that an abortion was best but they couldn't do it, they had no beds: 'I'm sorry'. She suggested having one done privately, they weren't very expensive - 'only about £40'. More tears and pleading to no avail; they'd write and tell my GP of their decision. The following day, assuming that he'd got their letter, I phoned him. The letter hadn't arrived, what had they said? 'The stupid cow said I couldn't have one', I said to my GP. Surprised, he said 'What? They can't do that, I'll get in touch with them. Ring me back on Friday'. When I did, the answer amazed me. 'You're going into .....hospital on Monday'. I was glad of the short wait (which really has to be for an abortion). I spent the weekend getting the baby fixed up and other things and had little time for changing my mind.

I cried in the waiting room when my husband left. I am terrified of hospitals and this would be the first operation I'd ever had; what would it be like? Would it hurt afterwards? The day was spent chatting with the other women, mainly D & C cauterisations (an operation very similar to termination, for the removal of vaginal ulcers) and hysterectomies; I'd never before realised how much women have to suffer because of their womanhood. There were two other women having abortions, which was a relief to me, and we talked quite openly about it. One's husband hadn't been bothered about contraception but walked out on her when she became pregnant - the other had three kids and was going to be sterilised at the same time. There was little guilt or shame felt by us, or was it me reflecting my feelings on them (did I just assume they felt like this because I did?). The nurses referred to the subject in whispers or avoided talking about it to the others.

The operation lasted 'no more than 10 or 15 minutes'. When I woke up I was retching and some nurse was urgently telling me to breathe through my nose, which I did and then fell asleep again. The next time I woke up, my husband was sitting next to me and an orderly was asking me if I wanted some tea, 'cheese and onion pie'. I was as stiff as a board (the stiffness lasted for days) but hungry. I felt marvellous, a few hours ago I'd been pregnant and now I wasn't and nothing to show for it but a slight loss of blood. We were given no instruction before leaving of what we ought to do, or not to do. I felt so well that it didn't occur to me to take things easy or refrain from sex, so some days later, after a long and strenuous walk, I thought I was dying when I haemorrhaged quite heavily; that passed O K but when I started bleeding again a few days later, I panicked and found myself in a hospital in Taunton, hardly bleeding at all, to my embarrassment, for they'd treated me as an emergency case. Repeating my story to one medic after another, I got the same bigoted response: 'I didn't realise abortions were so easy to get in Bristol now' etc. I don't (didn't) care what they thought; not being at the mercy of the NHS now, my boot-licking had finished.

Compiled by Monica Sjoo using material by Betty Underwood, Carmen Davies and Monica Sjoo

First published in ENOUGH No. 4, the journal of the Bristol Women's Liberation Group. 1972

Medical Mystifications

It has long been known that the diagnosis and treatment of mental illness leaves a lot to be desired. The growth of groups like People not Psychiatry, the Mental Patients Union and the writings of Laing, Szasz and others have made an appreciable impact on people seeking psychiatric help. Many more people are now aware of the ways in which psychiatric treatment seeks to make 'deviant' people conform, and the way in which it sweeps suffering under the State carpet with a bottle of Librium, or electric shock streatment. But if we have a pain in our stomachs, or a rash on our hands we go to our GP's, on whom the mantle of scientific objectivity sits quite comfortably, and expect a value-free diagnosis and a handy prescription. As women, we approach our doctors in good faith, sincerely believing that our complaints will be taken seriously and that, were we men, our reception in the surgery would be no different. Although we may be well aware of the workings of sexism in psychiatry and in the whole question of abortion, we are not particularly well equipped to identify it in the diagnosis and treatment of physical illness. It would be a mistake to assume that medical science is any more free from traditional assumptions about female inferiority than any other so-called 'science'.

Here are some everyday examples: a woman approaches her doctor with an intolerable discharge and, rather than examine her, he asks her if she is promiscuous' and dismisses her with the curt advice to wash more frequently. (This happened to me.) A woman of 20 complains of frequent blinding headaches to her doctor. He prescribes a pain killer and tells her that it's just 'pre-wedding nerves'. Six months later she is dead, having had a brain tumour. A young mother complains to her doctor of itchy hands and arms. He tells her this is very common among new mothers and that it's a result of her anxiety over her infant. He doesn't suggest an allergy test for Napisan or any other new product she's using. A woman complains to her doctor of depression and dizzy spells. While he's writing a prescription for Valium he perfunctorily asks her if she's worrying about anything. He doesn't note that she's taking the contraceptive pill and nor does he bother to check for anything else which might cause her condition.

These (and countless other) examples cannot be attributed to the shortcomings of the individual doctors concerned. These attitudes are endemic to the whole medical profession and are fundamental both to the teaching and practice of the great majority of doctors. Most disturbing of all is the complacency of the profession on these questions. Hooked on its own mystique, and with the aid of a top-heavy trade in boffins, the medical profession shores up its ignorance and continues to legitimise the outright oppression of women. The side effects of the contraceptive pill (debilitating headaches, nausea, loss of libido, thrombosis and death) are still described as 'minor'. Hysterectomies are performed for no other reason than that the junior surgeons need some practice (it is the second commonest operation in women and is often performed on relatively young women with *no* uterine disease, the justification being that they *might* develop some disease within ten years! - no serious consideration is being given, either, to the aftermath of this major operation, ranging from serious and long lasting depression to premature menopausal symptoms - see Jean Robinson's article on the subject in *Spare Rib No. 30)*; safe early abortions are denied, forcing women into back street abortionists from which several die, and mass screening of women for early signs of breast cancer is not thought important enough to administer though it would save 11,500 deaths per year from breast cancer and 37,000 mastectomies per year, if the technology developed were made available.

Recognising that the sexist practice of medicine is not just fodder for high table talk, but devastatingly and sometimes fatally affects women's health, two doctors, Dr. Jean

Lennane and Dr. John Lennane, took the brave step of attacking that practice in a formal academic paper called *Alleged Psychogenic Disorders in Women - A Possible Manifestation of Sexual Prejudice* (New England Journal of Medicine, Feb. 1973). They describe the medical profession's approach to three specifically female conditions - painful periods (dysmenorrhea), nausea in pregnancy and pain in labour as 'inadequate and even derisory'.

Painful periods

It seems that some 50% of women suffer from painful periods but the medical attitude to this condition, even when it is so severe that it totally disrupts normal life is, at best, dismissive, and, at worst, dangerous. Although the condition follows its own characteristic course and is similar for all women suffering from it (i.e. an almost 'invariable pattern' occurring two years after menarche, when ovulation begins, and ceasing with the birth of the first child or at about 25 years of age, and being alleviated by the suppression of ovulation) the exact cause of the pain is still unknown. The medical literature on the subject totally rejects the obvious - that it has a physical cause, and instead attributes it to female deficiency in whatever guise most suits the practitioners' prejudice. For instance:

It is generally acknowledged that this condition is much more frequent in the 'high-strung', nervous or neurotic female than in her more stable sister (1)

Faulty outlook ... exaggeration of minor discomfort ... may even be an excuse to avoid doing something that is disliked (2)

... very little can be done for the patient who prefers to use menstrual symptoms as a monthly refuge from responsibility and effort ... management must be directed at the underlying psychodynamics (3)

However, the classic explanation for painful periods is that the *mother* is responsible:

A dysmenorrheic mother usually has a dysmenorrheic daughter (2) (original italics)

As the Lennanes point out, in any other condition, it would be assumed that heredity had something to do with it, but where women are concerned, it is assumed that *they* are at fault, and not their genetic make-up. So, immediately, there is a watertight medical 'refuge from responsibility and effort'; how much easier it is for the medical writers to dismiss female complaints, without *any* substantiating evidence, as the product of hysteria, neuroticism, faulty outlook, laziness etc, than it is to do some serious research, research which doesn't take as its starting point the assumption that women are a lower form of life.

The Lennanes point out that, both in dysmenorrhea and nausea in pregnancy, there are 'organic etiological factors present', though, again, one would never guess it from the literature on either of the conditions.

Nausea in pregnancy

The results of treating nausea in pregnancy without prior thorough research are well known. Drug manufacturers and medical researchers must together be held responsible for the thalidomide tragedy, the first for exploitation and conspiracy, and the second for the savage neglect of female complaints which result in the indiscriminate prescribing of drugs, drugs which in no way are intended to cure or even treat the complaint, but which effectively prevent women from pestering their GP's. With this attitude prevailing, the way is clear for nausea in pregnancy to be attributed to the woman's 'resentment, ambivalence and inadequacy', her ' .. irrationally exaggerated fear of the obstetric hazards facing her'. Strange that her inadequacy and irrationality only begins in the fifth/sixth week of pregnancy (often before she is even aware of her pregnancy! and subsides around the 15th week, that she's more irrational in the morning than the evenings and that inadequacy is relieved by food - stranger still that ambivalence and resentment should cause the *same* symptoms in 88% of pregnant women. In fact:

The type of nausea and its usual duration are exactly mimicked by estrogen therapy and such nausea is a recognised *side effect of estrogen-containing oral contraceptives. Estrogen has been shown to be excreted in large amounts during pregnancy (*Lennane)

Since thalidomide-type drugs have been discredited and while there is no research into its exact cause, women will have to endure nausea in pregnancy as just another 'minor' discomfort.

It is horribly clear that whenever a condition or complaint is exclusive female, special anti-female criteria are put into practice. The research, practice and *industry* of contraception is, perhaps, the most obviously sexist and, second to abortion, has the most devastating effects on women's lives and health.

The pill

In 1973 the pill was brilliantly whitewashed by the Royal College of General Practitioners' interim report *Oral Contraceptives and Health.* A member of the reporting Committee appeared on television and soothed any 'neurotic' woman's fears with the categorical statement, not that the pill carried specific dangers and increases the risk of 62 conditions, but that women who take the pill are *healthier* than those who don't. (We must never forget how powerful the drug manufacturers' lobby is and how much money is at stake!) Mr. Denis Hawkins, a consultant gynaecologist who directs the birth control clinic at one of the largest London teaching hospitals has stated 'Expediency comes into medical practice as it does everywhere else'. ('Expediency' in the use of the pill is the cause of 24 deaths per million user/years) We might assume that a man in his position and with such experience would know better, but he joins ranks with those who legitimise prejudice as scientific fact. I know it gets boring but he describes the documented side effects of the pill - depression, headaches, loss of libido etc. - as, you've guessed it, 'psychosomatic'. The whitewash report went further than this. It dismissed the reported side effects of the pill because it was *women* who were reporting them and, as all doctors are taught in their training, women are quite unreliable and irrational. Only one doctor, a woman, spoke out against the Report.

She has maintained that

Even without it showing, the pill is altering the hormone balance and so affecting the body's natural immunity and resistance to infection.

Her own research has shown her that headaches, depression, migraine

are caused by the biochemical and enzyme changes in the lining of the womb which are reflected in the blood vessels in the head and elsewhere.

A biochemist friend and full time researcher into hormones has told me that they remain one of the biggest mysteries in medical science. Such ignorance, however, doesn't prevent drug manufacturers from making a great deal of money, or doctors from telling women that they should be thankful for the wonder pill of the age and that the 'side effects' are the cross they must bear for being born female, neurotic and inferior.

But the last word on this must be left to Denis Hawkins, the expert on female inadequacy. When asked about the possibility of a male oral contraceptive, he felt that it would pose not only ethical but legal problems: 'we don't yet know whether tampering with the sperm would create abnormalities' and he asserted that 'men are sensitive about fears of impotence'. So who's neurotic?

Lee Comer
November 1974

References

1. Menaker, J., Powers, K. Management of primary dysmenorrhea *(Obstet Gynaecol. 1962)*
2. Jeffcoate, T. Principles of Gynaecology. Butterworth 1967
3. Benson, R. Gynaecology and Obstetrics Current Diagnosis and treatment, edited by Krupp M. Lange Medical Publications, 1972.

The statements of Denis Hawkins were taken from an article/interview by Carol Dix which appeared in *The Guardian*, November 6th 1974.

Vaginal Politics

About 50% of our population is female, and, because women have the babies, they can be expected to make rather more use of the health service than men during their fertile years. Women currently live longer than men, so will need more health care in their old age. Women have more mental illness than men (a point to which I shall return). They are also known to consult their GP's — either for themselves or their children — more often than men do.

Yet of 20,208 GP's in the National Health Service, only 2,388 are women. Of 23,478 total hospital medical staff, only 3,336 are women. Few women are involved in the actual running of the health service via hospital management committees or regional boards.

The whole structure of the health service is a pyramid, with power delegated downwards, not upwards. And those many women who do contribute greatly to the service we use — nurses, midwives, occupational therapists, health visitors — are where they have always been — at the bottom of the pile in terms of salary and of course influence.

At the top of the pile, then, is the Minister of Health, and, below him/her a great many career administrators — almost invariably men, and, of course, the doctors, particularly the hospital consultants. The latter are still easily the best-paid health service workers.

Traditionally, we see doctors as men and patients as women, and this can be confirmed by any casual glance through a medical journal, to see the sex of the patient invariably given tranquillisers by the (male) doctor in the drug companies' advertisements. One particular ad shows a harassed woman bent over a sink with a pile of dirty dishes. The caption tells the doctor — 'You can't solve her problems, but you can give her 'X' '. Too true, alas.

51

Doctors are only human. Some of them would like to help. But in a society which prefers to hand out tablets to a woman whose only problem is she's stuck with two small kids 24 hours a day, 365 days a year — rather than act as a matter of urgency to give her a break, what can they do? Particularly when, as men, most of them have only the haziest idea of just how lonely and demoralising this situation can be.

Phyllis Chesler, in her book, *Women and Madness*, argues that the high incidence of mental illness in women is the result of intolerable pressures put on them by society. Many women crack up during puberty, after childbirth or during the menopause. Doctors mutter about hormones and admit them to mental hospitals, where, often enough, they are given drugs or electro-convulsive therapy against their will.

But the scale of the problem surely indicates that it is not so simple. Doctors seem to know remarkably little about endocrinology (the study of hormones), in any case. But until more is known, what about social support for women at these vulnerable times? Or does the natural life-cycle of a female strike a male doctor as too 'mysterious', alarming, or trivial to merit serious attention?

Mental illness is not the only field where women's special interests are ignored. You'd think that any doctor would be shocked into action by the sight of a battered woman. Yet, when I visited Chiswick Women's Aid recently, I spoke to many women whose husbands had inflicted appalling injuries on them and their children for years with the full knowledge of their doctors. Typical was the lady, blind in one eye, covered in scars, who'd been told by her GP that 'of course, you can't leave him, because of the children'.

Thus women are subtly brainwashed into playing the role of 'patient victim', helpless in the face of 'natural' male aggression. In these cases it was the man who needed the medical treatment — but the woman who ended up going to the doctor. The same all too often applies with rape and mental cruelty.

52

Angela Kilmartin, who suffers from chronic cystitis, a particularly debilitating and painful complaint which affects mainly women, got so fed up with the attitudes of doctors that she started the U and I Club for fellow sufferers to help themselves by exchanging information and acting as a pressure group on the medical profession. Many of the letters she receives constitute a shocking indictment of the way doctors think about us.

Cystitis sufferers are variously told to 'go home, you're imagining it', 'learn to live with it', 'get pregnant — it will go away when you've had a baby', 'have another baby', and even, in one case, 'find another man to sleep with' (the woman was married!). Complaints that cystitis has so crippled her that she can't have sex, produce such gems as 'try going without for six months', and 'are you married?'

But there is one area of medicine that is *supposed* to concentrate on women — gynaecology, which is still the most popular option for would-be consultants, and where a fair number of them are even female themselves. Traditionally, the specialty was, of course, the province of midwives. But a couple of centuries ago, the men started to take an interest, from which time we have been privileged indeed. Or have we?

Gynaecologists had to be bulldozed into accepting the idea of contraception despite their intimate knowledge of the damaging effects of endless pregnancies upon a woman's health. They had little hand in the liberalisation of the abortion laws. And many of them still seem more concerned with telling us what to do than ensuring that we're well looked after when we've done it.

A qualification in Obstretics and Gynaecology is supposed to mean that the doctor in question knows what can go wrong with our sexual and reproductive organs, and how to treat it, as well as simply how to deliver babies. The consultant gynaecologist in a hospital has a great deal of power, and, one would hope, a sense of responsibility to match. But the following are examples of what actually, all too often, happens.

A woman goes to see a handsome well-heeled gynaecologist about an NHS abortion. He doesn't offer her a seat. She's single, so he makes her feel so guilty about the whole thing that she starts to cry. He sees her once, briefly, after the operation, then hands over all 'aftercare' such as it is, to the registrar, while he sees his private patients.

A married woman with three children decides that she can't face the fourth that's on the way. Her gynaecologist makes sterilisation a condition of an abortion. She agrees, has the operation, and suffers thereafter from cystitis, due to hormone imbalance, which means she can't have sex any more. The doctor offers her no sexual counselling. A woman has a hysterectomy because of fibroids in the womb. After the operation, she is sent to walk around the ward and suddenly feels 'her insides giving way'. She tells the nurse, who tells her 'not to make such a fuss'. The gynaecologist discharges her. Ten days later she's re-admitted, in agony and with a high temperature. What she'd felt was her stitches coming apart.

A woman who's been in pain for months, and got no satisfaction from her GP, finally decides she's had enough and heads for the hospital to see the gynaecologist who delivered her child. He tells her 'yes there was thrush on your swab when we took it'. That was eighteen months ago, and nothing had been prescribed at the time.

A single girl wants a coil fitted and asks for a Copper 7 - the most suitable one for her. She is fitted with a shield, but the gynaecologist doesn't bother to tell her that he didn't have any Copper 7's handy. She bleeds for months before finally getting it removed and replaced.

A woman is asked how she feels immediately after her fourth (nine hour) labour, and says, 'tired'. 'It does you good to be reminded what a real labour is like' says the male consultant briskly.

An eminent gynaecolologist hits the headlines by saying that 'promiscuous young girls' are more likely to get cervical cancer. He fails to add that it takes co-operation to create promiscuity and that if infection is responsible, poor male hygeine might enter into the picture somewhere.

Indicative of the medical profession's general approach is its attitude to contraception. The provision of the pill or the sheath for family planning services is still regarded as a 'non-medical' matter. Most doctors therefore make a charge for pill prescriptions, and do not normally supply the sheath at all. I can sympathise with their reluctance to spend much time handing out condoms. But what can possibly be non-medical about a device which is one of the best protections against VD, infection and unwanted pregnancy.

And why is it that many more sterilisations are carried out on women than vasectomies on men? There are still so few facilities for vasectomy that men who want one are forced to wait, and there seem to be no plans to encourage more men to chose this means of contraception. Doctors clearly prefer to persuade women having abortions to be sterilised - a practice which in my view at least has absolutely nothing to recommend it.

Women, as we know, are reached from the moment they hit puberty (or even before), by a mass of propaganda aimed to persuade them that as they are, they won't do. They must be cleaner, sweeter, clearer, more antiseptic by several times over than nature made them, is the implication, before they can be acceptable to the male in search of sexual pleasure.

But real health education in sexual hygeine is almost absent from her programme and is never touched on during the education of her brothers. Thus what is probably the second largest women's health problem — vaginal infections — continue unabated. Cancer of the penis is unknown among Jews, who are circumsised at birth, and cancer of the cervix is much less common among Jewish wives. Circumcision is currently unfashionable in this country, though it is widely practised in America and Australia. But there is at least one doctor so convinced of its preventive role that he will perform the operation on men up to 50, on request. Meanwhile, what about health education for men?

Both the pill and antibiotics have ·been implicated in cases of vaginal thrush, yet women are rarely warned of this by their doctors. Coils often lead to infection unless fitted with the utmost concern for hygeine. During childbirth, it is still common to insert a catheter to draw off the urine, yet any instrument can carry infection which, once established, may be hard to treat. And women with cystitis or discharge are still sent home far too often without referral to both gynaecologist and urologist for tests which, if they had cancer, could save their lives.

The BUPA Medical Centre in London does a complete 'well-woman' screening, which includes cervical swab, breast mammography, and X-ray and instruction in self examination of the breast. They are trying to convince the Department of Health and Social Security of the need for widespread NHS facilities for routine screening of women. Despite impressive research results, they have failed so far.

Meanwhile most women whose breast cancer is diagnosed late are still subjected to the radical mastectomy they would never have needed had the disease been arrested at once. To add insult to injury, they are then unable to get the special bras they need on the NHS! Many women have unnecessary hysterectomy, which may leave them worse off than before. And a proportion of those women currently being told to 'stop worrying' by their doctors, will die of cervical cancer or kidney disease, spotted too late.

All doctors know that proper diagnostic tests, at the proper time, are vital to the practice of good medicine. What some of them don't realise is that, in order to judge the proper time, it is necessary first to listen to the patient. Yes, even if she is female, Sir, if you don't mind.

So, what exactly *do* our gynaecologists do for us? Well, we do have good ante-natal care, though cynics have have been heard to mutter that this is more for the child's benefit than for ours. And, some women say, good childbirth faciltities. True, we don't actually die these days, though, where there is a choice between mother and baby the mother is still not the one to be saved as *a matter of course*. But many of us suffer needless pain, anxiety and humiliation through the attitudes of those who attend us. There is still much to be achieved here.

How long are we prepared to wait to change the kind of medical care we are getting? Angela Kilmartin, whose career was in ruins and marriage on the rocks two years ago, had waited long enough. The U & I Club is historic in that it is the first organised women's self help group to make a real impact on the medical profession. It has used the press and television to draw attention to its members plight and already doctors are beginning to sit up and take notice. Chiswick Women's Aid is doing the same job for battered wives.

The Women's Abortion and Contraception Campaign hopes to get it through the thick skulls of all too many consultants that women *want* proper abortion and contraception facilities and intend to get them. WACC is currently fighting for us against the Society for the Protection of the Unborn Child (Production of Unwanted Children?) and other like-minded groups, who would like the 1967 Abortion Act repealed, yes, I said, repealed.

But the really interesting aspect of this whole question is, I think, ideological-political. Medicine, as we have seen, is a hierarchy, in which the female element is either exploited or experimented upon. I am irresistably reminded of those childhood games of 'doctor', when the little boy tells the little girl to 'lie down and take your clothes off', so that he can examine her. There's no harm in these things among children — but we're all supposed to be adult now.

A member of WACC who's a medical student reports in their newsletter that, at their first gynaecological lecture, the consultant addressed himself entirely to the male two thirds of the audience, with snide references to the variety of sizes and shapes of breasts and instructions to 'take a good look whenever you can!' And I have it on good authority that medical students have been solemnly warned against the awkwardness of having to examine that horror of horrors, an uninhibited woman! No wonder many girls prefer a female gynaecologist, who may at least have a chance of guessing what it feels like to be on the receiving end of this kind of thing.

American women's groups started to examine the sociopolitical background to these attitudes some time ago. Discovering how difficult it was to get any information out of gynaecologists about what, exactly, their discipline involved, they decided to find out for themselves. With the aid of plastic speculums, mirrors, basic textbooks, and each other, they set out on a journey which has brought far-reaching results.

Angela Briggs

This is a slightly amended version of an article which first appeared in SPARE RIB, December 1973 (19).

Sexuality

and Ideology

Notes on Ideology

The original reason for writing these notes lay in the discussion we had in the RED RAG collective about some parts of Beatrix Campbell's article *Sexuality and Submission*, notably the part where she writes about women 'colluding' in their own oppression. *(The version of 'Sexuality and Submission' appearing in this book has been revised in the light of these discussions - Eds.)* The use of this phrase seems to indicate that we understand history, oppression, and the struggle between classes and social groups in a very limited and mechanical way. So that we're able to talk in a surprised way about people colluding in their oppression - actively helping that oppression to continue as if we always thought that oppression was a matter of the oppressed being blindly tossed about like objects. We have reduced our understanding of human reality and human oppression to a narrow materialist one. By this I mean that we recognise that people have material needs and ways of satisfying them, defined by the relations of production of the system they live under, but what we tend to forget is that each person also has at all times a *consciousness* of that situation - a need to understand.

Just as there is a constant struggle going on between the ruling class, which has its hands on the resources, and the rest of us for our material needs, so there is a war going on in terms of *ideas*. Just as individuals have ways of seeing themselves and their situation, so do ruling groups have ways of explaining and presenting themselves. As the economic power lies in the hands of the owners of the means of production, so does the extraordinary power of defining how all the rest of us understand ourselves and the system we live under. I'll call this ideological power.

The cost of 'consensus'

As the advanced imperialist countries developed an increasingly complex commerce and technology, they developed needs for a workforce which gave them more than its unskilled physical labour (their old colonies could provide this commodity more cheaply), and began to exploit more of our mental capacities, training us to join a more sophisticated workforce with increasing consumer needs. At the same time, maintaining power by means of ideology became vitally important - if you can keep people understanding their situation in certain ways so that they accept them, go on accepting them, and pass on that acceptance to their children or to their pupils in school etc., then you have a system of exploitation which all classes consent to, vote for, and participate in. Reproducing the relations of production, to use marxist terms, is a main function of the modern capitalist state. A range of institutions currently pumps out ruling class ideologies necessary for the system to keep running smoothly with the mass of people consenting. The most crucial of those would be the family (of course, the family is *much more* than an ideological institution but it's as the place where our consciousness is first formed that I mainly want to give it importance here) and the school system, T.V. and press, with the Social Services, Nursery System, medical and psychiatric establishments supporting. Then there are other everyday institutions which also have importance in forming our ideas about the kind of lives we lead - the Church, political apparatus (the Party system, voting etc.), the legal system, the Trade Unions, culture/literature, football, bingo etc.

Consciousness raising

Late 1969/70. I'm a housewife living with man and child in an isolated family situation in a strange city. I make one trip per day to the supermarket, just for a change of scene. I try for jobs and fail because I can't get the child into a nursery. I try and write novels, I blame myself for not being 'strong' enough to make it in the world, I blame

*myself for not being consumed with interest for the child
and the man, I blame myself for not being sexually glow-
ing and happy. The conflict between the various ideas of
what I should be and the real trap I'm living in, makes
me constantly depressed and guilty.*

A woman friend took me along to a new women's liberation group, and in the space of an hour, the war that
was going on inside me began to show itself as a war in
which everyone was involved. Ideas I had about what I
should be, ways I had of understanding myself and the
world began to show themselves as aspects of *ideology*
which affected everyone (or all women, in this instance) -
sexist ideology, the ideology of competitive individualism,
and so on. That moment of seeing myself as part of a
social group with a history and shared oppression was the
same moment as seeing a system with a sexist ideology.
Though a partial realisation, it felt like, and of course
was, a real blow against the system and a step towards
freedom. The beginnings of political consciousness.

Had I been *colluding* in my oppression then, then, up
to that point? I had certainly been taking part in it - but
only because I had no weapons against it. Until that group
appeared, I struggled alone, understanding myself and my
needs in the system's terms, and perpetuating these terms
and the suffering.

The need for a total view

Obviously there are limitations to the kind of collective
consciousness raising and ideological struggle that were the
guts of the early stages of women's liberation (and still
an important part of its practice). When we discussed our
own experiences we located mainly one aspect of the capitalist system's reality - its sexism. When we went out and
took action against the system, we acted against its sexist
ideology - we covered adverts with stickers, we sat in on
male preserves where women were barred, etc. We were
more or less blind to our class position in a system which
was sexist. Our situations as middle class women made it

difficult for us to come to grips with the racist nature of capitalism. We could pinpoint a theory of sexism but not racism; in our early attempts to assess all these things and discover connections, we floundered and were constantly put down. We were still, unknowlingly, labouring away under various capitalist ideologies because we hadn't come to grips with the total, material and ideological reality of capitalism. And of course the women's movement alone cannot do this, nor can the male dominated left, nor the labour movement do it alone, nor the militant forces of black people but only a many sided revolutionary socialist grouping or movement which preserves the autonomy of its various forces, and organises at all levels in terms of ideological struggle and the development of new social relationships - a new balance and unity of our needs through struggle, which means the needs of the oppressed being set in total opposition against the needs of the oppressors to hang on to their power and keep us divided, materially, by sex, race, age, occupation etc.

While struggling through Louis Althusser's article on *Ideology and the State* I found myself thinking how much he was still blinded by being *inside* male supremacist ideology - so that he, of all famous theoreticians, while writing away about ideology, simply couldn't see the sexist aspects of capitalism and its ideology, because of his age, history and situation as a male intellectual. I wondered if he even noticed his housekeeper or wife come in and serve his tea while he was sitting perfecting his 'world view'.

Sexism and racism

One good point he makes, though, is that ideologies, like economic and political systems, don't just fall from the sky, of course, or emerge fully fledged from institutions. They arise at different times in history out of the struggle between different social groups and classes. I'll try and elaborate on this point. For instance, imagine the beginnings of the patriarchy, when the biological division between men and women hardened into a *division of labour*, and the control of production and ownership of resources (not just surplus produce, but women, children and slaves) settled in the hands of men. At this decisive moment, when one group appropriated social power and resources, the other group is denigrated as weak and inferior. So you have, in one move, a group with social power - *and* the ideology to justify having it. So much for the beginnings of male supremacism and private property. Similarly, with the uneven development of different civilisations and races, powerful nations took on weaker ones and made their first imperialist conquest, the ideological justification - the natural and absolute superiority of the white race - was born in the moment of victory (and elaborated and consolidated with every consequent one over the centuries, of course).

It's always the group with the economic, social and political power which has the ruling ideology - the ruled (if they want to stay alive and out of prison or whatever the repressive institutions are in any given society) have no option but to accept that particular explanation of reality. For women, say, who have to live out their women's lives, to have to live them by the idea that men are more important, men are more intelligent, men are more capable of running society etc. over centuries and to pass that on to our daughters (and sons), isn't *colluding* in our oppression, but simply the real and *total* nature of any oppression.

Men - the dream of power

I want to look now at how reactionary ideologies can flourish in groups which don't have the social power - for example, white oppressed men, men who don't own the means of production. It's necessary to see the *total* nature of their oppression, as well as the margin of privilege privilege they gained historically at the expense of women and black people and maintain now. (Simplistically - what strength and organisation male workers have developed against the ruling class has been won at the cost of increasing sexual division of labour, and thus women's toil and repression in the home, in childcare, and in the worst low paid work. And that very strength was a real push on the ruling class to find cheaper labour and higher profits elsewhere - the fruits of imperialism now, of course, benefit the whole working class materially). So much for the privilege. And the oppression? It has to be understood as total, and contradictory. There's a continual tension between the reality of boring, body grinding work for the bosses, bad food, consumer leisure, bad housing, sexual alientation - and the false ways of understanding that reality. Among these would be the ideology of equal opportunity and the freedom to compete (anyone can make it if they try), the James Bond sexual performance image, and the protective privatized bourgeois family dream. Apart from these obvious ruling class ideologies, there are other false ideas adding to this tension, new ideologies which reflect the extent to which the Trade Unions are beginning to be integrated, by way of the leadership, into the State, and become a part of the capitalist economic plan - for instance, the worker doing his bit for the national interest, the possibility 'honourable' bargains between (male) workers and bosses, workers' 'participation' in management, etc.

So you have the *fact* of individual powerlessness and deprivation in the face of a repressive system, coupled with the *dream* of individual male power and ownership (material and sexual - the Goods). This dream is worked out at the expense of women.

A mass of men living out this conflict provides the nourishment which the sexism and racism inherent in the structure of the system thrives on. (I am not at all saying that only men are racists - obviously all whites are - but just trying to get a grip on some connections between racism and sexism of ideologies). Racism or white supremacy, as the idea that whites are naturally superior, and the blacks naturally inferior, as I've said before, is the justification of the historically more powerful group for its privilege over the weaker, and as such is a constant among whites until black militancy challenges the status quo. But this ideology of superiority takes a battering when working class white people find the 'inferior' group vying for a place in the workforce or housing list. And in the frustration and anger of the contradiction I outlined above, the white supremacism which the ruling class can exude like a gentle rain from heaven, can explode into the bitterness of National Front type racism or fascism.

As long as oppressed white men retain their small privileges in helping to suppress women and black people, without being challenged, then the dream of masculinity and power will still keep men conservative, blinkered against the realities of their oppression under capitalism, and hide from them their unity of interests with all oppressed groups and in smashing it.

At this point I should say that there are some men's groups in existence which have started a kind of ideological struggle against this dream of masculinity. How far they will go towards refusing their real privilege and pledging their interests with women, I can't, of course, say. They have at least started to examine *more* aspects of the system (its sexism) and their oppression under it - more aspects of the class struggle, than has happened before with men.

'Private life' - the family and ideology

I'm going back a bit now to look at a couple of the ideological institutions which form us and which are crucial if we are to consent to the system and believe it's the only one which can satisfy our needs. To begin with the family - it's a crucial unit for servicing, production and consumption based on a division of labour which particularly suppresses women. And in the family, where men and women under pressure of material necessity, must meet and satisfy their needs for tenderness and sexuality and have their children - the sexist structure of society is embodied in miniature. This is where men and women live out their private lives and shield each other and their children from the realities, brutalities and possibilities of public life. This is where the child, under pressure of absolute economic dependence on her/his parents, receives its basic training, learns its needs and possibilities in terms of the system - that is, which of its needs are allowable and which of its possibilities are useful under capitalism.

In the micro-system of the family, then, the basis of the child's psycho-sexual formation is laid. The child's helplessness and complete dependence for existence on two adults is the first power structure it experiences, and in this state of vulnerability and anxiety, the child learns the power inequality between its father and mother, and the side of the fence it's destined to be on - its sex-role. As a way of understanding these realities, the child relies absolutely on the current ideologies her/his parents provide. The main ideologies which formed us as children in the West could be pinned down as competitive indiv-idualism and sexism. (Then there is the morality of 'clean-liness is next to godliness' and the work ethic. Both of these are very significant when it comes to any analysis of sexual oppression).

The restrictions the parents inflict on the child are mere-ly preparing her/him to consent to the material and sex-ual restrictions of her/his role in the outside world. The restrictions will be the restrictions of a particular class, as well as a particular sex role. The ideologies the parents use to answer the child's first demands for explanations of all this condition its thought processes and help it to *police* itself. And these idologies also vary to a degree with class. (Anyone who has gone from a working class childhood through 'classless' studenthood will remember the ferocious process of trying to throw off some aspects of ideology and adopt others more relevant to their new class position).

Everyone must have seen kids taking over this policing process in a big way and inflicting ideology on their young-er brothers and sisters - 'Little girls don't do that', etc. It's a pathetic and repulsive sight (and it happens every day). Is this kids colluding in their oppression? Well, no, once again, it's a matter of them *living* their oppression and making sure others don't escape theirs

Learning the commonplaces

Sometimes, of course, the family will begin to crumble under economic or sexual stresses - the well known 'prolem family' that housing departments talk of - and then its role will be bolstered by specific institutions such as Family Service Units, Marriage Guidance and so on, all with their dose of ideology. Or else the family will stay together as an economic unit, but perhaps has failed ideologically - the children haven't learnt to *police themselves*; Then a whole range of institutions come into play (!), from the gentle coercion of the Child Guidance Unit, to the Remedial School, Truant Officer, Juvenile Court, Borstal, Mental Hospital and prison. The class struggle goes on at all levels, from nudging your psyche into the correct shape, to direct repression.

For those of us whose families have trained us 'properly' so that we have a small prison in our heads (and for whom, therefore, real prisons aren't necessary), the school is the other major ideological institution we're subjected to. Here we sit and are force fed a mess of ideologies which explain and justify every aspect of capitalism - competitive individualism, private property, white supremacism, male supremacism, religion, morality, legality. And the more we're imprisoned and fragmented by these ideologies, the more easily we can sanction increasingly brutal repression in society. As the German comrades who set up Kommune 2 in 1967 wrote later :

As isolated individuals we were so restrained by fear of the landlady, the professor, the authorities, by the overwhelming power of the capitalist commonplaces that we let ourselves make accommodations with them. We knew that the mass murder in Vietnam belonged to these commo places.

Today, as I write, the army has set up a ring of tanks and roadblocks around Heathrow, and some dusty old ideologies are being dragged out from the wartime files of the Ministry of Defence and refurbished for 1974 - 'Military Aid in the defence of the civilian community'. Will people soon be seeing this as an acceptable face of Western 'democracy?

Classroom war

When we're at school, grading starts in earnest, and the ideology of competition helps us comply with it. We adjust our aspirations and capabilities to the various roles in the increasingly complex workforce that are offered to us. Teachers (not, of course, the radical ones who try to give their students the chance of developing their capacities for critical, independent thinking) and Careers Officers will have us sorted out according to sex, class background and degree of competitiveness before we know it. A trade, factory work, the army for working class boys, homecraft or typing for the working class girls, and for a lot of the rest, a promise of professionalism, a place in the new and expanding sectors of the workforce which carry out a more and more important supervisory or ideological role. The nursery nurses, Social and Community workers, primary and secondary teachers. Further Education teachers, psychiatrists, journalists, Television and film workers, Civil Service workers.

Luckily, training a mass of young people to be intellectual wage slaves and dealers in ideology, can backfire. In their prolonged apprenticeship in Universities and Colleges, they have little money and a lot of time to mull over the contradictions in their own lives and in the world generally, and a training in ideas can turn into a critical consciousness - a vital weapon against ideology. We've seen this happen massively in colleges throughout the advanced capitalist countries, and now, in the professions, more and more workers are refusing to be foiled by the bourgeois dreams held out to them, or at least are beginning to recognise that their privileges with regard to the rest of the working class are ambiguous and hardly worth preserving.

Ideology and consumer society

The ideology of individual freedom extends also to consumption. As the growth of capitalism depends more and more on everyone in the Western countries spending out on a vast range of commodities, and our needs are increasingly created by the advertising that the big capitalists bombard us with, this changing economic reality of capitalism is reflected in how we see ourselves today. As our material needs are artificially increased ('Simply *must* have that Biba's lurex jacket as well as the tweed one', Simply must fuck with that beautiful girl/guy as well as the old lady/old man'), so the ideology of *freedom to chose* from a wide range of commodities gets stronger and stronger. Of course we think we're free to buy or not buy - most people really believe that they're immune to advertising - but the reality is that we are not free *not to want* these commodities. The ideology of sexual freedom can be seen in this context as the way we understand our increasing needs to consume more, and better sexual objects.

Try on your love like a new dress
The fit and the cut, your friends to impress
Try on your smile, square on your face
Showing affection should be no disgrace. (Roxy Music)

70

Since sex (particularly women's sexuality) has been used tirelessly to sell all commodities to all of us (men *and* women), women have become more and more objectified, more and more confused about their sexuality. Are we to offer ourselves up passively to every man as objects to be consumed and compete with each other to be the most delectable object? Are we sexual consumers as Cosmopolitan would have us be, or are we to pledge ourselves to one man and his children in marriage and motherhood?

Having to grapple constantly with the force of these conflicting ideas of ourselves was certainly one impetus behind the realisations of the first women's liberation groups. And consider the pressures that maintaining the family now means to its members when men, forced by the economic structure to support dependent wives and children, forced by one set of ideologies to understand themselves in terms of 'good husband', 'protector and provider', are also stimulated constantly by the promise of sexual consumption, and the tantalising ideology of sexual freedom. We should examine how different classes try to reconcile these contradictory needs and warring ideologies - for instance, wife-swapping, as an upper working class or petty bourgeois practice, or the showing of home 'blue' movies among young working class couples. These are different ways in which, in my experience, people may be trying to do this. But obviously it needs more people's assessment to get a clear picture.

Our freedom to buy is all very well when capitalism is booming, but at a time like the present economic crisis, when the State has to move in with hob nailed boots to hold wages (our buying power) down so that the profits 'necessary for investment' can be kept up, and when simultaneously the price of all commodities soars, then we're faced with the State forcibly controlling the needs and desires that capitalism has developed in everyone over the last decade, and contradicting the ideologies that everyone has lived by, and that a whole generation has grown up with. The mass of people are increasingly able to see that the ideology of individual freedom, competition and plenty is a fraud - and that, in reality, they are manipulated according to the profit needs of the capitalists' or the economic strictures of the State. Especially for the generation which has no memory of the war, the ideology of 'tighten your belts in the National Interest' has worn dangerously thin this time.

Postscript

I hope that this article, however undisciplined and breathless, will be useful in stimulating more thoughts and discussions about the totality *of the system we live under which is, after all, no less than Capitalism, Imperialism, the Patriarchy. And about the depth and diversity of the contradictions people suffer living out their daily lives, about the many different ways people can begin to understand the dimensions of their oppression and mount a many sided passionate and rational opposition to it.*

Alison Fell
1974

Amended version of an article which first appeared in RED RAG, No. 6.

Cultural Influences on Female Sexuality

In the current debate about women's role in society, there are two opposing views. According to the first, men and women are fundamentally different; according to the second, men and women are fundamentally the same. Few people, however, would argue, that in terms of their sexuality, men and women are really equivalent.

The belief that 'natural' differences exist is a very common one. How are male and female sexuality thought to differ? In the first place, men are considered sexually aggressive, women sexually passive. Males initiate sexual contact, asking females to go to bed with them or marry them. Only males can, legally speaking, be capable of rape. Neither legally nor psychologically can women be capable of raping men, and this psychological passivity extends into the whole structure of their sexual relationships.

If men are thought to be sexually aggressive, women are considered sexually receptive. The vagina is simply there, waiting for the penis. Women are simply there, dependent, passive and submissive, waiting for men. In sexual intercourse itself, female sexuality means slow arousal and infrequent orgasmic satisfaction. Men, on the other hand, are easily and quickly aroused, and orgasm for them is a virtually automatic event.

Much of the assumed difference between their sexual attitudes and behaviour can be summed up by saying that men are thought to have a much stronger sex drive. Sex is something they find difficult to resist - so they begin masturbation earlier and practice it more, commit adultery more, indulge in a greater variety of sexual practices (including those society defines as perversions), as well as being

73

more demanding and aggressive in normal marital relationships.

To a considerable extent, these differences in sexuality represent stereotypes of behaviour which we consciously or unconsciously follow. Such stereotypes have an influence because they define the 'proper' way for people to behave, and what is 'proper' and 'normal' in a society is often thought to be 'natural' as well. But are these apparent differences in the sexuality of men and women in fact natural at all?

On a biological level men and women are much more alike than different. The genitals of both sexes emerge from the same structure in the foetus - a structure which is basically female. The penis and the clitoris both develop from a sexually undifferentiated 'genital tubercle'; the scrotum and the labia develop from the skin around the urogenital opening in the foetus; the ovaries and the testicles develop from the same rudimentary material which is sexually undifferentiated at first. The factor which determines whether genital development will be male or female is the chromosomal sex of the baby, which is fixed at the moment of conception. After about seven weeks of prenatal life, the male chromosomal make-up, XY, causes hormone production in the male foetus, and its urinary and genital system develop in the characteristically male way.

These elementary facts are very important in understanding just *how* male and female resemble each other. Far from being an inferior version of the penis (a 'stunted' penis, said Freud), the clitoris is an exact replica of it. Both penis and clitoris have a shaft and a glans (head), which is particularly sensitive to sexual stimulation, and the the same set of muscles capable of responding to sexual excitement in the same way. The penis has two roots known as 'crura', which become engorged with blood and contribute to the expanded size of the penis during sexual excitement, and the clitoris has these two roots, the same size in the female as they are in the male. The network of veins and nerves with which the clitoris is connected is at least as large and probably larger than the corresponding network in the male, so that the physiological capacity of the female to respond sexually is at least as great as the male's.

For these reasons, the discrepancy in size between penis and clitoris is hardly an explanation of the difference in the sexual response of male and female. Hormonal factors do not offer much of an explanation either. Both sexes produce male and female hormones. It is the male hormone which is associated with the sex drive, but women produce around two thirds as much of this as men. In any case, many studies have shown that psychological factors are much more important than the role of the hormone in determining sexual attitudes and behaviour.

When we look at the physiology of sexual response, there is again nothing which provides a basis to the belief in the 'natural' difference between the sexuality of male and female. As William Masters and Virginia Johnson have shown in their exhaustive study of *Human Sexual Response*, the body responses of male and female, *when sexually excited*, are virtually identical. Sexual tension in both men and women develops in four phases, which Masters and Johnson call the excitement phase, the plateau phase, the orgasmic phase and the resolution phase. Table I shows the general body reactions of male and female in all four phases.

The first specifically genital response to sexual excitement is erection in the male - taking between three and eight seconds - and vaginal lubrication in the female, which becomes established in between five and fifteen seconds. In the second, plateau, phase, there is extensive vasocongestion (filling of the blood vessels) in the pelvic organs and throughout the body in both sexes. At this stage, neither male nor female is able to respond effectively to minor non non-sexual stimuli. In the orgasmic phase, orgasm is marked by about eight to ten contractions per second in the relevant organs of male and female, though the female's may go on for longer. In the final phase, signs of sex tension disappear - slowly if the ascent to orgasm was gradual, quickly if the ascent was rapid. This process is again

HOW WOMEN AND MEN RESPOND TO SEXUAL AROUSAL

WOMEN	MEN
Excitement phase	
nipple erection	nipple erection (30%)
sexual flush (25%)	
Plateau phase	
sexual flush (75%)	sexual flush (25%)
carpopedal spasm	carpopedal spasm
general muscle tension	general muscle tension
rapid breathing	rapid breathing
heart rate 100 - 160 beats a minute	heart rate 100 - 160 beats a minute
Orgasmic phase	
specific muscle contractions	specific muscle contractions
rapid breathing	rapid breathing
heart rate 110 - 180 beats a minute	heart rate 100 - 180 beats a minute
Resolution phase	
sweating (30-40%)	sweating (30-40%)
rapid breathing	rapid breathing
heart rate 150 - 180 beats a minute	heart rate 150 - 180 beats a minute

identical in both male and female.

Masters and Johnson emphasise that the development of sexual tension in male and female follows the same course irrespective of whether the cause of stimulation is intercourse, masturbation or fantasy. They also show definitively that women only have *one* sort of orgasm - not two as Freud and others were convinced they did. *Female orgasm is essentially clitoral.* Another interesting finding is that sexual excitement which does not resolve in orgasm is physiologically just as frustrating for the female as for the male. One female studied by Masters and Johnson was exposed to multiple sequences of intercourse for six and a half hours without orgasm. During this time her pelvic organs were grossly enlarged and congested; she could not sleep and complained of pressure, cramp, pain and back-ache. At the end of six hours, she masturbated to orgasm. Pelvic vasocongestion disappeared completely within ten minutes.

In the light of these facts, how can the belief in differences between male and female sexuality be explained? There *are*, of course, clear and well documented disparities between the sexual responses of male and female *in our society.* Perhaps the most prominent of these is the difficulty women have in reaching orgasm during sexual intercourse. Estimates of total inability to reach orgasm in intercourse vary from 10% to nearly 30% of married women. Of 339 women treated by Masters and Johnson for sexual dysfunction, 88% suffered from the inability to reach orgasm in intercourse.

Why does this difficulty exist on such a scale? Two answers suggest themselves. Firstly, the relative infrequency of orgasm in women could be accounted for by the behaviour of their male partners in intercourse. Secondly, cultural factors could account for the 'blocking' of the orgasmic response in women.

In practice, both answers seem likely. Not only do we now know (thanks to Masters and Johnson) that the physiology and anatomy of sexual response is more or less identical in male and female, but we also know that masturbation is a much surer and speedier route to orgasm in the female than is intercourse. Kinsey asked 2,114 females how long they took to achieve orgasm in masturbation. About half took between one and three minutes, a quarter took four to five minutes and only 12% took more than ten minutes (some of these deliberately prolonged the time taken). The average man, like the average woman, can reach orgasm by masturbation in between one and three minutes. But whereas three quarters of males ejaculate within ten minutes of beginning intercourse, the time women take to reach orgasm in intercourse is usually considerably longer. Complete failure to achieve orgasm is also far more common for women in intercourse than it is in masturbation.

Clearly, therefore, orgasm difficulty experienced by women in intercourse has something to do with the sexual techniques used. The most common position used in intercourse - man on top of woman (and Kinsey estimated that 70% of American couples never used any other) - does not allow direct stimulation of the clitoris by the penis, although secondary stimulation does occur. Only the female superior (woman on top) and lateral (side by side) positions permit primary stimulation of the clitoris, with the female superior position being by far the best from this point of view.

No doubt in partial compensation for the inadequacies of the man on top position, marriage manuals advocate direct stimulation of the clitoris by the male before intercourse begins.

It seems, therefore, that some of the difficulty found by women in achieving orgasm during intercourse may be due to this conspiracy of ignorance against her. Sometimes the ignorance is complete, and men simply do not know enough about the female anatomy to locate or understand the function of the clitoris. Sadly, such ignorance may even extend to women themselves. To understand why this occurs, we have to go back to the beginning, and look at the way female sexuality is defined in our culture. As Simone de Beauvoir opens her account of women's situation in *The Second Sex:* 'One is not born, but rather becomes, a woman'.

Little girls are taught to sit with their legs together, little boys are allowed to sit with their legs apart. There is something inevitable about the small boy's manipulation of his penis, but something instantly reprehensible about the little girls exploitation of her clitoral/vaginal area as a source of pleasure. In adolescence, the sexual exploits of the male are ignored rather than forbidden by parents whereas those of the female are seen, and prohibited, as sinful promiscuity. A female who is a virgin on her wedding night is admired, but a male who retains his virginity is mocked. A man proves his masculinity by going to bed with women, a woman proves her femininity by *not* going to bed with men. Masculinity equals sexuality, whereas femininity is opposed to it. A man's sexual appetite is the core of his masculine role, but an adult woman with an appetite for sex is a 'bad' (unfeminine) woman.

Masters and Johnson describe one man whose inability to ejaculate in his wife's vagina was due to his disapproval of her multiple orgasms. He thought her one previous sexual experience had left a scar on her character, and perceiving her as 'bad', he was unable to let himself go inside her.

If men think of active sexuality in women as evil, then so do many women. A study by Eustace Chesser of sexual, marital and family relationships in a sample of 6,251 women found that over half the women had received the impression from their mothers that sex was something unpleasant, which women had to put up with. Those who got the opposite impression were much more likely to experience orgasm, and find sex generally satisfying (and also to have happier marriages).

Under these cultural conditions it is very difficult indeed for a woman to become aware of the fact that she possesses a sexual organ - the clitoris - and a physiological capacity for sexual excitement and orgasm which is equivalent to the male's. It is difficult for her to know her own body, and to have confidence in telling her lover

79

what she would like him to do to it. Sexual response to orgasm is the physiological capacity of most, if not all, women, but its achievement in our culture is conditional on the acceptance by women of their own sexuality.

Another factor which handicaps female sexuality is the kind of personality which our culture considers appropriate in females. Emotional instability and sensitivity, conformity, and lack of self confidence are all personality traits which are thought peculiarly feminine, and are possessed by many women. All these traits are also associated with a low capacity for orgams, presumably because they make self-assertion in the sexual act much less likely. Endorsing this association between personality and sexuality is the fact that the same relationship exists for men. Men with these personality traits tend to suffer from, or fear, impotence.

The ability to respond sexually is partly a function of experience for men as well as women. Cultural repression of female sexuality acts to delay the onset of sexual experience for women, thus providing another barrier to sexual equality. Premarital intercourse is rarer in girls than in boys - so is masturbation. During adolescence, masturbation in boys is practically universal, but, according to Kinsey, only 28% of 15 year old girls masturbated. However 40% of females aged up to 20 and 62% of those aged up to 40 had masturbated in Kinsey's survey. These figures demonstrate the increase in sexual activity which occurs with experience. For women, masturbation increases with marriage, with the rising age of the husband, and, notably, with divorce or widowhood.

The fact that women's sexual activity increases markedly with marriage is thus a reflection of its repression and inhibition before marriage.

During adolescence and early adulthood, marriage has a 'displacement' function in the development of female sexuality. While young men are concerned to achieve sexual success with girls, the young girl dreams of marriage, two children, a house, and all the trappings of domesticity. It is primarily with these goal in mind that she is allowed to show an interest in men and in sex.

This is one basic difference between masculine and feminine roles in our culture. While men have careers, women get married. More women are employed outside the home these days, but very few are employed continuously without a break for having and bringing up children. For women, the housewife, wife and mother role remains the most important one. Thus, differences in male and female sexuality in our society are associated with differences between their roles *generally*. Other cultures niether define the social and economic roles of the sexes in the same differentiated way as we do, nor do they necessarily perceive male and female sexuality as opposed and different.

For example, in one south-west Pacific society, it is men, not women, who are considered to need protection against the possibility of sexual attack. Cultivation of physical beauty is a male concern - only men wear flowers in their hair and scented leaves tucked in their belts to make them attractive. When fully adorned, young men are thought so irresistible to women that they run the risk of being seduced if allowed out on their own.

In their society, sex is an ordinary topic of daily conversation. Sexual intercourse is assumed to be intensely pleasurable, and deprivation harmful, for both men and women. When first married, husband and wife are reported to have intercourse twice daily. This consists of an extended period of foreplay, during which both partners stimulate each other's genitals, and a short period of copulation lasting 15 to 30 seconds which culminates in simultaneous orgasm for husband and wife. It is believed that once stimulated during foreplay, neither male or female can fail to achieve orgasm - women unable to have orgasm are unheard of. Either partner can terminate the marriage if sexual intercourse is infrequent - infrequency meaning about once every ten days. Between puberty and marriage both males and females are urged to masturbate to relieve sexual tensions, which are thought to be just as much of a problem for women as for men.

Clearly this is one culture which allows the female to discover and exploit her sexual capacity to the full. Malinowski, in his famous study of the Trobriand Islanders, reported a similar equality between the sexual attitudes and behaviour of male and female. Trobriand culture allows sexual behaviour throughout childhood and adolescence, so that children of four and five imitate intercourse, and girls at six or eight are having intercourse with penetration. Trobriand positions for intercourse omit the usual man-on-top-of-woman position used by Europeans - which they dislike because it restricts the activity of the woman in intercourse. (Not surprisingly, they consider that European men are inept lovers because they use this position, and ejaculate too quickly.)

The most usual position for Trobrianders is for the man to squat in front of the woman, pulling her towards him and, and, when orgasm is approaching, raising her body towards his. The expression used for orgasm means 'the seminal fluid discharge' and is used of either sex indiscriminately. (It also covers nocturnal emissions and female glandular secretions.) Masturbation is regarded as the practice of an idiot - in other words, someone who is incapable of having heterosexual intercourse.

Overall, Trobriander women appeared to Malinowski to be much more assertive and sexually aggressive than women in his own culture, and frequently took the initiative in sexual relationships. It is perhaps no accident that a society where there is a great deal of *practical* equality between men and women also recognises the disadvantages of the male superior position for intercourse. By contrast, our own society is still a patriarchal one, and where male dominance outside the bedroom is the rule, male dominance within it is more easily expressed in the male superior position.

Comparing sexuality generally in the two cultures, Malinowski believed that the Trobriander threshold of arousal was much higher than ours, with much more sexual stimulation needed to produce orgasm. The necessity for prolonged foreplay is commonly stressed as an exclusively feminine sexual need in our culture. In the Trobriander case, its importance to both men and women appears to derive from their identical conditioning in sexual behaviour throughout pre-adult life.

Many other cultures, like the Trobriander, recognise the right and ability of women to reach orgasm in intercourse, and the difficulty of achieving it in certain positions. Crow Indian women expect orgasm every time and are reported to obtain it usually by sitting on top of the man - if the man is on top of the woman they say he will ejaculate too soon. On many of the Caroline Islands, women are expected to have orgasm regularly in intercourse. If the man reaches a climax before his partner, she laughs at him and asks him to try again, and here also the best position is thought to be the female superior one.

Anthropology is full of examples of cultures which define sexuality differently. These examples show human sexuality to be culturally variable in the form it takes, rather than being fixed by nature or biology. So, although it can be said that female sexuality is culturally influenced in our own society, male sexuality undoubtedly is too. There are societies, like the Arapesh of New Guinea, which play down the aggressive and demanding element in sexuality for the male as well as for the female. The Arapesh develop tenderness and parental feelings in both male and female, devaluing the function of sex as a means of individual satisfaction. Neither men nor women are considered to have spontaneous sexual urges - sex exists for procreation, and childrearing is the main work for adults of both sexes. Men do not regard women as sexual objects, and parents do not fear that adolescents left to their own devices will indulge in intercourse.

The sexual role of the Arapesh male would seem very strange indeed to the male in industrial society. One of the most psychologically crippling disabilities from which the contemporary man can suffer is impotence - the inability to get or sustain an erection. The measure of his sexual success, of his success as a man, is the quality of his erection. The corresponding disability for the modern woman is her inability to achieve orgasm. Whilst 50 years ago it was thought improper for women to have orgasms or be sexually responsive in any way, now there is something wrong with a woman who is persistently non-orgasmic. Both these dysfunctions - impotence in the male and lack of orgasm in the female - are probably predictable reactions to the 'double bind' situation in which individuals today are placed. E.g., on the one hand, society expects them to make a sexual success of their lives but, on the other, sex is treated as something inestimably private and very little education or advice is offered to young people embarking on sexual relationships. The knowledge of how to make love is *not* instinctual - otherwise cases of infertility due to ignorance of the need for penetration in intercourse would not still occur.

Yet the female who cannot achieve orgasm suffers from a far more severe and deep-rooted form of sexual dysfunction than any that befalls the male. Masters and Johnson in their study of *Human Sexual Inadequacy* point to 'sociocultural deprivation' as the basic cause of this disability. Cultural influence, they say, makes women adapt, sublimate, inhibit and distort their natural capacity to function sexually, in the interests of fulfilling their culturally assigned passive, dependent (and inherently non-sexual) feminine role. *The experience of orgasm is resisted because women are still led to reject their sexual identity.* The treatment Masters and Johnson recommend for lack of orgasm hinges on the theme of telling women that the penis is theirs to play with, just as men have for centuries believed the vagina exists for them to use as they wish.

Masters and Johnson suggest, by way of explanation, that the repression of female sexuality is culturally induced (in a male-oriented society) to neutralise the physiological superiority that females undoubtedly possess in this respect. It is the female, not the male, who possesses an organ - the clitoris - whose sole function is sexual pleasure. In addition, multiple orgasms i.e. many successive orgasms in a short space of time, is a physiological capacity which only females have. Both these capacities quite possibly represent threats to the male, conditioned as he is by the need to feel dominant and superior. They also represent threats to the female herself, conditioned as *she* is by the culturally induced need to deny her sexuality.

Ann Oakley

First published in FORUM, Vol. 5 No. 6, 1973

The Suppressed Power of Female Sexuality

Sexuality, according to Reich, is life energy. It is, he says, *sexual energy which governs the structure of human feeling and thinking*. And it is for this reason that sexuality must be ruthlessly repressed if people's minds and feelings are to succumb without resistance to an authoritarian social order: If this is true of people in general, it is doubly true of women. It has been crucial, in creating the docile and submissive females required by our male society, to suppress and deny the existence of women's powerful sexuality. This has been achieved in a number of ways, from the propagation of myths purporting women's relative asexuality, to the denial of our right to control our own bodies. The reason for this is political. Its aim is to keep us 'in our place', to ensure our subservience, to render impossible our rebellion. But women are rebelling, and are reclaiming the control and ownership of their own bodies. To achieve fully this aim we must not only regain control of our fertility, we must also regain the right to our own sexuality, to use and express as *we* see fit. For too long women's 'life energy' has been suppressed or allowed only in the service of others. It is time we reclaimed it.

The colonization of women's sexuality

For centuries women have been made the sexual property of men. Our bodies have been taken from us and their ownership given either to an individual man or collectively to the political class of men. Barbara Burris writes:

Women, set apart by physical differences between them and men, were the first colonized group .... Our bodies were first turned into the property of the males. Men considered female bodies as territory over which they fought for absolute control.

Our bodies are our territory, our sexuality and fertility, our raw materials. In our male imperialist culture both are systematically exploited.

One of the effects of this colonization has been to cut women off from the inner core of their own sexuality. Women have a natural capacity for sexuality far in excess of that of men (see later). But thousands of years of patriarchal conditioning and exploitation has robbed us of our sexual potential and deceived us about the true nature of our sexuality. Women are forbidden to own and use their sexuality for *themselves*, as a means of personal self-expression. Our authentic sexuality has been taken from us, subjected to a process of distortion and mutilation, and then returned to us as a passive submissiveness which is held up as 'true' female sexuality.

In making the woman an object of sexual pleasure for men, patriarchal society defines her as a sexual object for herself. And like all colonized people she incorporates the definitions of the dominant culture. Her own experience and pleasure in sexuality therefore will be derived primarily from the effect she has on others rather than concern with her own subjective desires and experiences. It is through *experiencing* ourselves primarily as objects in the lives of others that we have lost touch with our own subjective sexuality

The distortion of female sexuality is achieved through defining it exclusively in terms of its complementarity to men's, and never in its own right. Male sexuality is defined as the 'given' and female sexuality is then defined in relation to it. Anything which does not correspond with this is then dismissed as either perverted or sick. Because men have defined themselves as sexually active, dominant, and sadistic, they have in turn defined women as sexually passive, submissive and masochistic. At no time have women been allowed to define their own sexuality. Anna Koedt has referred to this as the myth of the invisible woman.

One of the elements of male chauvinism is the refusal or inability to see women as total, separate human beings. Rather, men have chosen to define women only in terms of how they benefitted men's lives. Sexually, a woman was not seen as an individual wanting to share equally in the sexual act, any more than she was seen as a person with independent desires when she did anything else in society. Thus, it was easy to make up what was convenient about women; for on top of that, society has been a function of male interests, and women were not organised to form even a vocal opposition to the male experts.

And so women's intrinsic sexuality is suppressed and replaced instead with a counterfeit male ideal of what he would like her to be. This stereotype of the compliant, passive female is so ingrained in our male culture, that in spite of considerable evidence to the contary, it continues to be accepted, by and large, by both sexes.

Women's sexual potential

In 1966, Masters and Johnson published the findings of their eleven year study on human sexual physiology. Their findings have been particularly significant for women and have exploded many myths, in particular the myth of the vaginal orgasm. However what is particularly relevant to this paper is their discovery of the vastly superior sexual capacity of women to that of men. After studying 7,500 female sexual responses they concluded that multiple orgasm was the biological norm for most average females, and that their capacity to go on having orgasms was only terminated by physical exhaustion.

The average female with optimal arousal will usually be satisfied with 3-5 manually induced orgasms; whereas mechanical stimulation, as with the electric vibrator, is less tiring and induces her to go on to long stimulative sessions

*of an hour or more during which she may have 20 to 50
consecutive orgasms. She will only stop when totally exhausted.*   (Masters and Johnson)

It was also found that, in general, 'a woman's orgasm
lasts about twice as long as a man's' in terms of effective
contractions. Although the overall duration may be the
same in men there are three to four very strong contractions followed by less intense ones. In women there are
eight to fifteen contractions of which the first five to six
or more are the most intense. In an analysis of the Masters and Johnson findings, Mary Sherfey comments upon
women she has encountered in clinical practice who,
through the use of an electric vibrator have also achieved
up to fifty orgasms in a single session. She says that she
had considered them 'cases of nymphomania without promiscuity', and that although that label may be correct from
the standpoint of our cultural norm, '...from the standpoint of normal physiological functioning, these women exhibit a healthy, uninhibited sexuality - *and the number of
orgasms attained are a measure of the human female's orgasmic potentiality.*' She comes to the conclusion that most
women are completely unaware of their own orgasmic
capacity.

'A woman,' quotes Masters 'will usually *be satisfied with
3-5 orgasms...'. I believe it would rarely be said, 'A man
will usually be satisfied with three to five ejaculations.'
the man* is *satisfied. The woman* usually wills *herself to
be satisfied because she is simply unaware of the extant
of her orgasmic capacity. However, I predict that this hypo-
thesis will come as no great shock to many women who
consciously realise, or intuitively sense, their lack of
satiation.*   (Sherfey)

Much of the mystification surrounding female sexuality has
come from our male culture's virtual denial of the existence of the clitoris, or at best dismissing it as unimportant
or immature. But in actual fact, all female orgasms are
located in the clitoris, and it is no accident that male
society did not wish this independent organ of female sex-

ual pleasure to be recognised or acknowledged. In fact the sole function of the clitoris is that of sexual pleasure. The penis on the other hand, has the dual function of urination and the transmission of semen. The clitoris is the *only* human organ solely designed for sexual pleasure and as Mary Sherfey comments 'our myth of the female's relative asexuality is a biological absurdity.'

The suppression of female sexuality

With such a tremendous sexual drive and capacity, it is extraordinary that our male culture has been able so to distort the true nature of female sexuality, that the woman herself has been largely unaware of this fundamental biological capacity within her. It is interesting therefore to consider some of the ways in which this has been achieved. Firstly, one of the most common physical components which stands in the way of full female sexual satisfaction is the male's inability to delay his ejaculation long enough for the woman to attain even one orgasm during intercourse. Premature ejaculation is the most common sexual dysfunction in men and is considered to affect millions of men and their wives. (Belliveau & Richter). The extent of this problem can be seen in the fact that 'according to Kinsey three-quarters of the average male population reach orgasm within two minutes.' Unlike females, who have an unlimited capacity for sexual activity which ceases only when physical exhaustion intervenes, men have a strictly limited sexual capacity, and having once ejaculated, are rarely able to achieve another erection without at least some interval of time. In view of this, the woman in such circumstances never has an opportunity to get in touch with her greater sexual capacity, because the whole exchange is over before she has had a chance to begin.

Fifteen to twenty per cent of all [American] women have never had an orgasm. About fifty per cent can reach an orgasm on a 'now and then' basis, meaning that they experience full culmination about one sex act out of three. Thirty to thirty five per cent of American wives say that they 'usually' reach orgams, meaning that they get there two out of three times or thereabouts. Only a very few women can claim that they have an orgasm every time they take part in sexual activities (Woodward).

If a woman has never experienced sexual excitement or climax, she can come to believe that it is she who is lacking in sexuality and will see herself as asexual. This view is generally confirmed by men who ejaculate prematurely, as they often tend to see the fault as their wives' lack of sexuality and never consider that the problem is their own sexual incompetence. These men also put a low evaluation on female satisfaction and see sexuality mainly as a male prerogative, with their wives fulfilling the role of 'sexual receptacles who are not supposed to have or to express sexual feelings of their own'. *(Belliveau & Richter).* Many women, whose husbands were successfully treated for preature ejaculation, found that they attained orgasm for the first time in their lives. It is also worth mentioining that male problems of premature ejaculation are greatly increased by the male superior coital position (i.e. the man on top). It is probably no coincidence that men who hold a derogatory attitude to women prefer to maintain the male superior position, and thereby further decrease the woman's chances of attaining full sexual satisfaction.

Secondly, the male culture itself forbids the woman to 'accept herself honourably as a sexual being'. It decrees that the female requires special permission for the expression of her sexuality. She is conditioned in her formative years to dissemble 'much of her developing functional sexuality in response to societal requirements for a 'good girl' facade'. She is allowed to retain only the 'symbolic romanticism which usually accompanies these sexual feelings'. It is only in specifically prescribed conditions that her inherent sexuality is allowed to emerge, namely when it is accompanied by strong personal commitment, and is directed solely towards one man. 'These studies which demonstrated the sexual capacity of women, added to Masters and Johnsons contact with women in treatment of sexual problems have shown them clearly the role of our

91

culture in inhibiting female sexuality'. *(Belliveau & Richter)*.

Thirdly, the male culture not only distorts female sexuality to the point of absurdity, it then draws up a moral code based upon that distortion. This has come to be known as the double standard , that is, a moral code 'which has offered a set of permissive attitudes for men and another set of restrictive ones for women.' The double standard was particularly blatant in the Victorian era, but Geoffrey Gorer, writing in 1971, in his study of *Sex and Marriage in England Today*, comments that it still has fairly wide currency. The extent to which women have incorporated these distortions can be seen when he concludes that 'it is predominantly women who maintain this double standard'.

Lastly, if female sexuality should survive the problems of premature ejaculation, the lack of societal permission for its expression, and the unjust condemnation of the double standard, it is then considered indecent. In the last century 'if a woman showed an active interest in sex, it was thought she had become depraved'. *(Rover)* Even as late as 1955 when Gorer undertook his study *Exploring English Character*, he was not allowed to ask concrete questions about female orgasm because 'the editors thought that it might cause unnecessary offence, and would anyhow be too embarrassing for the young women coding the questionnaires!' The assumption being, presumably, that female sexuality is offensive.

If in spite of all this a woman refuses to accept her subservient sexual role, external enforcement is resorted to, including the threat of physical sexual violence.

...it is interesting to see the continued recurrence, in conversation about a snobbish or aloof woman, of the phrase, 'She ought to be raped', as if this were the ultimate humiliation that would bring her to her (psychological) knees and thus allow the man to feel superior. (Maslow)

But probably the most effective form of external control of female sexuality is our male society's refusal to allow women control of their own fertility. The fear of pregnancy has always been used to deter women from engaging in sexual activity not sanctioned by society. At the same time pregnancy has also been used as an excellent way of keeping woman 'in her place'. As Nietzche so aptly put it, woman is 'a problem solved by pregnancy'. *(Sullerot)* And the capacity to fertilize therefore is one of the most prized possessions in the male's armoury of coercive weapons against the female. It serves to reassure him of his power over her.

Studies in the US of lower class (male) adolescents show a clear relationship between an assessment of their own masculine potency and getting a girl pregnant. The boys say quite openly that they 'like to ride bare-back and get a girl pregnant'. (Ciba)

If they are prevented from doing this by the girls' use of contraceptives, they find the situation almost intolerable. Dr. Derek Miller of the University of Michigan Medical Centre claims that 'late adolescent males may find it almost intolerable to feel their fertility is absolutely controlled by women. Many such men report intercourse as being more enjoyable when their partner discontinues the contraceptive pill. Others are furious when a girl goes on or off the pill *without permission.'* (my emphasis). *(Guardian)*. For the woman who lived before the advent of the pill, there was no protection from the ribaldry of the males over her wretched subjection. Laurence Housman wrote of a scene he witnessed 'on the borders of one of our great London Parks'.

A poor working woman, about to become a mother, was on her way home when unexpectedly her pains overtook her, and she could go no further. A policeman came to her aid, and went to find a conveyance; and while she waited a crowd gathered, men and boys; and as they watched her they laughed and made jokes. She was a symbol to them of what sex meant; some man had given her her lesson, and now she was learning it; and to their minds

93

it was a highly satisfactory spectacle. *(my emphasis)* (Rover). She was a symbol to them of what sex meant; male dominance-female subjection. It meant sexual intercourse as an exercise in power; male power-female powerlessness. But we now know that women are not powerless and that their sexual capacity is far greater than men's. It is time for a redefinition of sexuality.

Social control

In spite of all the evidence to the contrary, the myths about female sexuality continue to flourish. Susan Lydon in her article *The Politics of Orgasm* says,

To anyone acquainted with the body of existing knowledge of feminine sexuality, the Masters and Johnson findings were truly revolutionary and liberating in the extent to which they demolished the established myths. Yet four years after the study was published, it seems hardly to have made much of an impact at all. Certainly it is not for lack of information that the myths persist; Human Sexual Response, despite its weighty scientific language, was an immediate best-seller, and popular paperbacks explicated it to millions of people in simpler language and at a cheaper price. The mythology remains intact because a male dominated culture has a vested interest in its continuance.

Mary Sherfey argues that it took 5,000 years or longer for the subjection of women to take place. 'All relevant data from the 12,000 to 8,000 B C period indicate that pre-civilized woman enjoyed full sexual freedom and was often totally incapable of controlling her sexual drive'. In order to establish a patriarchal social system based on property ownership and inheritance women's sexuality had to be crushed. 'With the rise of settled agriculture economies, man's territorialism became expressed in property rights and kinship laws. Large families of known parentage were mandatory and could not evolve until the inordinate sexual demands of women were curbed' *(Sherfey)*. And this suppression has continued ever since, reaching perhaps its highest point during the last century, when women were viewed merely as child bearing machines, and all sexual drive was claimed to be male.

By robbing women of their sexuality, male society has created a certain kind of 'female' personality. Cut off from our strong sexual energy we are also cut off from, as Reich puts it, our 'life energy'. We become submissive, compliant, unsure of ourselves. We lack confidence and we rely on men to make the rules and tell us what we have to do. Without our sexuality, our self esteem is low. Maslow has found that sexual behaviour and attitudes are much more closely related to feelings of high self esteem than to 'sheer sexual drive'. It seems that a vicious circle is set up - robbing us of our sexuality diminishes our self esteem, and low self esteem diminishes our sexual drive. Kept permanently on the horns of this dilemma, women remain inactive, unsure of themselves, and therefore easily socially controlled (i.e. oppressed). To break out of this dilemma, we need to create a new 'female' personality, in which our powerful sexuality is fully integrated. This would mean not only reclaiming our sexual drive, but also re-discovering our assertiveness, our self confidence and our personal autonomy. Through this re-making of our female personalities we would be propelled into re-making our 'female place in the world'. Studies of the psychological make-up of persons who become involved in social action have found that the activist were those whose behaviour and attitudes were governed by feelings of 'inner-directed-ness' and personal autonomy *(Wilcox)*. Denying women their full sexual autonomy is one of the ways in which male society ensures that women experience themselves as powerless and unable therefore to change the conditions of their lives.

The power of female sexuality

Faced with the threat of more and more women demanding their sexual rights, our male society has tried to absorb and neutralise that threat. It has appeared to accept the demand as legitimate and allow women more apparent sexual freedom but *only* while our sexuality remains firmly within the original male definition. The only freedom we have been allowed is the freedom to make ourselves more readily available sexual objects. 'Young women by the score still limp away bruised in spirit from sexual encounters they initiate under the banner of sexual freedom, but with an archaic stance of 'Take me' that acknowledges the male as actor and themselves as objects.' (*Rossi*). To engage in more sexuality within the framework of a male definition, can only further reduce our self esteem, and thereby trap us ever more firmly in our powerless female role. The way out of this is to find ways in which sexual involvement no longer *reduces* our self esteem but increases it. Freedom of choice and complete sexual autonomy must be basic prerequisites of any attempted redefinition.

We must come to see quite clearly that 'women's sexuality has been suppressed in the name of monogamy at the service of a man-centred civilisation'. (*Rossi*) We must understand the connection between suppressed sexuality and social powerlessness.

When we reclaim our sexuality we will have reclaimed our belief in ourselves as women. When this intense and powerful part of our nature is no longer suppressed we will refuse to do meekly as we are told. We will refuse to be compliant, submissive and weak. We will demand and achieve our rightful equality. A woman who is directly in touch with her own forceful sexual capacity would no longer tolerate being told that she is inherently passive, essentially masochistic, and that she will only find true fulfilment in submitting to a man. To such a woman, these ideas would be absurd. She would no more be prepared to suppress her sexuality than to suppress or subordinate herself in any other sphere of her life. Having finally come to realise the reality of her own power, she would never again relinquish it.

Angela Hamblin
1972

First published in SHREW 1972

References

Belliveau F. and Richter L. *Understanding Human Sexual Inadequacy* Hodder 1971.

Burris B. *The Fourth World Manifesto* in *Notes from the Third Year* N. Y. Radical Feminists 1971

Ciba Foundation *The Family and its Future* Churchill 1970

Gorer Geoffrey *Sex and Marriage in England Today* Nelson 1971

Guardian *Report on the Third International Congress of Psychosomatic Medecine on Obstetrics and Gynaecology* 30. 3. 1971

Koedt A. *The Myth of the Vaginal Orgasm* in *Voices from Women's Liberation* Ed. Leslie B. Tanner Signet 1970.

Lydon S. *The Politics of Orgasm* in *Sisterhood is Powerful* Ed. Robin Morgan Vintage 1970.

Maslow A. H. *Self-Esteem (Dominance-Feeling) and Sexuality in Women* Journal of Social Psychology 1942

Masters W. H. and Johnson V. *Human Sexual Response* Little, Brown & Co 1966

Reich W. *The Sexual Revolution* Vision Press Ltd 1969

Rossi A. *Essays on Sex Equality* University of Chicago Press 1970.

Rover Constance *Love, Morals and the Feminists* Routledge & Kegan Paul 1970

Sherfey Dr. Mary Jane *The Evolution and Nature of Female Sexuality in Relation to Psychoanalytic Theory* The Journal of the American Psychoanalytic Association Vol. 14 Jan 1966 No. 1.

Sullerot E. *Woman, Society and Change* World University Library 1971.

Wilcox R. C. *The Psychological Consequences of Being a Black American* Wilney 1971.

Woodward L. T. *Sophisticated Sex Techniques in Marriage* Lancer Books N. Y. 1967.

* * *

Sexuality & Submission

It is in woman's privatised domestic role that we see the roots of her social position. The family remains one of the many institutions through which the State perpetuates the social order in which we live, and the family is particularly important for analysis in the women's movement since it is the woman who is the fulcrum of the family and her destiny is most closely associated with it.

While family forms have changed over the generations, the assumption that woman's place is in the home has persisted, and despite the erosion of many of its functions, the ideology supporting it in combination with the changing needs of capitalism perpetuates its material basis.

It is clear, for example, that Social Service cuts carried out by both Labour and Tory administrations, while being a direct attack on the living standards of the working class, also shore up the belief that ultimately family units must look after themselves without relying on the collective responsibility of society. The effect is to reassert the primacy of the nuclear family.

This demonstrates the need to understand just how much the ruling class has invested in the perpetuation of the nuclear family unit; not the least of it being the inevitable confinement of women to an isolated domestic world, hived off from the more naked class antagonisms experienced in the area of social production.

This article attempts to look specifically at only one facet of private life - sexuality.

Submission from within

It is useful to note first how repression of sexuality has

often been used by capitalism as a vital weapon in the conditioning of workers to submit, apparently spontaneously, to an authoritarian labour system. Edward Thompson in *The Making of the English Working Class* illustrates the ideological restraints imposed on the poor by methodism, which penetrated deep into the ranks of the working class, and which specifically attacked sexuality. A classic instance of the potency of ideology - by generating compulsion and submission- from within it obviates the need to impose it from without.

This lesson is not lost on the ultra right in our own era. The *East-West Digest*, a journal which sees itself as 'a contribution to national security, and to the furtherance of freedom in Communist countries', recently had an article regailing everyone from the Yippies to Left-Labour MPs and Women's Liberation for eroding authoritarian social values.

Anything that breaks down the family and traditional morality helps break down law and order just as surely as do demos or illegal picketing.

Clearly the ruling class makes the connection between sexual morality and submission to the established order - but do we?

Self determination

To return briefly to the family, the economic dependence of a woman on a man does not only leave her economically dependent, it impinges on her whole identity. And just as the perpetuation of private domestic economy denies women economic self determination, so does it ultimately deny them political and sexual determination.

Within the male dominated domestic world woman's identity hinges on her relationship to a man. She is not seen as a worker, she is seen as a wife. By the same token, her sexuality is defined by men, and her experience of herself as a sexual being tends to be derived from a male

100

experience of her.

She is a sexual object. In general men are not sexual objects for women because our whole culture has focussed on a male concept of womanhood.

Thus woman's sexual pleasure tends to be felt as a response to man's pleasure in her, so that her pleasure is assumed to lie in being related to, rather than in her own sexual self expression and in her response and relationship to him as another sexual being. Taken a stage further women can be seen as sexual objects both for men and for themselves.

Women's sexual credentials are primarily derived from their physical appearance, how they look, how they move, how they perform as sexual objects - and it is herself as a sexual object that woman has to promote.

Most of us us fail as 'successful' sexual objects. But the dynamics of failure may be no less important in the repression of women. How better to undermine us, than to infiltrate into our very identity the fifth column of inferiority and self hatred.

Objectification erodes independence, active expression of women's physical and emotional potential - which must necessarily impinge on our general capacity to function as social beings. In sexual terms, it is most likely simply to prompt activity, love, lust or whatever in someone else, and this has often been assumed to be sufficient for women's sexual gratification. If women are passive, it is because objectification prevents them being otherwise.

Of course things have changed over the years; we don't just endure sex any longer. It has been converted into a wonder of the world. We used to lie back and think of England. Now we lie back and think of the heavens, a cosmic cavern yawning open revealing glinting lights stretching into infinity or maybe it is a consuming fire which inflames our whole being. 'It's the most beautiful thing that can happen to you,' said one of my teachers. Precise-

101

ly, it happens to you. You don't do it, it's done to you.

One of the problems in looking at this subject is the great difficulty in actually defining what women are, want, or can do. What is so characteristic of so much that is written of women's sexuality is that it is never really defined at all. It is worth taking a look at some of the most typical strands of thought on women's sexuality. Often the crieteria which seem to be applied still derive from male experience. An examination of women's sexuality is thus simply comparative. As a result of such comparison women's sexuality is only seen in the negative. It is simply something which men's is not.

Emotional not physical

Men's sexuality is described in our culture as real, concrete, urgent, visible. By comparison women's sexuality is seen as the opposite. Consequently, instead of applying completely different criteria which relate specifically to women, analysis of women's sexuality avoids physical experience and often relies solely on their supposed emotional responses.

Thus women's sexual climax becomes a fire, a raging eruption, a fever seizing mind and body, a heavenly excursion into some ethereal dimension. But it isn't physical. It isn't quite real.

Even Simone de Beauvoir's *The Second Sex*, regarded as one of the most comprehensive works on women's sexuality, often fails to transcend male orientated definitions, and tends to sink into swamps of almost metaphysical symbolism.

Male excitement is keen but localised, and - except perhaps at the moment of orgasm - leaves the man quite in possession of himself; woman, on the contrary, really loses her mind; for many this effect marks the most voluptuous moment of the love affair, but it also has a

magical and fearsome quality.
Magical mush.

It is worth looking at the implications of what she is saying here. Firstly, it is doubtful if many men or women would experience it that way. Secondly, the nearest we get to a definition is that woman 'loses her mind'. No definition. Only an elevation of mental abandon, a non-physical mental convulsion.

Power without responsibility

The crucial import of this is that she perpetuates acquiescence in woman's passivity. Indeed she admits that it is still true that the sexual role of women is largely passive, but she strives to invest this with approbation, and superlative propensities.

If man,

lusts after the flesh while recognising her freedom, she feels herself to be the essential, her integrity remains unimpaired while she makes herself object, she remains free in the submission to which she consents ....the man's potency reflects the power she exercises upon him.

So the object has power. But power without responsibility. In an age of escalating expectation of sexual activity and excitement, the persistence of women's passivity can give rise to violent contradictions - at least at a subliminal level to rape. Not simply the violation of the unwilling maid. But the violation of the 'magic spell' of women's sexual silence.

There is no lack of imagery to reinforce the merging of phallic conquest with rape. The Beatles, to think of one of the most universally consumed commercial-cultural phenomena of our time, more than once express the phallus as a murderous weapon. 'Happiness is a warm gun' and *Hi Hi Hi*, the Wings single, declares:

I'm going to do it to you, do it to you, do it to you,

103

like it's never been done.
Lie on the bed, get you ready for my body gun.
This is reminiscent of posters shown in London Tube
Stations recently advertising a skin flick called *Maid in
Sweden*. They showed photographs of a woman lying
on a bed, hair scattered across the pillow, with a look of
what one presumes was supposed to be ecstacy on her
face, which was taut and gasping. Ecstacy but no joy.
Ecstacy submerged in agony. Being fucked hard, so hard
that it hurts.

Perhaps this is all stretching a point too far. Perhaps it
is a media myth, which does not correspond to most
people's reality, which is at least mediated by affection.

But at least at the subliminal level, it suggests a compulsion to bust through the dead hand of passivity, which
could understandably provoke violence in the male, trapped
by the predictability of dominance. Certainly, for current
generations of young people reared in an age in which
sexual satisfaction for women is seen as being important,
women have expected more of sex, and concessions have
been made.

Even the enlightened 'tasteful' approaches of, for example,
the eastern love manuals like the *Kama Sutra* and *The
Perfumed Garden* remain entirely within the pale of sexist
sex. They also run the risk of both detaching the physical
from all other facets of personality and, by offering universal blueprints, separating the practise of sex from individual needs and desires, and from spontaneity. The whole
concept contained within them of lovemaking as an art
reduces it to a mechanical routine albeit a more inventive
routine than might be proposed in more banal sex manuals.
Lovemaking as an art is no art - it is painting by numbers.

Another danger lies in simply acknowledging the need
for 'foreplay' and 'stimulation' of women, because they are
still little more than what a man does to a still largely
passive woman.

The mechanical approach to the nature and function of sex can lead in its extremes to the dislocation of people's sexuality from their communication with and pleasure in each other so that it becomes an industry within itself, committed to ever more extraordinary permutations, an industry in which both men and women are reduced to objects. Thus the *Kama Sutra* and the endless pursuit of novelty can conspire to reduce sex to a kind of bedroom Olympics, in which the protagonists can donate each other medals for doing it endlessly every night sixty nine different ways, invoking whatever artifacts come to hand from Mars bars to Coke bottles.

Implicit in all this is the spirit of competition, both between the protagonists themselves and everyone around them. How often has the seed of sexual doubt been sewn because we don't 'do it' a million times a night swinging from the light bulb.

Symptom of the system

The pathological pursuit of novelty, of stimulation, as if it could rescue people from the banality and alienation of their psychological reality is not only an expression of de-humanised sexuality, it is also a symptom of a social system in which waste and consumer renewal are important factors. Compulsive consumerism impinges on all facets .of aesthetic and social life, so that intimate human relationships in turn mirror the transience and planned obsolescence of capitalist society.

The frantic search for sexual novelty should also be seen in a context of the contradictions within an established puritanical, anti-sex morality in which the right to free pursuit of sexual commercialisation vies with anti-pornography, pro-censorship reaction.

Certainly, some men and women have managed to eke out of this contradiction a greater measure of sexual freedom. With the erosion of some guilt and taboos, some women are able to enjoy increasing respect and love for their own bodies, and those of men and other women.

It is vital, therefore, that the women's movement should begin to articulate both women's social and sexual aspirations. It seems that little has been written in great depth from within the movement of the nature of women's sexuality (despite the allegation hurled at us that we are only obsessed with our orgasms or the lack of them). And it also seems that although consciousness raising has expressed man's 'private' problems as symptoms of political oppression, sexuality has not been so easily discussed or understood.

One of the few, and one of the earliest of the women's movements examinations of female sexuality is Anna Koedt's pamphlet *The Myth of the Vaginal Orgasm* which asserts that the 'establishment of the clitorial orgasm would threaten the heterosexual institution because it would indicate that sexual pleasure was obtainable from either men or women, thus making heterosexuality not an absolute option. This opens the whole question of human relationships beyond the confines of the present system.'

A couple of comments on this could be that while the claims of the clitoris *may* be threatening to heterosexuality and indeed probably are for many men   they *need* not be. Furthermore, it would be a mistake to confine consideration of sexuality to the achievement of orgasm and to an obsession with the erogenous zones, for this would deny an important intervention that could be made in taking sex beyond the tyranny of orgasm and the concentration on the genital area at the expense of a more generalised sensuality. The danger of the genital obsession is that it can create objects within objects. That woman - the object par excellence - becomes simply a compendium of erogenous zones. For men, this can mean that the prick is almost detached from the rest of his physical personality, and may be the sole source of his physical involvement.

As for women, this lays to waste the rest of his physical geography. This is compounded because since women tend not to be sexually active, not to make love, his body is often left largely ignored and unloved. It also perpetuates a form of sexual activity which, far from being a totally sensuous experience, limits it, in his case to a narrow progression from erection to ejaculation. Furthermore, because of the determining role men play in sex, this means that instead of enjoying what could be described as an open ended intimate physical conversation, sex can be confined to a kind of time and motion study in which lovemaking is reduced to a restrictive industrial practise involving simply genital stimulation and climax.

At least now, within the women's movement itself, and among men who are informed by and sensistive to, the women's struggle, more and more people are striving to discover not only their own capacity for coping with sexuality, but changing the whole nature and function of sex, whether it be heterosexual, homosexual or bisexual relationships.

Clearly the solution is a political one - one in which the destruction of capitalism as an economic system is wedded to the erosion of a authoritarian and repressive sexual relationships in which women's self expression in particular is denied. This is not to say end capitalism and all else will follow, because too often women's liberation and the transformation of personal relationships have been glibly attached as an afterthought to the 'real' revolution. This one dimensional view of the real revolution derives from an economist view, which fails to analyse the real extent to which all our institutions and relationships manifest and purvey bourgeois, sexist values. It is, therefore, not committed to the simultaneous transformation of all human relations; economic, political, psychological and sexual. If revolutionary change is to be comprehensively socialist, it must include all these dimensions. An inescapable function of revolutionary and feminist movements must be to express the need to change not only domestic organisation - to collectivise the hitherto privatized functions of the family - but to confront at every point the sexist definitions of womanhood which arise from this.

It is certain that unless this ideological confrontation takes place, not solely in the privacy of our own homes, but in the public, political arena where it belongs, then socialist movements will continue to acquiesce to some degree or other in bourgeois institutions and thought.

Sexuality has no mean place in this struggle because it is embedded in the whole formation of our character structures. Women's sexual passivity and objectification undermines their functioning as autonomous individuals.

Needless to say, this struggle will pass through many stages, including for some women practises which may not seem intrinsically desirable. Acknowledgment of lust, acceptance of so-called promiscuity must be recognised as potentially inevitable stages in some women's escape from sexual conformity. At best, perhaps, we can have more room to explore and maneouvre, and at worst shore up and mystify persisting and pervasive oppression.

It is important in this context to be alert to the short-sightedness of seeking absolute personal solutions which neglect the need to integrate private change with overall political change. Our lives will change, must change, as we struggle within capitalism. But the limitations of possible individual achievement can only be recognised in a collective political context of struggle, analysis and support.

The seizure of superficially alternative life styles is too often posed as a solution. Without wishing to diminish the significance and courage of some of those alternatives, it is important to remember that since they coexist with capitalism they can be distorted because they mirror its moraes and often amount to 'the same only different'.

Yet it remains important to acknowledge the value of a plurality of relationships and forms.

The Radical Lesbians wrote in *Notes from the Third Year* that 'what is crucial is women disengaging from male defined response patterns'. But there is more to it than that - for the intervention of women in determining how sexuality is to be expressed need not simply end in evolving 'new response patterns' for this can just as easily end in exchanging one mechanical blueprint for another. The potency of women's intervention in the sexual arena lies in the possibilities of shedding the whole mythology of masculinity and femininity.

Beatrix Campbell

This is a revised version of an article which first appeared in RED RAG No. 5, 1973.

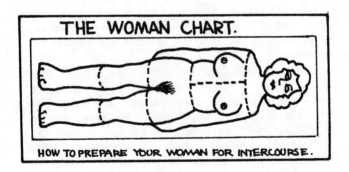

Gayness & Liberalism

Ever since the Bristol Women's Conference it has seemed important that there should be some discussion of the role of gay women in the women's movement. Since I am myself gay, it's natural that I should have thought a lot about this this, but, although I don't think my personal life gives me any particular right to speak on the subject, in another way I feel that perhaps I do have a responsibility to at least try to explain why I, as a Marxist, am not a Radical Feminist and yet do, at the same time, feel it's important to see homosexuality as more than a mere matter of private choice. I decided to begin by describing some of my personal experiences not because I want to exhibit myself, but in the hope that this might make clearer why a liberal attitude to homosexuality isn't enough, and is, in fact, insulting to homosexuals. There is increasing liberalism towards homosexuals not only in the whole of society, but also in left parties and groupings, and, within the women's movement, it is, at a superficial level, very readily accepted indeed, but this makes it harder rather than easier to confront.

I grew up during the late fifties - the affluent society of Macmillan's 'You never had it so good'. My own home was far from affluent, yet my mother and grandmother with whom I lived, though reduced to genteel poverty, and letting rooms by a series of disasters, divorce, ill health and bad luck, operated on assumptions of privilege left over from the grandeur of my grandmother's past. She lived on memories of country houses, servants, the Indian Empire and a luxurious Edwardian heyday.

Their unhappiness made me ill at ease and peculiar. I couldn't cope with the contrast between them and the liberal academic private school I had been sent to, where the other girls came from the families of well off London intellectuals. These girls were sophisticated and many of them had boyfriends when my fantasy life still centred largely around girls and women. Partly because I was a social misfit I came to feel I was a sexual misfit too; and this came to seem very exciting, strange and evil. To be attracted to another girl seemed unmentionable, horrifying. I also came across the theme of the homosexual as damned in the books I read (e.g. French 19th century literature and novels). These seemed to confirm a vision of myself as Satanic, doomed and alone. Yet of course, this pose gave me a certain feeling of superiority. At least I would never be ordinary.

Other people sometimes react to homosexuals in this way too. Because homosexuality faces them with something they find threatening, they can cease to see you as human, and instead you become sinister; disturbing because you seem, whether purposely or not, someone who doesn't respond or conform to the deep 'natural' laws of family and procreation. To give an example of the way in which homosexuality is still equated with evil and madness, the Sunday Times (19.8.73) ran a sensational article on terrorism which set out to prove that all terrorists were mad, mentally sick perverts ...

In Britain, more than one member of extremist organisations ... has been convicted of offences involving sexual abnormality ....

Sexual confusion

I progressed to the ritual ridden world of Oxford student society. There, there was a certain amount of furtive sex, along with the walnut cake for tea and six o'clock sherry parties (it really was like that). At school I'd been totally isolated. In the more unreal world of Oxford I found it easier to achieve the semblance of relationships but I could never feel at ease or come to grips with myself because the competition for social and intellectual success made it impossible for me to ever know what I really wanted.

When I first arrived I was shocked to discover that what

most of the women wanted was marriage. I was really stunned by this, my brain being the only aspect of myself I'd ever been taught to respect or feel positive about; and also I'd somehow got hold of Simone de Beauvoir's book *The Second Sex*, and she did after all, whatever we think of her now, rightly argue the necessity for women to fight for economic independence. And in a way I was right - though what I wanted, not white tule and wedding bells, but the vague, imaginary kind of success, to be on a par with the men, was no better. Anyway, I think it was really only possible to succeed in competition with the men if you, as a girl, had terrific self confidence and could succeed both 'as a man' and as a sex object.

I told some of the women in my college that I thought I was a lesbian and was upset and humiliated when they reacted either by brushing it aside as a phase or else by looking on me as neurotic rather than sinful. This attitude of 'you are sick' rather than 'you are wicked' was actually the more undermining of the two.

This is still the most usual attitude in society today; in this scheme of things, the homosexual is an inferior being unable by reason of his or her hangups to achieve a relationship with a member of the opposite sex. A homosexual is to be pitied for he or she is less than the 'normal' man or woman. As Anthony Storr, well known psychiatrist and apologist for sexism, puts it: *Lesbians do not know what they are really missing. (Sexual Deviation,* Pelican). This view lacks the positive strength of wickedness. I certainly felt I was ugly, awkward, wrong; but I was no longer magnificent and tortured ('Evil, be thou my good'), just a squalid social casualty, victim of my socially embarrassing background. If only I'd had a Daddy, everything would have been OK.

Men did take me out, of course, and I told some of them too about my 'problem'. They, understandably, were even less able to help than my friends, for they were either alarmed or aroused by the information - interestingly, they *all* saw it in terms not of me, but of their own virility. I'd hung the label 'lesbian' round my neck before I came to university because I was so obsessed by my feelings about women, yet what that label did, once I was there, ws prevent me from developing any understanding of my feelings towards men. Because I could only have men, I could only want women. Men attracted me sexually, but I hated the relationships they expected to have with me, in which I was expected to be totally passive yet responsive, vivacious and charming, putting on an act of entertainment for them the whole time. I think I should have liked to have men who were friends, but this was not possible, for me at any rate, so I ended up by being what was then called tarty. I could roll about on sofas and in punts with men I hardly knew, - and usually didn't want to know because that was satisfactorily unreal and unimportant. And while I was doing it, I was *always* saying to myself inside my head 'I'm really a lesbian' - whatever that meant, since I'd never had a complete sexual relationship with a woman.

When I did finally meet and start an affair with another woman, I immediately became very dependent on her, because, believing as I did, that homosexuals were all doomed to misery (because that is what you read in all the books on the subject), a happy relationship was something to cling to as hard as you could.

Sexual typecasting

We entered the Swinging Sixties together and became the 'white negros' of a rather pleasure seeking, but mildly political group of academics in the midlands. What she and I gave each other that was positive - and there was a lot - was always subtly distorted by our living in this liberal, heterosexual world. I did not, in the beginning, see her as male, but everyone else did, largely because she had a higher status job than me. The men she worked with gave her recognition as a honourary man. She could fancy birds and drink pints, but I remained 'feminine'. Yet I still preferred women or could only find a woman, so I was the woman's woman, which made me the lowest of the low. This world, where we imagined we were freed from the domination of men, was shot through with male assumptions and male values. And it was the men, I think, who liked our company; most of the wives and girl friends either saw us as manless and therefore to be pitied, or else a special kind of rival and thus not to be trusted. But we were so grateful for being accepted that we never even noticed the price we were paying (and nor did anyone else, since there was certainly nothing deliberate or malicious about all of this).

This then was our place in the permissive society - to make our friends feel liberated and progressive by 'accepting' us, without their having to feel any challenge to their own sexual identity.

We had a second separate social life centring around the 'gay scene' in London. There we were also typecast, as a stable couple, in a group in which stability was much prized; and here too we were pressured to play the roles of male and female, 'butch' and 'femme', even though in the class conscious scene such role playing was much more open and exaggerated among working class than among middle class women; the more middle class we were, the more you emphasised equality and sharing - but only in the way 'straight' middle class couples do. That was still the standard we measured ourselves against.

This scene too was drenched in liberalism. That is, we *said* it was OK for everyone to do their own thing; you could sleep with who you wanted and you shouldn't be jealous; a good relationship was an open relationship; you shouldn't make moral judgments about sexual behaviour - an extreme of liberalism that clashed violently with the wish to 'succeed' as a stable lesbian couple, and often led to hysterical exaggerations of feeling, while at the same time, a kind of shallowness in a world from which children were almost wholly absent, so that what is usually the *material* reason for fidelity was missing, gave an air of unreality to the scenes and dramas.

Many of us were obsessed with clothes and our image.

There was one particular group of women who seemed to associate together on the basis of all being very rich and beautiful. They all had affairs with one another - a tiny incestuous clique. I remember a party of theirs we went to in a Dolphin Square flat where there was no furniture at all except an enormous bed surrounded by mirrors and hundreds of bottles and jars of make-up and scent - just like something out of a movie.

For lesbianism, while remaining unacceptable, can still become a mask of assurance to hide behind. I myself did not have many extra marital 'affairs'. I was on the whole timid and faithful, and hid behind my lover, while feeling more and more resentful of her. We developed many of the worst features of a 'straight' couple. Having lived through this, I am suspicious of women in the movement who proclaim lesbianism as a solution to sexism in men, for lesbianism too can be sexist. When either of us did have an affair, these relationships, instead of challenging the nature of our coupledom, actively reinforced our mutual dependence - sometimes we even ganged up on a lover, whose belittlement or destruction strengthened us. Of course, this was never deliberate. But outside affairs are very far from necessarily challenging the dependence of the couple, or encouraging personal autonomy. Indeed, a whole literature has grown up of 'swingers' (couples who exchange partners on weekends or go in for group sex) and 'horizontal enrichment' (i.e. affairs on the side), the *stated* purpose of which is to strengthen the 'open marriage'.

Along with our friends, we drifted towards Marxism as the sixties wore on. This was, to begin with, a largely intellectual conviction and when the women's movement arose we at first rejected it as petty bourgeois. This, at least, was what we said, but I think it must have been more a result of our feeling cut off from the experience of most women, cut off, perhaps, from ourselves as women. With the gay movement we did, however, on the other hand, immediately identify, and this led to great changes in our lives. We separated and formed new relationships and were somehow freed to be politically active.

I think one reason for this was that in its beginnings the great explosive positive thing about gay liberation was the feeling that there were hundreds of homosexuals who were not afraid to assert their homosexuality. It no longer had to be discreetly hidden. That was a truly liberating experience, and although perhaps gay liberation was essentially a liberal movement, its slogans *Gay is Good* and *Gay is Proud* are important in challenging the oppression and repression of homosexuals. Gay people really are oppressed, although their oppression is a peculiar one since it rests partly on the possibility of always remaining hidden and invisible. This was the reason for the stress on 'Coming Out' in gay liberation.

The lesson to myself of my life during the decade of the sixties is that I could be tolerated as a homosexual provided I could be stereotyped. That way I did not challenge society, by wanting, for instance, to bring up children. One of the Dolphin Square women I mentioned earlier did transgress this unwritten rule by privately adopting a baby. The Welfare Officer concerned discovered her lesbian relationship and it was only because the adoption was a private one and had already gone over more or less all legal hurdles that it was not reversed, and indeed the Welfare Officer did try to bring a Court Action to do this.

Mothers who subsequently become gay not infrequently have their children removed from them. It is as if women are so deeply repressed sexually, that should they themselves try to divorce their sexuality from their reproductive function, they call down a terrible retribution from society. Indeed, the whole way in which lesbians are treated illustrates the extent to which women still are not seen as having a sexuality of their own. Even lesbian pornography is produced for men; to see female sexuality as autonomous would presumably be too threatening.

Bisexuality

Occasionally, when we lived in the Midlands, we did sleep with men, and that made us feel even more liberal and liberated.

I want to say more about bisexuality, since to be bisexual is perhaps to reach the high point of sexual liberalism. It's important to recognise that bisexuality is ambiguous politically as well as sexually.

A distinction, in my view, must be made between bisexuality in the 'future society' and bisexuality in the
present. If we see sexuality as a line drawn from pure
homosexuality at one end to pure heterosexuality at the
other (the way Kinsey saw it), we might suppose that in
a freer society than ours more people would be nearer
the centre of the line and fewer driven to the extremes
at either end. And although this two dimensionsal view of
sexuality perhaps blots out some of its complexities and
the differences would be greater than this, even as things
are, many, perhaps even the majority of us, are capable of
being attracted by individuals of both sexes. Ideally perhaps
we should all be able to relate sexually to a much wider
variety of people of both sexes and all ages, but this remains an ideal for the future, rather than a present
reality.

Individuals on the left who do not wish to condemn
homosexuals sometimes express the view that people should
be free to choose whether they are heterosexual, bisexual
or homosexual, or even say that people are actually able
to do so. This is liberal because it is based on incorrect
ideas about the possibility of free choice. It is simply not
true that these three categories offer the same possibilities
and I don't see how they could as things are. Heterosexuality *must* remain the norm so long as we retain the
narrow nuclear family. In our society the nuclear family
harnesses sexuality and reproduction firmly together. This
disciplines men, women and children, and is one reason
why homosexuality, in challenging this, is seen as threatening and subversive. It *is* subversive, it *does* challenge authoritarian gender roles, and gay men or women, sexist
though they can be and mystified as they often are, do
objectively have less stake in the status quo than adults
who are harnessed to a family in its present depleted
form. The family man is the reliable worker, and homo-

sexuals, in spite of increasing tolerance, frequently find it impossible to 'come out' at work - i.e. where they depend economically upon capitalism. Who, for example, has ever met a gay health visitor, shop steward, judge or secretary?

And in spite of more tolerance, gays are still, to a great extent, relegated to the rather dingy underworld of the 'gay ghetto' where the worst features of straight society are exaggerated — sexual exploitativeness and competition for example — or else exist in secrecy. For secret homosexuality is perhaps the most common of all — married men who 'cruise' when they're away from home; married women who sleep together when their husbands are away — homosexuality as a substitute, as wholly alienated, or as co-opted and contained.

Sexual consumerism

Bisexuality is different again, as it exists at present. It has no social recognition — no 'role' — and is often used as a cover up for something else. It usually means a secondary liking for one sex in the context of a primary relationship with the other sex. It can be a kind of sexual consumerism in individuals who are largely straight but want more and better of everything, orgasms included: or worse, it can be a way of avoiding 'coming out' and confronting the fact that you are actually homosexual. It is often used as a put down to gay people (if you were really liberated you'd be bisexual). Bisexuality is the Permissive Society's solution to homosexuality, and the extent to which it can be political is therefore very limited.

I feel that some women who have hitherto been heterosexual do see in an exploration of sexual relationships with other women a way of both personal and political development. While this is not to be put down, I think it would be a mistake to see it as a solution, and it may even be a very different *experience* from that of women who have always felt they were gay. For example, the following quotation is taken from a *Guardian* article on Women's Liberation (29.11.73). The words are those of a young woman being interviewed.

118

Not long ago I made the intellectual decision to become bisexual. I've had sexual relationships with two women, both of whom were close friends anyway. It's slower and more relaxed with women - more like a mirror image - with men the emphasis is always on doing so it's different with women....I'm in love with a bloke just now...

My own experience in no way relates to what this woman is saying, since I have always experienced my sexual feelings for women as more, not less, voilent, compelling and active than my feelings for men.

But obviously, each individual develops differently. I am not saying that one set of feelings is 'correct' or that some gays are more equal than others. Lesbianism cannot, however, solve the problems of women under capitalism. At the Bristol conference, there was an entertainment on the Saturday night — the Sister Show — which suggested that lesbianism is the highest expression of sisterhood and the ultimate way forward. Some women were upset by this and by a blanket anti-men stance that ignored or rejected class struggle. On Sunday afternoon there was a debate about this. While it was going on, I happened to want a cup of coffee and on my way to the canteen I passed a small room on the doorway of which was pinned a notice saying 'Gay women's meeting'. Looking in I recognised women I had seen or known in Gay Liberation, women who lived out homosexuality before the Women's Movement decided it was respectable. These women presumably did not see that debate about the Sister Show as relevant to them, and I feel there must be something wrong with this very loudly voiced and ideological gayness if women whose first identification is as gay find it irrelevant.

In any case, the point isn't whether we should be nice to men and help liberate them the while we're all fighting capitalism, nor whether we should kick them out of the present and future societies altogether. The real point is the liberation of all women to find their own autonomous sexuality.

Having seen the seamy side of a world in which every-one is officially 'normal', I could never want everyone to be officially gay, so that straight people were hidden out of sight in an underworld, or cut off from their sexuality altogether. Those on the left who assert that this is what all homosexual activists do want are simply wrong, or feel-ing threatened. In claiming that homosexuality is a form of bourgeois decadence they are confusing cause and effect. The life I led in the sixties was decadent, not because I am gay, but because all bourgeois life is in a state of de-cadence, and gay people are the poseurs, the camp jesters, the extreme manifestation of that decadence. And to say that there will be no homosexuals under socialism also seems very unlikely to be true, since a socialist revolution presupposes an upsurge of energy, and a release of all kinds of feeling, as happened in Russia for a few years, not more repression and stultification. Obviously in a truly socialist society there would be a much wider variety of possible relationships, not a blanket imposition of one part-cular kind.

I'm not sure why the traditional left has got caught up in these puritanical myths, nor why many of them seem to believe that no working class people are gay, which is very far from being the case. They are just more oppressed and repressed than middle class homosexuals.

I have experienced homosexuality as a romantic ideal, and as a prison. It is only during the last few years that I have been able even to begin to experience it as a form of freedom. I do not want lesbianism distorted into some kind of ideal in the women's movement or anywhere else. I simply want us all to fight to free ourselves so that we can apprehend our real feelings more fully, whether we are straight or gay.

****

Postscript

Since I wrote this piece, Lesbianism has been further discussed in the women's movement. There has been another National Women's Conference, this time in Edinburgh (in June 1974) at which two further demands were added to the original Four Demands of the women's movement. One of these demands was for the recognition of the validity of lesbianism, and for the recognition of each woman's right to her own autonomous sexuality. The feeling that there should be a demand related to the position of lesbians stemmed from an earlier conference, for gay women, organised in the spring, and before the demand was adopted at Edinburgh an afternoon was spent by the whole conference in a discussion of it.

It seems too that the position of Radical Feminists, or Separatists, is now more forcefully articulated in the women's movement. Separatists are those women who believe that the oppression of women springs primarily from the patriarchal power position of men, and that this domination of women by men precedes any form of class society and is more fundamental than class struggle. The belief in the sisterhood of all women transcends the notion of class solidarity between men and women who share a particular relationship to the means of production. Women should therefore devote their energy to living and working with women, rather than dissipating themselves in party politics and left groups.

On re-reading my original article, I feel that I failed to explain my opposition to Separatism. For me, Separatism is an over-simplified position, though it expresses a very real gut feeling many women have about men: 'Get lost — we've had enough.' The trouble is, this denies the reality that, in practice, women's interests diverge. The woman screw (prison officer) perceives herself as on the opposite side from the woman prisoner, and vice versa. Seldom, if ever, will these two groups unite in sisterhood; their power relationship prevents this. And in practice, women agitating around the question of women's conditions in prison will also find themselves in conflict with the screws. White women can be racist about black women. Or to put it another way, do we want the Queen at women's liberation conferences?

If you are a Separatist it follows quite naturally that lesbian relationships become an important part of life-style politics and, excluding men as they do, may be seen as a solution to the dominance of women by men in society. 'If all women ejected men from their beds and their lives — the general strike of women — then the battle would be won.' A few Separatists take it further and see in 'cloning' and other experimental forms of reproduction the final solution, since were such methods to be used to reproduce the human race, there would no longer be a biological need for men's existence at all.

It is important to stress the advantages and all the good things about sexual relationships between people of the same sex, if only because homosexuals have been so put down and belittled by those who dominate our society — represented in the past by priests, today by psychiatrists and criminologists etc. But I found it difficult in my article to stress this and at the same time to say that I still feel heterosexual relationships also have validity. I found it difficult because I attempted an intellectual justification of what must I think remain a feeling: my life experience has not brought me to a point of hating all men, and I do believe relationships between men and women can express genuine love and warmth, even though I also believe that sexism and male attitudes of domination and superiority run very deep and express themselves in many different ways, both crude and subtle.

My personal experience of relationships is that all the people I know, men and women, straight and gay, experience problems as they try to get beyond the traditional male and female roles. You do not have to be in the women's movement or part of the left to notice — as bourgeois sociologists have done — that we demand so much of the couple, while it is not an especially flexible social form. It is only common sense to say that of course we all have difficulties, lesbians like anyone else; and those in the women's movement who see in a lesbian relationship the solution for their own and society's problems will be disappointed.

Perhaps this is a liberal position! I don't know how significant it is that my article aroused no interest whatsoever from Separatists, but many bisexual and heterosexual women felt uneasy about it. Did I mean that all women who hadn't been lesbians all their lives were necessarily liberal in their attitudes? Was I putting down the experiences of bisexual women as somehow less 'authentic' than those of lesbians? I think they sussed out an ambiguity in the article, which was that I was trying to say at one and the same time that I don't feel superior to bisexual women, but that I do feel they should recognise that my experience - as someone who felt she was a lesbian in her adolescence with all the isolation that that entailed - is a *different* experience from the woman who begins to have lesbian relationships in the relatively supportive environment of the women's movement, especially if she is continuing to relate to , even to live with, a man, which does inevitably shield her from the hostility of society.

Perhaps all I can say is that there does exist amongst lesbians a recurring resentment towards bisexual women who seem to be having the best of both worlds. Some lesbians speaking at the Edinburgh conference expressed a bitterness about women they felt had been 'experimenting' at the emotional expense of 'real' lesbians. Another woman expressed her positive feelings about the lesbian relationships she was able to have in a small group of women students, but said that she wouldn't be gay if it meant having to put up with 'oppressive straight-gay scenes, the gay ghetto of the clubs etc.' This also annoyed some lesbians who feel they would *have* to be gay, no matter how unpleasant the circumstances.

These are feelings, emotional responses, and perhaps we can only recognise the validity of all of them. We all need to be more sensitive about one another, so that we can respect and understand one another's very different experiences more fully.

There is also an ambiguity about any definition of bi-sexuality. My own belief is that most individuals eventually opt in practice for either heterosexuality or homosexuality. Even if, as Freud thought (and as I believe) we are all potentially bisexual in our responses, the constraints of the way in which social life is organised usually means that a choice must be made in the long run.

It is difficult to define liberalism, especially in any discussion of sexuality which is a very unclear and private area of our lives. I would question generally the way in which the women's movement has approached the problems of sexuality. Perhaps the kinds of sexual freedom and liberation we have been seeking are based on bourgeois notions of individual freedom. Perhaps, far from expressing a revolutionary attitude to sexual love, Alexandra Kollontai simply took the bourgeois ideal of romantic love to its logical conclusion. (E.H. Carr *Socialism in One Country*. Section a) The Family) But this should not throw us back onto the alternative offered by some Left groups of a kind of socialist monogamy, which just seems like ordinary old bourgeois monogamy with the problems ironed out. Such a view, which feels that if there were better nursery care and equal pay for women this would solve all *sexual* problems (which are in fact not mentioned), is puritanical, because it denies, by ignoring, the profound change a woman must undergo when, as she becomes independent and freer, she can no longer accept the *way* in which most men make her a sexual object. Surveys undertaken by Slater and Woodside (1943), by Geoffrey Gorer (1971) and by the French Magazine *Elle* all show only around 50% of women even claiming that they regularly 'achieve orgasms'. This is an unfortunate way of talking about sex, but surely does indicate a real problem.

Are women with equal pay automatically going to enjoy sex more? Will men become more considerate and less repressed as lovers when their wives have a good job and the kids are in a nursery school? Are there more orgasms per head in socialist countries? How much does it matter?

We have hardly even begun to think about sexuality. My article is only part of a very small beginning, and I certainly don't have any answers. But, while I don't feel lesbianism is the solution, I do feel that it must and should be part of any freer society we might hope to make.

Elizabeth Wilson
1974

This article first appeared in RED RAG No. 6 which was published early in 1974. The postscript was written for this book in Oct/Nov 1974.

The Patter of Tiny
Contradictions

Learning Sexism & Femininity

In the process of trying to merge two practices - that of teaching and that of being in women's liberation - my thoughts on women's oppression have always tended to arrive back at the same point: 'masculinity' and 'femininity'. Not as the answer to the crucial question of how it happened or of what came first - but as an explanation of how and when it takes place now.

The question is central to any consideration of girls and education. We experience discrimination as women explicitly on the economic and legal level but it is more important to understand how our oppression becomes entrenched in the way in which we come, from an early age, to interpret and understand our place in society. Various agencies (family, school, mass media) convey a range of meanings to us. We acquire psychological characteristics in keeping with the rigid dichotomy we see between male and female behaviour patterns. We learn to relate in a socially acceptable way. An assumption prevails that the differences we observe derive from biological difference, and that this justifies differential treatment, when in fact the treatment itself causes the difference. The question 'Are men and women necessarily different kinds of people?' is clouded by the fact that they are subject to different cultural influences and moulded into different personality patterns.

Most of us aren't allowed to discern the difference between being female and becoming feminine. Learning our femininity, however imperfectly, is a process of internalising a male culture's definition of our destiny as wives and mothers. All the qualities intrinsic to femininity - docility, submission, altruism, tenderness, striving to be attractive, not being forceful or bold or physically strong, active or sexually potent - also qualify us for a lifetime of servicing, maintaining and comforting men. Whether or not we manage to acquire all these characteristics is not the point; we confine ourselves to sexual and family functions and collude in limiting our possibilities. The carrot dangled in front of us, those female traits which are valuable, those which guarantee immediate success with men, shouldn't blind us to the high price exacted from us by a male culture for them, our freedom, dignity and self respect. To see sex role stereotyping as underpinning women's oppression is one thing, to understand why is another. In *Sex, Gender & Society* (Maurice Temple Smith), Ann Oakley shows the need to distinguish between gender and biological sex when thinking about femininity, and is surprised at *the way in which arguments long believed in have a tendency to remain suspended in thin air by a slender string of passionate and often irreconcilable conviction. They seem not to need foundations to survive.*

But she misunderstands the nature of our social existence. The underlying foundations which stimulated and provoked the arguments are still with us. Far from being suspended in mid-air, they rest on the very real foundations of our economic and political structure.

Female status and definitions of femininity have undergone change, and new ideas corresponding to these changes have arisen, and with them new arguments for sex differential. The most important force affecting this is the differing requirements of the economic system. For social values and attitudes arise out of the social structure which is based on the production process. How woman fits in determines how her role is viewed and how she views herself. But confusion arises when her labour is embodied in people and not in commodities and when it is not waged. This conceals not only the economic importance of what she is doing, but the fact that she has a relation to the economic system at all. A good illustration of this connec-. tion between production and ideology is provided by the period of the second world war.

The war economy demanded that women relinquish their 'traditional role' in the home, that being taken over by state nurseries, restaurants and so on. Even the evacuation might be looked upon as freeing the urban female labour force from domestic duties. But with the end of the war, and demob, this was no longer necessary.

The status quo was to be asserted. Beveridge was quite frank: domestic work, he said, was 'vital though unpaid' but without it 'the Nation could not survive.' The nurseries were closed - maternity wings flourished. And, to add weight to this reaction. psychological 'science' was enlisted, providing dire warnings that the traits required for success in industry and the professions would 'distort the character' of women.

The corollary of these mores was the establishment of 'vocational education', the notion that girls should be educated for femininity. This corresponded to the Tripartite system instituted by the 1944 Education Act which justified provision of different types of education for 'different' children. It was ratified 15 years later by the Crowther Report, which recommended that

the prospect of courtship and marriage should rightly influence the education of adolescent girls, their direct interest in dress, personal appearance, in problems of human relationships should be given a central place in their education.

Later on Katherine Ollerenshaw, a contributor to the Newsome Report, wrote:

the incentive for girls to equip themselves for marriage and homemaking is genetic.

Newsome was also important in stating the distinction to be made for the 'clever girl'

More able girls have no time for education specifically related to their careers as women, but the less able do have.

'Less able', within the framework of education, usually means 'working class'.

In school the education transmitted to the female child is connected to the wider process by which she is encouraged to 'hold herself in and become feminine'. (Sheila Rowbotham *Women's Consciousness, Man's World* Penguin). The method used to reinforce internalised notions the child already has are both explicit and hidden. Teachers' expectations, attitudes, atmosphere, curriculum, teaching methods all contribute. In some ways school acts as a double-sided mirror providing at the same time a faithful reflection and a vast distortion of reality. School books, particularly early readers, are a powerful example. They present not just a male dominated world, but one more so that present reality. Glenys Lobban *(Forum)* has just finished research into reading schemes. She shows that in them the female world consists almost entirely of domestic activity and child care. Only one showed working mothers - this in a country where most women have paid jobs outside the home. The only physical activity for girls are skipping and hopping, and there is the usual surfeit of heroes. Following the usual pattern, boys take the lead whilst girls watch. The male world they depict lies outside the home and allows for neither expressive nor caring behaviour. Male toys suggest future careers. She summed it up like this:

Reading schemes show the real world peopled by women and girls solely involved in domestic activity, and whom adventurous and innovatory males might occasionally allow into their world in a helpmate capacity.

The structure of the school itself is another factor which ratifies the dominant position of men. School is a hierarchical and bureaucratic institution within which women are subordinate to men. They are the assistant teachers, secretaries, auxiliary workers, cooks, cleaners. Men are the headmasters, heads of departments and caretakers. Although women have traditionally held key posts in female secondary and infant schools there is now a disturbing tendency for them to be ousted from these jobs, given the trend towards comprehensive and co-educational schools. In 1974 out of the 994 mixed comprehensive schools only 53 had female heads. Whilst co-education and the entry of male teachers into primary schools can be positive in undermining sex roles, we must challenge the assumption that 'being a man' alone qualifies you for promotion. And of course the higher up you are, the more status and prestige is attached to your job, the less likely it is that you will be a woman

Many women are drawn to teaching because it provides the least amount of conflict with the role of wife and mother. It is hardly surprising that children show a certain confusion between the two, frequently substituting 'Mum' for 'Miss'. The connection between the two is that both entail a constant drain of emotional energy. Teaching, like housework, is not clearly defined in terms of hours, you are constantly on duty. In both, the emotional commitment to other people is exploited. Seen in this light, it's not difficult to understand the rabid antifeminism of the National Association of Schoolmasters. Deeply committed to turning the profession into a nine to four job, they resent the women who provide a natural blacklegging force. Having concluded that salaries are low because so many women are employed, they oppose equal pay, camouflaging their attitudes beneath an emphasis on better pay for career teachers. They try to divide teaching unions along sex lines, work to preserve headships and administrative posts for men, and, blatantly stating that the training of women is wasted, they are the one section of teachers openly in favour of discrimination against women. Victims of divide and rule tactics, in the long term their policies can have disastrous effects.

The consciousness of female teachers reflects their subordination to men and is consistent with their motivations to teach and the content of teacher training. This, the lowest sector of higher education, in terms of prestige, is probably that area which could least stand rigorous examination. The bulk of all those women in higher education is concentrated here. The steady trickle of girls through to universities in the sixties seemed to confirm that equal opportunities existed whilst compounding the inferiority of those women who didn't go. Those of us in teacher training were there almost by default - we'd entered a race, kept up a steady pace, yet refused to make the final spurt at the end. The fear of losing, and thus reinforcing our inferiority, completely immobilised us. Most of us thought we had actually decided to do it, so this clouded the issue.

My college, like most, had academic pretensions but underlying and undermining it was an environment which cocooned you securely from any real mental effort. Right from the beginning we accepted that marriage would be on the agenda long before a teaching job. Student culture, from 'freshers week' and the emphasis of the words of that all too familiar song 'How do you feel when you marry your ideal' to the spoon banging which broke out spontaneously at dinner after news of an engagement, rising to a frenzied crescendo like some primitive initiation rite, only emphasises it more sharply. We examined, with a mixture of curiosity and jealousy, those girls studying with the university men we went out with, subjecting their appearance to harsh scrutiny, not realising, of course, their handicap, having much less time to do what virtually all our existence at college centred around. Three years of filling in time, soaking up ideas second hand, never reading anything in the original, even the Plowden Report. Because somewhere in the space of a childhood tinged with poverty and unhappiness I had invested my trust in the power of education and because the obvious failure of my parents' marriage served as a bitter reminder that it wasn't always 'happy ever after', I resisted some of these pressures. I began to realise that teacher training was second rate and worthless, yet I wasn't able to make the connection between being female and being there. I couldn't understand that the reason we despised men at a similar college so much was because they represented a mirror image of our inferiority. I emerged painfully from college with the dreadful presentiment that I was trapped qualified to work in a woman's world I had grown to despise. For me this meant identifying even more with men clinging parasitically to them, letting them feed me with ideas, living my intellectual aspirations through them.

To a greater or lesser degree this experience affects most female teachers. The National Institute of Industrial Psychiatrists recently surveyed the attitudes of female teachers.

They found that, on the whole, women thought men better in authority, fairer, more patient and generally gained more respect. One third of the sample admitted that they thought that the opposite sex was generally superior, hardly surprising then that female teachers should reinforce sex roles. Given little positive encouragement to examine anything in depth, anything which is so much an accepted part of our existence that it seems insignificant is transmitted unquestioningly. Though they don't create girls' attitudes and interests in feminine role playing they encourage it implicitly by their very attitudes and behaviour.

A further factor is the conflict between femininity and academic motivation. At first sight girls' development seems contradictory. In primary school they learn faster and certainly have verbal superiority over boys. At this stage experience more conflict (*Journal of Educational Pyschology*: Asher & Gottman). Taught to be assertive and autonomous outside, school demands obedience and passivity. Girls don't pose the same behavioural problems but the characteristics useful in early education have repercussions higher up. Girls approaching adolescence become aware of femininity and have lower motivation whilst those facets of femininity which encourage girls to accept rather than question impose restrictions. They lead to learning patterns geared to exam preparation, like learning by rote, which are not conducive to later academic success.

Female children themselves collude in this. At play they exclude those of the opposite sex, and exclude themselves on the basis of sex. Even at this point they seem to understand their future position and have learnt to relate in a particular way to men. Pressure from mass media creates even more insecurity and uncertainty. It has certainly increased the pressure on girls to project themselves as sexual objects. If your raison d'etre is to spark off a response in someone else this must inevitably have debilitating effects on your intellectual development.

But there is some resistance. Research into role behaviour in the young shows that boys show significantly greater preference for their role than girls, who often opt for the opposite sex role or accept components of both. It seems that workers' children are more aware of sex differences earlier than middle class children, especially middle class girls. The pressures to conform on girls from professional backgrounds are not so great and divergence is more acceptable. Conflict usually comes later. At university they experience a high degree of anxiety - in testing and achieving situations, women will worry not only about failure but also about success. If you fail you are not living up to your own standards of performance; if you succeed you're not living up to the social expectations of the female.

And those who succeed despite the odds face even more obstacles. The anger and disillusionment of women graduates in the late sixties who discovered to their cost that, whatever equal opportunities were presumed to exist, they would still be relegated to the traditional role was one of the contributory factors in the emergence of the women's movement. Although this has been a stick used to beat us with, it is inevitable that it should be these women who saw those contradictions first.

Girls from poorer families who have had to cope with streaming, selection and a cultural gap, are usually the ones who have the greatest difficulty resisting the pressure to adopt the female role and who enter traditional female servicing occupations. Legions of third and fourth year secondary school children testified to the fact that they have assimilated their femininity only too well. The lack of purpose, apathy and alienation they show in the school situation is an indication of their realisation that their future position is dependent less on academic achievement or qualifications than on displaying themselves in relation to a man. Writing love letters to pop stars, or drawing pictures of the shoes they have just bought or dream of, are symptoms of this. Desiring more money with which to achieve this end product means that they drift out of school and into boring nine to five jobs, exploited to the hilt in a boutique, or joining the hordes of girls servicing industry in the typing pool, or exploited and alienated on the production line. Adolescence, the time when pressures to conform are the greatest, is also the time when girls begin to underachieve. The trouble is, that having once accepted the stereotype of their own inferiority, girls underestimate themselves, are unable to judge their own performance realistically and become afraid of failure. Their expectations, if not already compounded with the differential treatment of the sexes earlier on, and implicit discrimination all the way up the school, will now be reinforced by the rigid separation for vocational courses which takes place at this time.

Having understood the all persuasive way in which sex role stereotyping infiltrates in the minds and self images of girls, not to mention its entrenchment in the school structure, what needs to be asked is: can it be successfully challenged? Even a factor such as the 'sort of school' you attend can affect your possibilities. If there is a differential in the facilities available to girls and boys this will affect their performance. There is now emerging a body of information that shows that at co-ed schools the likelihood for achievement for girls is substantially than at single sex schools. Up to the age of sixteen it is as good as that of boys in all subjects except maths. Within single sex schools, the environment tends to reinforce outside pressures on girls, with an increasing tendency for them to leave school earlier.

It is in this context that the question of overall control of education becomes important. Taken out of the general framework of education, the question of girls and education can become distorted. Education, always at the mercy of the prevailing economic climate, is at this point in time being subject to cuts. The policy of expansion witnessed in previous decades is now being replaced by one of restriction. The choice is between getting mixed schools to give girls access to courses already provided or persuading girls' schools to use their limited resources to introduce courses traditionally regarded as only for boys. The first seems the obvious strategy. Though some women will argue that in mixed schools the differential changes from being rigid to becoming more subtle, the potential is there to undermine the polarity which at present exists between boys' schools, at one pole, with an overtly authoritarian and rigid atmosphere, and, at the other pole, the docility and compliance intrinsic to that of girls' schools.

The women's movement, and those teachers within it, have to resist the 'educational fatalism' affecting some elements in the schools, i.e. the idea we have that teachers are helpless in the face of powerful forces that we cannot change. In the last analysis, the changes in education demand the important social reform which will only accompany economic change. In the meantime, we can work towards creating a situation where such a change is possible. We are aware that education, at the moment, contributes to girls' self perceptions. Do we allow this to continue unchallenged? What we could be doing is examining how we can develop a new consciousness.

There is already an important ideological battle being waged within education that we must be part of. Recent studies indicate the way in which a female child's self-identity determines her ability to learn, have brought several responses from educationalists which illustrate the contradictions and struggle between opposing views. Between those who think that education should fulfil the function of allowing and enabling all children to learn, and those who use it in a deterministic way to make people adjust all the better to the status quo. What Crowther said in 1969 is not so far from expressing the reality of the rearguard action.

We try to educate girls into becoming imitation men, and as a result we are wasting and frustrating their qualities of womanhood at great expense to the community.

He was right in identifying the values inherent in educational achievement as conflicting with the female role. Those girls who achieve success in this situation may feel themselves forced to imitate men and acquire their characteristics. But he uses this not as an argument for changing and eliminating roles to remove this conflict but as a justification for women only being encouraged to concentrate on their 'natural' role. Margaret Thatcher, when she was Secretary of State for Education posed this even more explicitly when, in answer to a letter from the NUT, when she expressed the opinion that:

The role of the education service is to reflect rather than to lead society in that its major task is to prepare its citizens to take their place in it.

A more sophisticated version of the same argument is that used by Sally Oppenheim, Conservative MP and co-sponsor of the Tory Anti Discrimination Bill in 1973, who sees the sex roles as complementary. Demanding legal equality and expressing the need to change attitudes and prejudices, whilst at the same time refusing to attack the sex roles underlying them:

Every woman wants to overcome discrimination, wants equality of opportunity in jobs and training in education and under the law, but not every woman wants fundaemental change of role.

A recent newcomer to this controversy is Corinne Hutt's book *Male and Female* (Penguin) which uses evolutionary theory based on animal evidence to prove that characteristics are biologically determined. In marked contrast to this camp is the statement made recently by the education officer of ILEA, one of the leading progressive education authorities (though fraught with contradictions) who links under-achievement of girls to their traditional sex role stereotyping, and suggests possible measures to combat these attitudes by broadening the concept of women in society, campaigning to change books, encouraging better careers advice for girls and informing teachers in training colleges. All of these ideas, if put into practice, can contribute to changing the consciousness of girls. Teacher and parent attitudes would also have to be changed to match the philosophy of these reforms.

Schools who do resist pressures to act as agents for the status quo, rubber stamping prevailing oppressive ideas and attitudes enabling children to fit all the more exactly into the correct social and occupational slot, but who, instead, insist on every child having the fullest opportunity for learning, provide, like the free schools, an important alternative model. Not enough in themselves to bring about fundamental change, for concepts of masculinity and feminity underpin the economic structure, they can accompany struggles being fought on the economic level.

The original demand of the women's liberation movement for equal education and opportunity was prefixed by the following:

We don't just demand an education equally as bad as that of men, we want equal resources not equal repression, we want to fight for real education to make our own jobs and opportunities.

It is important to remind ourselves of this, for it acknowleges the fact that, within the education system, the possibility for either sex to develop and learn are limited. Within our schools, the success of some children is only achieved at the cost of rejecting and alienating others. Although boys are groomed for a dominant outgoing role and encouraged to have aspirations of success, their psyche is at the same time, damaged by being forbidden to acquire qualities such as tenderness and sensitivity. The demand questions what has in the past been a safety valve for those women who couldn't conform to the expected femininity, the possibility of becoming like men. It suggests an education of a qualitatively different kind. This demand, by no means short term, has implications that are far-reaching, that would seem to challenge the very way in which social relations are organised. In the meantime, we need to look at the demand and expand it with detailed plans for organising campaigns around specific issues it raises. These, in order to be successful, must be educative, focusing on a specific demand, e.g. provision of technical courses for girls, which people can identify with, and, taking them further, to explore the framework in which these limitations exist, i.e. the sexist ideology which underpins the economic system.

It means working to inform teachers likely to be affected and moved by discrepancies between girls' education and wider educational ideals, linking up with teachers concerned about education in relation to race and class yet not aware of sexism, making the Trade Union movement aware that their demand for equal pay is linked intrinsically both to the education opportunities girls have and their wider conditioning into male and female roles. Hardest of all, because they usually tend to defend authoritarian methods and be suspicious of progressive innovation in education, is to get parents interested in campaigning around the issues this raises and raise their expectations of their own female children.

Maria Loftus
1974

An amended version of an article which was first published in RED RAG No. 7

Sex Roles in Children's Literature

Liberal minded teachers, librarians and writers recently became aware that children's books reflected a one-sided view
of life, that of the well-to-do middle classes. All children
in books were well educated and played out their adventures against a background of parental understanding and
concern. Few, if any, adventures happened to working class
children. It became a cause for concern that there were so
few stories in which the working class child could see itself depicted and it was realised that this might be one
reason why working class children do not read very much.
If the working class child was a determined reader and
overcame the problem of identification, he/she soon realised that the world of significant people, that is, people
who do exciting things and influence events, did not include him/her. The bright child who could read absorbed his
his/her lesson about his/her place in society.

The same people who awoke to the fact that the working class child would feel discriminated against in his/her
reading were blind to the fact that there is another large
section of child readers who are alienated by the main-
stream of children's fiction. Girls find that there are very
few books where girls play a crucial and satisfying part.

Small girls are no different from small boys. They like
to get dirty, play rough games, climb trees, scrap, run, jump,
and swim, and they like to read satisfying stories about kids
like themselves having adventures. Adventures can either be
of a fantastical kind, or simply about children getting
deeply involved in a new experience. The child's involvement and positive action are really more important than
the scale of the adventure. The plot could be a trip to

Jupiter or a quarrel with the people next door. Whatever the adventure, children can identify totally, and extend their own experience into the realm of their choice.

Choice for girls is limited. Children's books comprise boys' books, girls' books, and books supposedly meant for both sexes, but the latter, I suspect, are largely read by girls. Both boys' books and girls' books emphasise the polarity of the sexes but boys' books at least statisfy children's need for adventure, while books for girls tend to suppress it. Many women I know remember the hunt for suitable heroines to identify with. We longed for books about women pilots, women divers, women explorers, climbers and space travellers, or even about girls who were unrepentantly naughty and rebellious. It wasn't that we couldn't identify with boys in stories, we just wanted to be reassured that we were not to be excluded from the world of action. We ended up reading Biggles and William and like other girls, we soon got the message that the people who have the adventures and scope to determine the course of their own lives, are men.

In exactly the same way that the working class child absorbs the lesson about his/her place in society from his/her reading, the girl reader learns lessons about the role she will play as a woman. Before they reach their teens, many girls rebel against the feminine role they see ahead of them. (I am talking from my own experience and from that of numerous friends). They see no evidence in play or at school that they are less equipped for an exciting and active life than boys. Some are as strong physically and many are at that stage more advanced at school, and yet they are learning all the time that a woman's role is to be an adjunct to a man's life.

Stories for girls show no sympathy with the conflict between the developing awareness of self and the experience of the female role which goes on in many younger girls. Girls and boys in books behave in ways which are stereotyped according to adult concepts of male and female behaviour. Sex roles are rigidly emphasised, denying a child's feeling that she is a person in her own right, independent of sex.

Polarity of the sexes

The worst offenders in role preparation are books exclusively
for boys or girls. Both stress the polarity of the sexes and
exaggerate the sexual stereotypes. Girls books are, however,
more inhibiting to the development of the child's imagin-
ation than are books meant for boys. Boys' adventures
take place in all-male societies of motor racing circuits,
the services, cargo boats etc. The selection I looked at
were about smuggling, rallying, motor racing and trapping.
The stories roved all over Europe, America, Northern Can-
ada, and the China Seas. Extraordinary feats of physical
endurance and skill were involved and the resources of the
hero were stretched to the limit. One thing common to
them all was the hero's high degree of technical compet-
ence in his particular field - the technicalities of motor
cars, explosives or traps were all described in detail, and
the adventures, though hair-raising enough to be satisfying,
were based on a firm grasp of real life.

Books especially for girls are set in predominantly female
societies like schools, pony clubs, ballet school, and among
secretaries, nurses or air hostesses. Adventures are reduced
to a kind of social extravaganza. In a school setting, this
could be the achievement of Angela Brazil's 'Sunshine of
popularity', by the proper exercise of feminine qualities.
In the more sophisticated stories for older girls, the aims
are social success in the adult world and the capture of
the inevitable husband. Lorna Hill has written a whole
string of books about different girls at Sadlers Wells. Dance,
however, plays a minor part in the stories, which are concerned with the social lives of the characters. There are
illustrations of the girls doing various ballet steps, but no
real sense is given of the rigorous life a dancer leads, and
the technical detail, so emphasised in boys' books, is stud-
iously avoided. The difficulties are entirely in adapting
to the rarefied world of balletomanes. Other 'girls only'
books describe the girls overcoming their desires for ad-

venture and feelings of rebellion (described as their cap-
riciousness and wilfullness) and transforming them into
acceptable feminine qualities, like inner strength and imag-
ination. Remember Jo in *Little Women* and Katy in
What Katy Did. Another common plot tells how the girl
heroine overcomes the motiveless malice of another girl.
These female Iagoes appear surprisingly frequently and encourage the belief, subscribed to by women themselves, that
there is a suspect quality in all women.

Current booklists promoted by publishers 'for girls' show
a preponderance of books about love, dating and romance,
with a sideline in problems, like spots, glasses and so on,
which interfere with romance. Dating is a teenage and sub-
teenage preoccupation, and should be considered in children's
books, and so should the physical problems which manifest themselves in the teens. However, the implication in
these books is that romance is the purpose of a girl's life,
and problems exist insofar as they hinder romance. Boys
are interested in dating too, but they are not expected to
read books about it. It is a minor part of their lives. Girls
are not allowed the comforting assumption that sex and
dating need play only a part in their lives. They read that
it is of crucial importance, and learn to think about very
little else. Dating literature is habit forming - I remember
from my own teens reading quantities of the stuff to find
the recipe for dinding a man.

Out of date ideas about woman's capabilities

Career books absolutely reinforce the traditional, out of
date ideas about woman's capabilities. Bodley Head concede
that girls can be air hostesses, beauticians, fashion buyers,
journalists, farmers, library assistants, policewomen, teachers,
almoners, booksellers, dental assistants and therapists. They
may play a part in the processes of publishing, television,
advertising and broadcasting. Other publishers have similar
lists. Why are there women almoners, nurses and therapists
in hospitals, but no doctors? Why is Sheila a dental assistant but not a dentist, when these jobs are done by many

women? Juliet in publishing turned out to be a secretary to a publisher, and left to get married. Joan on the farm became a herdswoman, and left to get married. Jane, young authoress and failed doctor, did not succeed in getting anything published. The following quotations are typical:

A girl confident that with A certificate typing, her ugly mug would not impede her career - Juliet in Publishing.

Daddy: I know it's a bit of a bore, but shorthand typing never comes amiss - and later

Julian: I think it would be silly of you to give up this job of yours. Obviously you like it. It's going to get you out and about all over the world and teach you to stand confidently on your own two feet. But maybe in say four years time you might feel that you've got all you can get out of being a ship's officer and that a home of your own might be a good idea? - Hester, Ship's Officer.

Broadly speaking, books for boys extend the child's desire for adventure and involve him closely with the technical aspects of the development of the plot. Girls' books minimise adventure to social play acting and skate over the technicalities of adult life, clouding them in romance. I think that the great popularity of the school story must lie in the fact that the girl heroine is allowed considerable scope for adventure and rebellion against authority. There are no men present, indeed, within the terms of reference of the story, men hardly exist, except in very menial capacity of gardeners and grooms. There is no need therefore to inhibit the girls to maintain a standard of femininity. Even in school stories however, the girl does not rebel for the sake of rebelling, or because she questions the authority imposed upon her. It is always revealed that she was acting to uphold the honour of the school.

The solution is to 'fall in love'

A book which combines most of the topics of 'special interest to girls' is *Portrait of Margarita* by Ruth M. Ar-

145

thur, (Gollancz 1968). This book purports to tackle the colour problem. Margarita, a young coloured girl, is living at boarding school when she is given the news that her parents have been killed, and she is sent to live in a village in the country. John, her guardian, is a brilliant, handsome, enigmatic lawyer, and Margarita falls in love with him. Anonymous notes warn her to leave the village and threaten her life. At first Margarita assumes that the villagers will not tolerate a coloured girl in their midst, but it turns out that the writer of the notes is an old woman who nursed John. Finally, the old lady tries to kill Margarita, but herself falls victim to her own trap. John takes Margarita abroad to solve her problems, and she falls in love with a young fisherman, who is really a student of architecture with a brilliant future.

At the beginning of the book, Margarita has real problems. She has to adjust to the fact of her parents' death and adapt herself to life without them, and she has to establish her relationship, as a coloured girl, with her new surroundings. The solution she finds to both problems is to 'fall in love' with John, who is conveniently available as father figure, comforter and male ideal. The facts of the case may be psychologically realistic, but the writer does not show any attempt to come to terms with Margarita's problems on a realistic level. Her feelings about her parents' death are only mentioned twice, and her other problems are glossed over. Margarita makes no attempt to come to terms with her problems herself, her big decisions are made by John. Her second love affair is both a new way to evade present problems and a solution to those of the future. This affair is horrifying in itself in that this child who has not yet even finished school with almost no experience of life, is willing to see her future finalised in the form of this young prince/fisherman with a fat bank balance in his glass slipper. The final objection is to the old nanny, who is sharply contrasted to lucky Margarita as the old woman who never found love, and who went mad when her only love object was threatened.

Traditional ideas about sex roles

Books especially for one sex blatantly reinforce traditional ideas about sex roles, but there is another group of books which purport to be for both girls and boys but which are, perhaps, more pernicious. This is the family or group adventure story. These books represent a supposedly balanced view of reality. Girls often play a crucial part in the adventure, but the leader and final decision maker is always a boy. The male and female roles are invariably stereotyped when it comes to physical prowess. Boys and girls of similar ages vary a great deal in physical accomplishment, but it is always the girl who jeopardises the safety of the gang by falling over a tree root, or by her strength giving out half way up a rope. And it is always a boy, not another girl who comes back and rescues her. Emotionally, too, girls are a liability in a group adventure. They may, like Anne, in *The Famous Five* be cry-babies who need constant encouragement from the others, or their impulsiveness may thwart the plans of the boy leader, or their extra sensitivity may allow them to sympathise with the other side too much. In all cases, girls become an extra hazard, an old man of the sea for the boys to deal with.

Even the best imaginative adventure stories maintain the traditional roles. In *The Shield Ring* by Rosemary Sutcliffe, the central character is a girl, Frytha, but through her we feel the experiences of a boy, Bjorn. Bjorn is always active, carving, making toy boats, while Frytha lies in the grass, watching. He is the talented one, a brave fighter and a gifted musician.The battle sequences are experienced by Bjorn, but made available to the reader through Frytha. Both children are refugees in the Viking camp, but while Frytha settles into her woman's round of duties, Bjorn maintains his apartness and separate identity finally taking Frytha away to make a new life on his terms. In all things Frytha passively follows Bjorn, but as she follows him into some really good adventures, it is one of the more satisfying books for girls to read. In the last analysis, unfortunately, it maintains a traditional attitude to women.

From the Mixed up Files of Mrs. Basil Frankweiler is the story of a brother and sister who run away from home in a New York suburb, and go to live in the Metropolitan Museum. It is the girl's idea to run away and initially she organises the escapade, manipulating her little brother into accompanying her. Once the boy gets enthusiastic about the adventure, he takes over most of the organization. His sister cannot handle their modest sum of money. She wants to spend it on non-essentials like the laundromat, going to restaurants with waiters travelling in taxis. In short, her adventure is still in the realms of fantasy and it takes a boy to make it work practically. She is also upset by the fustiness of the four-poster bed they sleep in and insist that they take baths in the fountain in the museum. Once the boy has become concerned to make the escapade work, he determines a plan of action and insists they keep to it, while the girl is distracted by events as they arise. They behave in what are considered to be typically male and female ways.

In *The Hidden Road* by Leila Berg, Jeremy and Nicola, two oppressively middle class children, move to a new house in a secluded road, which represents paradise for both of them. The council move in with bulldozers and build council flats right next door. The whole family is shocked that their road could be violated. Nicola is especially affected as the privacy and exclusiveness of the road are identified with her own developing feelings of awareness about herself. Working class and middle class finally come together in a fight to bring a man to justice who crushed a child's trike with a car, and prejudices on both sides are demolished. Sex roles are rigidly adhered to on all levels. Nicola responds to the newcomers emotionally and from an entirely selfish point of view. Jeremy is sensible and acknowledges that people have to live somewhere. Nicola has great difficulty in coming to terms with the new people during the course of their action together. She sees them as noisy and crude and even assumes that working class mothers don't know how to care for their children. It is Nicola's female emotionalism and self orientated approach which makes her behave in this way. Her brother's responses are rational. The adults who appear are old-fashioned by any standards. The working class flat is always full of the smell of home baking, and the middle class mum, when not baking herself, spends the afternoons sorting through the family sheets for possible holes, then prevails upon Nicola to help her fold them and put them back. Both mothers are cuddly secure figures and fathers appear briefly to dispense wisdom and get things organised.

A stereotype has already emerged from the last two examples mentioned; that of the girl who reacts in an emotional and impulsive way and who is restrained by the common sense of her little brother.

Media image of happy families

The books I have described above, which were chosen completely at random, maintain established sexual roles rather than reinforcing them. Career books and one-sex only books operate a harder sell, providing girls with an image of their future lives which reflects the general media image of happy families seen in the commercials. Mother is happily engaged in keeping the home spic and span, father appears in the evening, smoking his pipe, and the kids are clean and charming, if a bit boisterous. We all recognise the falseness of the world of commercials, because we know that they are trying to put one over on us, to sell us something. Books of fiction should have no interest in selling an image, but the media world is immediately recognisable in teenage romances and other books. Marriage and family life is an area in which there are no problems. The problems in the stories are about getting married, and looking right in order to get married. The popularity of the dream world of *Valentine*, *Jackie* and *Marilyn* has been recognised by the publishers. Saleability is the prime motive. The good imaginative book, on the other hand, combine a genuine reflection of what the writer sees as the actual situation, with a shrewd idea of what will sell.

Some writers may wish to make their girl characters more positive, departing from the formula slightly, but feel that this would alienate their possible boy readers as girls will tolerate a boy hero but few boys will read books with girl heroines. I feel that this picture of the market is probably accurate, and few boys would want to read about girls having adventures. The conclusion I would draw from this is that the male role, like the female role, is a source of doubt and insecurity to kids, who cannot take a flexible attitude. Writers are right to feel that they cannot hope to challenge the sex roles and sell their work. Children are going through a difficult period of adjustment to sexual roles, and do not wish to read books which challenge areas of behaviour which they have been led to believe are of supreme importance.

Most writers of books read by girls are women, who are writing about society as they experience it and as they think their readers want to see it. Many of them may have rebelled against their femininity when children, but must have come to some sort of terms with it in adult life in order to survive. Feelings of rebellion, once despatched, are seen as undesirable, and the writers' work reflects their successful coming to terms with their problems.

An interesting concession to young girls' rebellion is the tom-boy. She appears in the younger age range, where little girls are still unsure about accepting female status, and do many of the same things that little boys do, like playing rough games and climbing trees. Tom-boys are allowed to play a prominent part in an adventure, even to take over leadership for part of the time, to be tough, resourceful, and to make decisions. They also openly attack the female role that outside people like parents, and relations, expect them to play. George, in *The Famous Five* is openly scornful of the idea that girls are in any way weaker than boys. Nancy in *Swallows and Amazons* fiercely defends a girl's ability and right to do anything a boy can do. Unfortunately, a tom-boy's scorn for the trappings of femininity extends to girls themselves. George treats Anne in exactly the same way as boys do, patronising her weakness and kindly looking after her. Anne maintains the feminine ideal, while George is considered as a boy. Peggy and Susan in *Swallows and Amazons* spend their time in the galley being good girls, allowing Captain Nancy to have her aberrations. The tom-boy seems to be a kind of safety valve for girls who are unsure of their role. She allows free reign to their fantasies of adventure, but, at the same time, she is sternly contrasted with the real girls. She is allowed no concessions to femaleness, dressing, acting and looking like a boy, and while she herself will not accept the fact that she is a girl, she is not toally accepted by the boys. Her world is ultimately unsatisfactory. Perhaps it is better after all to be a real girl.

It is interesting to note that the roles are never reversed the other way. Arthur Ransome never puts John and Roger in the galley.

It will be argued that many of the books I criticise merely represent society as it is. This is true. But I am writing from a point of view which is critical of the way society is, particularly in its attitude to women. While it is representative and safe to write books showing women in traditional passive roles, books of this sort show no encouragement to girls who have not yet totally accepted second class citizenship. One of the many reasons that girls accept their passive, secondary sex role is because they are not exposed to the idea that they can be anything else. Though it is unrepresentative to write a book called *Jill, Test Pilot* Jill will never think of becoming a test pilot until someone writes such a book. In the same way that the working class child learns from his reading that the world of significant people is made up from the middle classes, so the girl sees that the significant people are men. The working class child may be spurred on to reject his class and rise in the world, but no girl can aspire to change her sex.

Sexual stereotyping

It is not feasible or desirable to ask that children's fiction be in the vanguard of revolutionary change in society's attitude to sexual steretyping. It is a far too sensitive area to start pushing propaganda - but this is exactly what we have been doing so far - pushing the idea of female subordination through children's stories to the confusion of little girls who are trying-to come to terms with roles for which they see themselves destined, but for which they feel themselves unsuited. Nobody wants to replace dominant men in literature with dominant women. That would simply be substituting one stereotype for another. We simply want to see books where boys and girls behave as people, not according to pre-set patterns, which have no relevance to the way children feel when they read the books. The concepts of male and female behaviour are adult ones and are sources of insecurity to all children, and frustration to girls, as the female role is more restricting.

I think a change of attitude in kids' stories will only follow a change in attitudes in society unless some feminist women start writing books. One thing that can be done, however, and is being done, is to compile lists of kids' books which do not stick to the adult pattern and which show kids as people. They are not necessarily recently written books, or books written in a modern context. In fact, older fiction escapes the media image of women, and often makes an honest attempt to deal with the problems faced by girls. Outside Georgette Heyer, people in historical settings do not have to behave in prescribed ways any more than they do today. Joan Aiken's *Dido Twite*, Helen Cresswell's *Gravella Roller* and Rosemary Sutcliffe's *King's Daughter* exist at different times in the past and are in no way restricted by being female. The word has no significance for them except as a physical description.

Characters in adult fiction are not necessarily restricted by sex. It is something which seems prevalent in children's stories and it is difficult to escape the idea of a sell. The way out must be to create an awareness that kids in stories are nearly always stereotyped according to sex, but to point out that this need not necessarily be so, by using illustrations from authors who have consciously or unconsciously avoided the trap.

Cammilla Nightingale
1972

First published in the ASSISTANT LIBRARIAN, October 1972

The Ideology of Sex Differences

The conventional ideology of sex roles puts emphasis
on sex differences, not similarities; it fails to say 'there
are some similarities and some differences' but says
instead 'there are differences'. Two aspects
of the arguments are interesting; first of all, it is
couched in terms of the female's inferiority to the
male ('women are different from men' not 'men are
different from women') and, secondly, the supposed
biological facts dragged in to support it are a perfect
reflection of (male-dominated) social reality. In terms
of the politics of women's liberation, it is necessary
to look at the evidence on the biological and cultural basis of sex roles. The argument that biology
determines important social differences between female
and male roles has to be refuted.

The argument in favour of sex differences begins
with a citation of the 'obvious' distinctions between
female and male - differences in genitalia and the
related fact that women and not men bear children.
On the first of these - genital differences - the evidence
is twisted to suit the argument. It is a case of men
being different from women rather than the converse;
maleness is brought about by the production of male
hormones in the foetus. Thus the basic human form is
female, and biological maleness is something added. The
biblical myth in which Eve is created out of Adam
is mistaken; biologically speaking, Adam is made out
of Eve.

Rather than there being clear distinctions between
the sexes, the groundplan of female and male bodies
is identical. This means that, for example, every normal

man has a womb and a clitoris. The male womb, ('uterus masculinus'), is a collection of vestigial tissue which usually only draws attention to itself in old age when it is often the cause of prostate trouble. With the decrease in male hormones which occurs with age, the vestigial womb increases in size, blocks the bladder outlet, and demands surgical intervention. The male's clitoris is his penis; this way of putting it is simply to reverse the conventional order of precedence, in which women are assured that they are 'just as good' as men because their clitoris is really a penis. The clitoris is a socially inferior organ, its lack of prestige deriving from the inferior stereotype of woman. Yet another reason why men are not told they have a clitoris has to do with size. The intrinsically superior value of greater size is one of the male oriented values which runs all the way through the debate about sex differences. In the genital context, a preoccupation with the size of the penis is a common theme in pornographic literature and in masculine psychology generally. Perhaps it is interesting that the human clitoris was only measured for the first time forty years ago.

However, it is not the area of sexual response, but rather that of reproductive capacity from which the argument about sex differences derives so much of its 'evidence'. The fact that women have children and must endure the associated processes of menstruation, gestation and lactation, is held to be reason for multiple forms of discrimination against them. This is a convoluted, culture-bound argument. Different cultures define parenthood in different ways; modern industrial societies are unusual in attaching a great deal of importance to *social* motherhood, and the traditional argument about sex differences reflects this preoccupation. It is very difficult, if not impossible, to find a non-industrial society which lays so much stress on the one-to-one mother-child relationship, and in which women are as tightly bound to their children in an emotional/psychological sense as they are in industrial cultures today. But in small-scale societies, women do not have the relief from constant child-bearing and breast feeding which contraception and the feeding bottle offer. The paradox is that cultures are so much more closely caught in the web of biological processes than we are, yet they are free from the ideology of motherhood which restricts women in our culture, and which is reflected in the traditional male-oriented argument in favour of natural differences between the sexes.

In Alor, a small island between Java and New Guinea, women carry the kind of economic responsibility which is common in small-scale societies throughout the world; they are agriculturalists and are responsible for the basic daily supply of community foodstuffs. They work in the fields throughout pregnancy and there is no idea that physical exertion is bad for pregnant women. It is only 'bad' in societies which view pregnancy as some kind of pseudo-pathological process. Most small-scale societies do not in fact ban physical exertion during pregnancy, lactation or early motherhood, so the Alorese are fairly typical in this respect. A week or ten days following the birth, the Alorese woman returns to regular field work, leaving the infant in the village to be cared for by its father, an older brother or sister, a grandmother or other relative. The mother breastfeeds the child when her work permits, but other women also breast feed it. It is not thought peculiar for a baby to be breast fed by someone other than its biological mother; every baby is fed by a number of women, and breast feeding is commonly continued until the child is two or three years old. This 'communal lactation' is not confined to Alorese society, but has been reported by many anthropologists studying a range of different cultures.

It is perfectly possible, in other words, to have a society which reproduces itself effectively and in which babies are fed on human milk, but in which the division of labour does not follow the woman-housewife and man-provider model. Biology itself is flexible, and does not 'determine' any particular version of the *social* role of mother. To argue that women's capacity for motherhood is an obstacle to their participation in a world outside the home is a spurious argument, based on the prescription that the proper place for women *is* the home. Many of the disabilities from which women suffer in modern industrial society, such as post-natal and pre-menstrual depression, painful periods and so on, are unheard of in small-scale societies. This is not to say that such syndromes are not very real for many women who experience them in our society today: they are. But they are not biologically inevitable.

The same biological flexibility that is found in cultural notions of parenthood is found in the area of personality and temperament. In the ideology of sex differences propounded, a whole range of behavioural differences between the sexes is attributed to biology. Since the pattern of behavioural sex roles is very different in other cultures, the influence of biology here has to be questioned. The hysterical, emotional, sensitive and intuitive nature of the feminine stereotype in western culture belongs to the man in Iran (a notably patriarchal society); women are expected to be the practical, cool and calculating sex. Among the Tchambuli of New Guinea, the intelligence and enterprise of the female far outweigh those of the male, who lacks the ability to concentrate, is introspective, and cannot come to grips with anything. In many societies, women are said to be stronger than men, so they carry the heavy loads and do all the strenuous work: physical exertion is a 'feminine' activity. In Anglo-Saxon times, within western culture, women were self-assertive, and independent, and one writer said of France at the time of the crusades:

Men had the right to dissolve in tears, and women that of talking without prudery...If we look at their intellectual level, the women appear distinctly superior.

157

*They are more serious: more subtle. With them we
do not seem to be dealing with the rude state of
civilisation that their husbands belong to....As a rule,
women seem to have the habit of weighing their acts;
of not yielding to momentary impressions.*

These are only a few, isolated examples. But they
serve to illustrate the kind of flexibility that the ideology of sex differences does not take into account;
they serve to confirm the proposition that the power
this ideology accords to biology in the shaping of sex
roles simply mirrors the norms of our own culture.

Any field in which sex differences/similarities are
examined is likely to reflect these social norms. Thus,
in the area of intelligence, sex differences are found
in a number of abilities. Females excel in verbal ability
especially early in life. This is often explained with
reference to the close tie between female parent and
female child, but the cultural stereotype is generally
one of verbal fluency in females. In mathematical
ability, there appear to be no early sex differences,
but after eleven the male's ability to perform well on
tests of arithmetical reasoning becomes consistent and
marked. On the criterion of analytical ability, males
seem to perform better. One test which asks children
to think of ways in which toys could be improved
obtains the following results; up to about seven, children
of both sexes score better on toys appropriate to
their own sex; after this age, boys are able to
think of more ways of improving both feminine and
masculine toys. The masculine image is one which emphasises activity, exteriority and constructive activities
(compared with the feminine one which is focussed on
the home). Thus the male's conditioning exposes him
to an outward-looking, rather than inward-looking perspective.

None of these differences in intellectual ability has
been established outside the western cultural context.
Observations of anthropologists studying other cultures
would strongly suggest that they are culturally and

not biologically determined. The influence of culture can be very easily discerned within our own society. Many studies show a stronger relationship between measured IQ and achievement for boys than for girls. One follow-up study of gifted children demonstrated a close relationship between IQ and occupational level for men, but virtually no relationship for women: both men and women in this sample had started in the same high IQ range as children. The occupations of the women were undistinguished: two thirds of those with IQ's of 170 or more were housewives or office workers. Females thus seem to be particularly prone to under-achievement in relation to their measured IQ.

Female under-achievement begins at puberty, at a time when the pressure on girls to 'act feminine' suddenly accelerate. The cultural standard in female-male relationships is that the female should not be as assertively intelligent as the male. This is the stereotype which girls confront. Since the life chances of women are so strongly affected by their relationship to men, it is easy to see how many girls may choose a traditional feminine role at this time, rather than the pursuit of more self-oriented intellectual goals.

In the argument for sex differences, a great deal of importance is attached to aggression. Indeed, aggression has become the main quality used in defining masculine and feminine behaviour. As one might expect, its converse - passivity - is hardly discussed at all. Instead of it being said that men lack passivity, it is said that women lack aggression; while one quality - the masculine one - is positively valued, the other has a negative value. Like size and strength, aggression is a key masculine value. What is the biological evidence here?

Male hormones injected into animals make them more aggressive. When two male mice meet, they usually fight, but females and castrated males do not. Animal experiments have suggested that hormones may have a pervasive effect on behaviour because they cause some

159

kind of sex-differentiation in brain patterns in the period before or shortly after birth (dependent on species). It is not known how far this is applicable to humans, but certainly the relationship between hormone levels and behaviour is a complex one. The whole business of generalising from animals to humans is dangerous. Two experts have said:

In view of the enormous dependence of the human species on learning processes, it seems quite unlikely that the early exposure of hypothalamic [brain] cells to androgen [the male hormone] would establish fixed, complex patterns of aggressive behaviour for a lifetime.

The process would be much more subtle than that. However, this issue remains hypothetical, until a great deal more is known.

There is strong evidence that much of the male's aggression in society today is a result of cultural, not biological, influences. An interesting survey was conducted by an American research institute on 45 females and 44 males over a period of about 20 years. Researchers found that the male's adult aggression could be predicted from his aggression record in childhood, and the same was true of the female's passivity. But the passivity of boys and the aggression of girls in childhood bore no such relationship to their adult behaviour: the effect of social conditioning was to reduce sex-inappropriate behaviour. Passivity in boys is frowned upon and discouraged: so is aggression in girls. Another American study, this time of child-rearing patterns in 379 families, found the greatest and most consistent difference in parental behaviour towards boys and girls in the area of aggression. Boys were allowed far more aggression in relationships with other children than were girls. If a girl behaved aggressively towards her parents she was likely to be punished; a boy had a greater licence. To be a real boy meant fighting back, but femininity consisted in a non-retaliatory attitude. Moreover, the punishment of boys was likely to take the form of physical aggression - an activity often left by the mother for the father when he came home. In contrast, girls tended to be punished by the withdrawal of love.

To talk about sex differences or similarities in passive and aggressive behaviour is, of course, silently to concur with the appropriateness of these categories. The ideology of sex differences *does* hold up female/male categories as dichotomous, black-and-white (perhaps a relevant turn of phrase here), as mutually exclusive. In reality they are not. Virtually every sex 'difference' that is discussed is not a dichotomous classification. Thus there are many girls who play with cars and trains, many boys who play with dolls (given the chance); there are women who are good mathematicians and bad cooks, men who are hopelessly impractical and given to bouts of 'feminine' hysteria. Patterns of IQ scores show some sex variation, but the majority of all female and male individuals fall in to the same group, and so on.

This lack of polarity even extends to biological sex categories themselves. Experts studying inter-sexuality have said that in the end it is impossible to define femaleness and maleness; they are merely ends of a continuum.

So far as aggression is concerned, therefore, some males are passive, some females aggressive. The sex difference, even for those people socialised into very traditional sex roles, is not one of discontinuous grouping. Coming back to the issue of male bias, it should be noted that the aggression to which so much importance is accorded is *physical* aggression. This is rarely stated, because it is implicit in the whole tone of the argument. But another sort of aggression - verbal aggression - is a female speciality. Girls display a lot of 'prosocial' aggression - they are fond of stating rules together with threats of punishment for breaking them. Much of the sex difference in aggression is manifest rather than latent. Females feel more guilt and conflict over their own aggressive behaviour than males; this is because the female's sex role training includes an inhibition of aggressive behaviour which in turn is liable to induce anxiety and guilt. Differences of this kind are clearly cultural, not biological, since females would not have problems with aggression, were they 'naturally' unaggressive people.

In a society which brings up the sexes differently, to different complexes of expectation and reward, female and male are bound to be different to some extent. This is a truism which the ideology of sex differences conveniently ignores.

Sex differences created by early conditioning permeate many patterns of adult behaviour. Crime statistics and social stereotypes of criminal behaviour are one of the areas in which the different upbringing and situations of the sexes reveal themselves. The most typical female crime is shoplifting. The majority of offences are for stealing low-value items; the typical shop-lifter is not only female, but likely to be over 40 and suffering from some kind of difficulty or stress. Shoplifting is a female crime not because women are naturally predisposed to this kind of behaviour, but because the stealing of food, clothes etc. is a response to stress that 'fits' with other qualities of the feminine role. In a sex-differentiated society people on the whole want to excel not as people, but as men or women, and when they deviate from 'normal' behaviour, they want to deviate in specifically feminine and masculine ways. Hence the criminal ethic of aggressive masculinity; boys brought up to equate maleness with acts of aggression and violence are exposed to a situation in which criminality is a perpetual possibility.

Many sex differences can be traced back to the sex-discriminatory nature of the modern family, which is probably the most powerful force acting to conserve traditional sex role patterns. Not only is it obvious that parents behave differently towards female and male children, but it is known that they do so even towards very tiny babies. The male child is treated with a respect for his autonomy and independence which is not afforded to female children. Mothers have a tendency to transmit their own socially conditioned lack of confidence to daughters; fathers may evoke in sons the same brash self-assertiveness that they were brought up to believe was the sign of a 'real' man. In these respects parents are behaving as the (usually unaware) agents of culture-transmission; they themselves are the perpetuators of sex polarity.

Particular social differences between the sexes are also traceable to the family, and to the maternal system of child rearing. Thirty years ago it was noted that the male children of over-protective, dependency-encouraging mothers resembled females in school achievement and intellectual ability. These boys had not made the break between mother-identification and father-identification which is necessary for the inculcation of traditional masculinity. In the field of sex differences in intelligence, one tendency that has been described is the lesser ability of the female to 'break set' or to re-structure a problem. (Commenting on the male bias in the sex differences argument becomes monotonous, but why is it not said that males have lesser ability to stay within the context of a problem?) It has been suggested that the male's need to change from an identification with mother to an identification with father is the reason why he finds it easier to break set, whereas the female does not acquire this ability because she continues to model herself on her mother. This interpretation certainly makes sense.

A recurrent problem in discussion about the biological and/or cultural origins of female and male roles is a confusion between 'sex' and 'gender'. Sex is the biological classification 'female' and 'male', while gender refers to the cultural feminine and masculine identity which individuals acquire. Convincing evidence that sex and gender do not always overlap comes from the study of individuals who have some physiological sex

- anomaly. Some of these people are of one chromosomal sex, but are given by their parents the label of the opposite gender, through an ambiguous physical appearance. Thus 'boys' become 'girls' and vice versa. Robert Stoller, a psychoanalyst who has made a particular study of gender identity problems in such people, recounts various fascinating case-histories. In one, a biological female was reared as a male, believed herself to be thoroughly masculine and played the male role as effectively as any normal man. 'She' was spectacularly successful as a lover; with the help of an artificial penis she was capable of intercourse, and one girls she made love to accused 'her' of getting her pregnant. Another of Stoller's patients was biologically neuter, but her gender identity was feminine and she sought medical help when her breasts fail to develop and menstruation had not started. Her external genitals were female, but she had no womb, ovaries or vagina. She had been brought up as a normal female, and was as feminine in appearance, interests, personality and behaviour as other girls of her age in Southern California. Like other girls she wanted marriage and motherhood. Her sister said of her:

She had a doll that she got when she was eight, and she always said that she was going to save it to give to her little girl after she got married. She still has that doll and it's in perfect condition....She was nine years old when my son was born and she always loved to take care of him and was very, very good at handling him....You can't kid her about not having children.

The patient was told she could have a vagina surgically constructed, but her parents opposed this. They felt it would lead to promiscuity - although, of course, they knew she could never get pregnant. These reactions illustrate how 'normal' the parents' treatment of their 'daughter' was - femininity to them, as for most parents, entailed the repression of sexuality.

In a large series of hermaphroditic patients, 95% of

the cases were ones in which the sex of rearing
(rather than biological sex) corresponded with gender
identity. If brought up as a girl, the individual felt
feminine; if reared as a boy, 'he' felt himself to be
male. Gender identity is established early - primarily
in the first two years of life - and is usually irrev-
ersible. Even in cases where sex of rearing and gender
identity contradict biological sex, it is less psychologically traumatic to change the individual's biological sex
than to alter 'her' or 'his' gender identity.

Most of the arguments about the naturalness of
sex differences collapse under the weight of this kind
of evidence; cross-cultural data on female and male
roles fails to support them, and all, certainly, are discredited from a feminist point of view when the bias
of masculine values is uncovered. There is also the
question of relevance. Whatever their biological make-
up, women are socially oppressed in a multitude of
ways. The issue of biological sex-differentiation is simply
not relevant to the question of social, economic or
political oppression.

Ann Oakley
1973

The Patter of Tiny Contradictions

Child care is and always has been a central issue for the women's liberation movement. The liberation of women is inseparable from, among many other things, the development of different ways of caring for and relating to children.

Considering the centrality of the issue, attention given to it has been both incidental and underdeveloped with few exceptions. Before attempting a description of one of the exceptions, the Children's Community Centre at 123 Dartmouth Park Hill, London N.19, I think it's necessary to examine the dominant features which influenced the formulation of the first women's liberation child-care demand for 24 hour nurseries for all, and to understand the difficulties involved in the campaign which followed and how its ultimate failure influenced the setting up of the Children's Community Centre (CCC).

A report presented to the National Conference of Labour Women in 1970 detailed the number of nursery schools and classes, admitting that in 1967 nursery education was available to only 6% of 3 - 4 year olds:

Some areas provide for as many as 20% while others as low as 1% or less.

1968-69: 26 of the 83 county boroughs and 18 of the county counils provided no nursery places. Large towns such as Grimsby, Rochdale, Doncaster and Darlington provide no places at all, neither do the county councils of Berkshire, Kent and the East and North Ridings of Yorkshire.

Most outstanding is the absence of a single local authority in Wales providing nursery places.

These statistics do not include day nurseries which are

run by Health rather than Education Authorities and which are therefore staffed by nursery nurses rather than teachers. They are open long hours and take children from 6 weeks old. But they are in similar short supply and, in the main, only cater for priority hardship cases.

However, despite the extreme national shortage expressed in the report, there was no public outcry! Not surprising in a society divided horizontally by classes and vertically by sex, each division subdivided into a multiplicity of races, religions, and occupations and each believing itself to be at odds with the rest.

Not the best situation for united action against injustice or exploitation, but super-efficient at reproducing the capitalist system whilst containing the most hair-raising contradictions and illogicalities for working class people, especially women. For example, we are penetrated with an ideology, with all its component parts, which says a woman's place is in the home looking after her husband and children. This ideology co-exists with a reality of 9 million women making up over one third of the workforce and being paid approximately half of the average national male wage.

The only logic for these apparent contradictions lies in the economic needs of the system which this duality specifically expresses.

Thirty years ago, during the last war, the dominant ideology made it desirable for women to leave their children in nurseries and join the workforce. The ideology of the late 60's, refined and cemented with pseudo-scientific evidence from Educationalists, Sociologists and the media, all nicely situated in the middle classes, clearly operated (and still does) to make women almost totally responsible for the pre-school care of their children.

Time and time again, TV and radio programmes and magazine articles discussed the 'deprivation' of 'latch-key' children whose mothers worked outside the home.

There was status attached to the family where the woman stayed at home; some men boasted of how they wouldn't let their wives work outside the home once they were married or had kids.

John Bowlby had it all sown up. He was the authority of the day on infant deprivation and wrote that to avoid serious emotional disturbances the child must have a one-to-one relationship with its mother or mother substitute for the first few years of its life.

The flimsiness of his experiments has since been exposed and discredited (see *The Myth of Motherhood*, a pamphlet by Lee Comer (Spokesman) and *Maternal Deprivation Reassessed* by Michael Rutter (Penguin)).

When reality conflicted with the ideology, it was concluded, with blind consistency, that the mother was at fault. The Plowden Report openly stated its disinclination to persuade the Government of the day to provide nursery places for the children of mothers who were not economically obliged to work. So, expensive private nurseries, childminders or relatives filled the gap, depending on the economic status of the mother.

The Playgroups Association had been growing by leaps and bounds during this period and for very understandable reasons. Playgroups are run on voluntary help and therefore are of minimal cost to the government and local authorities. They are 100% motivated by the educational development of the child which is ideologically acceptable and, because they operate for such short hours, in no way 'threaten' the mother's role in the family.

Even the National Campaign for Nursery Education, in its concern for popular support, stuck firmly to a child-centred motivation.

When, in the late sixties, the Women's Liberation Movement burst onto the scene, it naturally approached child care problems with women in mind. The audacity of this simple step produced reactions of incomprehension and embarrassment (I'm not exaggerating). By 1970, the Women's Movement consisted of a collection of small but different organisations, the largest one being the Women's Liberation Workshop. These were linked by a quarterly meeting of representatives which was called the Women's National Co-ordinating Committee. This committee was responsible for formulating the four demands of the women's movement which were

Equal Pay
Equal education and job opportunities
Free contraception and abortion on demand
24 hour nurseries for all under 5's

The WNCC had tried to work out a set of demands which touched broadly on all the points at which women experienced discrimination. The demand for 24 hour nurseries in common with the other demands, was intended to cover the immediate needs of the most hard hit women, including women night workers. It was saying, if we are to have nurseries for everyone they must be open around the clock. Unfortunately, the wording was ambiguous and many people took it to mean that the same children stayed there for 24 hours a day.

Socialised child care is a crucial concept for the women's movement and the left to introduce, but in the form of a demand isolated from the support of a total socialist system and simply plonked onto an alienating capitalist one, it created formidable contradictions, as we discovered when we tried to launch a national campaign around the demand. We could have overcome the problems of inexperience, lack of funds, family committments, had other aspects been clearer. As it was, one of the main stumbling blocks was that the demand was quantitative and in no way qualitative, which meant we were simply asking for more of what already existed and, though serving its original purpose in covering the most hard hit women's immediate needs, it had very limited appeal for those with a remnant of choice, both in and out of the movement.

Women who were not in the movement frequently argued that all the problems of caring for children in the isolation of their own home were preferable to the daily grind of some rotten job, given that money wasn't the deciding factor. It was impossible to relinquish easily the only justification. But even where work was preferable, the

169

conspiracy of guilt, created often by other women, who had similarly been kept in their place, was hard to confront.

Women in women's liberation were confused, suspicious, uncertain. They didn't want nurseries for everyone if the nurseries remained hot beds of sexist ideology and authoritarian organisation. Support was impossible, action was impossible without a large well organised and powerful movement behind the campaign. Where would pressure come from to force the government to provide a service they already got for nothing.

It must be implicit in any campaign demand that it is achievable, in part at least. This wasn't! But, paradoxically, this was its sole positive feature; it served an ideological role in exposing that the simple notion of child care for all pre-supposed a multitude of other progressive changes in society before it was even conceivable.

So the Women's National Co-ordinating Committee's national campaign for 24 hour nurseries proved to be a non-starter, though many went grey in the process of not starting.

However, early in 1971 an opportunity presented itself to work in a completely different way. Not so majestic perhaos but a good deal more feasible. It was an opportunity to explore in a real way the viability, in a full time nursery situation, of all the concepts which were bandied about like non-sexist, non-authoritarian, collective childcare.

Some women's groups in Camden offered an idea to the council that short life property should be used as childcare centres run by women's liberation. Camden Council lived up to its liberal image and accepted the idea. It took 20 months negotiating before the first centre was opened on December 4th 1972 at 123 Dartmouth Park Hill in the redevelopment area of Highgate New Town.

Description of the house
The centre is in a four storey house facing directly onto

the street. There are two rooms on each floor with a back addition on the two lower floors. The open plan basement and minute back yard are the main play areas for paint, sand, water, clay and climbing, jumping, sliding. Toilets and washbasins are in the back addition. The main room on the ground floor which adjoins the kitchen is used for eating, reading and clean play. On the first floor, the largest room is an office used also as a children's rest room and, in the evenings, as a meeting room. Adjoining this is a smaller living room used so far by the part time worker in lieu of salary.

The upper floor is a flat for a woman and child so that the building is always occupied.

Money

The council gave a capital grant of £1,500 with which to equip the centre and an annual grant of £3,000 for all salaries and running costs. Out of this the parents employ a full-time qualified worker, a part-time worker and a daily cleaner. The only charges for the children are 10p per day which covers morning and afternoon snacks and lunch.

Staffing

Apart from the paid workers, all staffing consists of voluntary help, mainly from parents carefully organised on a rota system. There is a high ratio of staff to children, usually four, never less than three to fifteen kids. Most days there is extra help at lunch times and every day a very welcome person gives up her lunch hour to read stories to the children, allowing other people to have a break.

Selection

Twenty one children pass through the CCC in a day between 8.30 a.m. and 6.00 p.m., but only fifteen are present at any one time. The children fit broadly into three categories.

1) Seven are the kids of the 7 women who negotiated for the centre of whom 6 are teachers and work part-time and 1 is an ex-librarian. All these mothers give time at CCC- and in addition so do 3 of the fathers.

2) Five are the kids of women with full time jobs; a bar maid, an office worker, a student and a ground hostess for Ghana Airways.

3) The remaining 9 kids come from 6 sets of parents out of which 3 mothers give time at the centre. Their occupations are student, clerk and teacher. Out of those who give no time at the centre, the fathers' occupations are postman, house painter, and shopkeeper and the mothers' occupations are houseworker, houseworker and shopkeeper.

Months before opening we wrote to and visited all local families with children under five whose addresses we could get from the local Neighbourhood Advice Centre. We informed the local Tenants Association of our opening and invited applications for places.

Since opening we had so many applications for places we realised we had to have a very strict policy on selection. We have to limit our intake only to those in the greatest need from immediate streets. Definition of need is an on-going discussion which necessarily considers the needs of the parents as well as the needs of the child.

Journal

A daily journal has been kept since the opening of the centre where events and non-events are minutely re-corded. Everybody who works at the centre is encouraged, not always successfully, to summarise their daily experiences and impressions. This has several purposes; the very action of formulating one's thoughts in order to write them down gives a greater sense and understanding of what's happening. On a very practical level it is necessary that different people working each day can know the happenings of previous days. It is particularly important that the development of the children can be observed over long periods.

Men

During the 20 months preceding the centre opening, those women in the negotiating group who were members of women's liberation strongly resisted the inclusion of men in the group, on the grounds that if the centre were to operate in the interests of women, which was its reason for being, then the definitions and control must be kept in the hands of women during the formative stages. However, the same women felt equally strongly that it was in the interests of women that men should take an active and equal role in child-care. Therefore, as soon as the centre opened, efforts were made to involve male parents and helpers wherever possible.

There are now five men who work regularly at the centre, some of whom admit to extreme feelings of insecurity and awkwardness, in the early days, due to being a minority group in an occupation dominated by their opposite sex, in which they had little experience and therefore expertise.

Collectivity

If one had to isolate the most important single element at the centre, that element must be collective organising. It would probably be the slowest, hardest and least efficient form of organising in a time and motion study but that is not the criteria. The purpose is the development and strengthening of the people in the collective by gradually breaking down oppressive divisions and passing on each other's skills and knowledge. Theoretically, all have equal rights. In fact, due to unevenness of experience, some people are more vocal than others and consequently play a larger part in defining directions of the centre. It's necessary always to explain all references so as not to exclude people from the discussions which often go on for months. But the constant interchange of ideas, questions, criticisms means a very rapid and progressive development of the people involved.

It seems to be the only way to confront competition and egomania within a group, for collective organising presupposes the value of and concern for each individual and this is important, especially for women who have been under-valued all their lives. But, even more simply, it is the only way we can hope to pass on to future parents at the centre all the ideas and aspirations we have for it.

Contrary to what many people think, non-authoritarian organising (if it is to work) means very careful, systematic organising and this is a characteristic which runs through every aspect of the centre. We find time and time again that lack of organisation is oppressive and disruptive and allows unfair dominance of some over others. This is true among the adults as it is among the children.

The meeting

The centre functions through a weekly meeting of the collective, where all decisions and organisational problems are thrashed out. It is the point of interaction between the centre and home, where parents can discuss how and what their children will learn. It's often hard to utilise this free-dom after years of being prevented by the mystique and impermiability of institutions. The more parents feel at ease with ideas expressed at the CCC, the less chance of their children experiencing a double standard between the centre and home.

Tensions related to the meeting have arisen from some parents simply not attending. Many forms of persuasion have been tried as non-attendance is seen as a very serious problem for several reasons. It has been a growing area of resentment among parents who work at the centre and attend meetings to see other parents doing neither. Unless those who can't give time attend meetings there is no way that the centre can extend its knowledge of the child or communicate to the parents what it's about.

Without the meeting the centre is, in the experience of those parents, no different from any other nursery, and not least of its justifications for existence is that it should provoke awareness and development on all questions of child-care among everyone who is connected with it.

174

The collective is divided on how to deal with the very real problem of non-attendance of meetings. Some think attendance should be a pre-condition for having ones child at the centre. Others resist this, believing people should be persuaded rather than forced to attend. So the discussion goes on.

Practice

Anyone who has worked with numbers of small children knows that the wear and tear on ones psyche is tremendous and we were trying to organise the learning and exchange with the children in ways which were often uncharted.

Our early experiences of 'collective' child-care were pure torture for many of us. We were relating to children out of the privacy and protection of our own homes. Those of us with quite long experience in women's liberation realised with shame how little that had penetrated our daily relationship with our children. We were publicly exposed. We watched each other minutely; instinct was ridden with pitfalls. It took a collective situation to make us painfully aware of each expression of our continuing authoritarian sexism.

Many of us were in misery those first few months. What could we do? How could we change years of relating to children as a controller and server? We felt we had been caught with our knickers down and frequently we fled to the kitchen, an area of security, and got madly involved with the washing up. But as time went on a routine evolved and as habits changed things got less tense, though the level of criticism has heightened if anything.

The children

We are trying to break away from the traditional authoritarian mode of relating to children and are attempting to offer them as many choices as possible and as much independence as they can cope with. All activities are made available for children of both sexes but it's not enough simply to treat all the children equally. The boys have

175

frequently already learned their advantage and are quick to make capital out of it. There has to be positive support in favour of the girls, who are generally already less adventurous. So we go further and actively encourage the boys to do traditionally female activities like cooking and shopping and encourage the girls to use hammers and saws and to fight back when attacked. In doing so we hope to counter the rigid role definition our children are forced into by society and to give them the confidence to challenge it. At the centre the children sometimes see men cooking the lunch and women putting up shelves or changing plugs and hopefully the children will form less conventional images of men and women than those perpetrated elsewhere.

The Centre is carefully organised to allow the children to do things for themselves. All the toys and most art materials are kept on shelves at child height, so that the kids can help themselves to anything they want without having to ask a grown-up. A routine was devised for meal times, after an opening week of chaos, which allows them to serve themselves, pour their own drinks (and wipe up the spills!), clear away their dirty dishes and scrape the plates. At first we all lunged forward to heap food onto their plates and hovered around whilst they ate, but we are slowly learning to restrain ourselves from always doing things for them and are being continually surprised at how capable they are. Everything doesn't always run smoothly, but on the whole they respond to responsibility and seem to be thriving on it.

Whilst encouraging independence from adults we are also encouraging greater dependence on the peer group and suggest to the kids that they do things together and help one another. We don't want to breed competitive children always seeking adult approval and praise. The children often paint together on one long sheet of paper, they move the tables together ready for snacks, they help each other on and off with their coats and they comfort and hug each other. Slowly they are growing more sensitive to one another and are learning to work together. Like the adults,

176

they are finding out that things get easier when they are shared.

In choosing equipment for the children to use we have deliberately brought in many improvised materials. Large cardboard boxes and old drawers allow much more scope for imaginative play than most of the glossy, expensive and badly made toys in the shops and the children can take apart an old camera from a jumble sale and examine the bits without being told to 'stop because they're breaking it'. In providing them with real things to examine and play with, instead of always toys created by purely adult fantasy, we are allowing them to better understand the world around them. The basic activities mentioned earlier are always available, but in addition we organise other 'special' activities around a weekly theme, in order to maximise the number of different experiences we can offer the children. Themes we have had include living things, the senses, colour, shape, size and measurement, how things work, and printing. Having a theme helps to bring continuity from one day to the next for the children. It also makes us feel more secure when we work at the centre if we know that there are plenty of activities planned, as it is often hard to think of fresh activities on the spot. We go out with the children a great deal to try and relate what they experience at the centre with their knowledge of the world outside. The same local park can be used to illustrate several different things, perhaps colour one week and plants the next. Sometimes we take more ambitious trips to places like Kew Gardens or the Science Museum and create quite an amusing spectacle on public transport.

Our experience has led us to feel very positive about the use of a house as a child-care centre rather than a purpose-built institution. The size and distribution of the rooms is not so different from the children's homes and the function of each room is visible. Wherever possible the children are involved in everything that happens at the centre. The kitchen is not a magical, mystical place out of which ready cooked meals emerge at lunch time. Instead, the children are in there grating cheese, cutting up fruit, making jelly or bread, not simply 'helping' or hindering, but being genuinely useful. Food doesn't just appear on the shelves, the children go out to buy it with an adult. The washing doesn't clean itself, the kids take it to launderettes and learn about conepts of hot/cold, dry/wet in the process. The day at the centre may be a long one, but it is not often that anyone is bored.

Training Scheme

Our biggest problem at the moment is that many people at the centre find the work difficult and feel ill-equipped to cope in a creative way and we've realised that if we are to survive in the way we want to, then we must supply our own training scheme or learning situation for people who work at the centre. We have to implement a real course of study and exploration into the practicalities and theory of the sort of child-care we want to practice. Daily we have recognised the urgent need for this. Plans are in motion and it is at present our greatest priority.

Future struggles

Already out of the short experience of the centre, future struggles are predictable. First and foremost, to get an increase in our grant so that more people at the centre can get paid and ultimately everyone. Secondly, a working party is already forming to begin negotiations with the council for permanent re-housing, especially to include facilities for under two year olds, a most neglected group in terms of nursery provision. Also, to include a women's centre with facilities for overnight stay, a need we have been made very aware of since opening.

Relationship to community

Having short life property in re-development areas can be a source of antagonism with long-standing residents in that area, who see their locality being allowed to decay for many years before re-development actually happens. In Highgate New Town some houses will have been empty for nine years before they are finally demolished. Shopkeepers flee the area and amenities generally decrease. With empty properties everywhere the area soon becomes rat-infested and filthy. The council fails completely to assess and supply the needs of people during this period, failing even to maintain repairs on council houses.

Bitter resentment is therefore levelled at transient groups, organisations and squatters who are seen to take advantage of this situation and in a real sense can represent permanent takeover of a working class area by the middle classes during redevelopment. In our case, there has been criticism on the grounds that we provide *free* child-care when the long term residents had to pay for their children's nursery education in the past. The reasoning is that they are now paying through the rates for us to have free child care and this is hard to take when on the one hand they are so neglected by the council and on the other it is seen that *some* parents could clearly afford to pay. However, it is conveniently ignored that other parents can clearly not afford to pay.

From the beginning we have voiced the principle that charges and shorter hours would mean effective discrimination against the children of working class parents, and it goes without saying that we believe that good child-care *should* be available to every child.

There is a notion, held by some people in the women's movement, that alternative childcare should not be council financed on the grounds of vulnerability if that finance is withdrawn. But surely a centre has less chance of survival if it has the crippling problem of continually raising its running costs by its own efforts. The logic of the argument escapes me. People pay rates and taxes and have a right to expect that this money is used to provide services which operate in their interests (albeit that they may have an understandably short term view of their interests). The very existence of our centre is evidence of the failure of local councils to provide adequate child care. I see no reason to let them off the economic hook as well.

The fact that the children's centre is council financed is one of its most important features. If we were dependent, in whatever shape or form, on private finance and enterprise, any remnant of political justification we might have would evaporate.

Strengths and weaknesses

It has always been implicit in the politics of the Children's Community Centre that part of our activities should be to stimulate and help people to start other centres. From the beginning we have made all our information as accessible as we could. When we opened the Centre we produced a pamphlet describing the struggle up to that point. After three months we had a press conference for local and women women's liberation journalists. In may 1973 we had a very successful public meeting which increased our solidarity as a group and where we invited all other groups and individuals interested in starting similar projects. We write and encourage articles and go to speak to other groups when invited. There is a second, more comprehensive pamphlet in the pipeline and a film in the making. Visitors are welcomed whever it's convenient.

Naturally, we are under close scrutiny from many quarters. Do we stand examination? Are we a legitimate experiment in an overall move towards an improved child-care system? Can we build policies and structures in the CCC which ensure that the progressive political development of everyone involved outweighs the cheap service we give Camden Council, or are the contradictions too great? We *are* a cheap way out for the local council but that is also our bargaining power, slender though it is at present. Councils are under pressure to provide decent child care facilities and they are looking for ways out. Their willingness to encourage all forms of voluntary help is sufficient proof.

Meaningful expansion of national nursery facilities in the interests of working class children must include enormous changes in both the ideological and practical content. For the right to control a miniscule experiment in this field we pay in vast amounts of time and energy.

There's no way of knowing at this stage what the larger implications of this experiment will be. We know our existence means positive support to those directly involved and indirect support to those working along similar lines. But we are walking a tightrope and we have no way of knowing if it will break before we reach the other side. But anyway there's a lot more reality in this project than there was in the abortive campaign of two years ago.

****

Valerie Charlton with the CCC Collective

First published in RED RAG, No. 5 1973

Personal postscript

It's now a year since *The Patter of Tiny Contradictions* was written and it seems to me that the patter has turned into thunder. Nevertheless, it is becoming possible to see the roots of the problems we felt in embryo at that time. It's been a year of endless discussions about the politics and survival of the centre, culminating in a comprehensive pamphlet which describes everything but the agony that went into producing it. Confusion about the issues, lack of time, lack of energy meant that it took eight or nine months to produce. However, it was worth it.

Perhaps the most pressing of our problems this year was the need for more paid labour. Inflation has meant that more women are being forced *out* to work and this has put pressure on us to take a higher percentage of children of 'working' parents. We were forced to take another full-time paid worker who we could barely afford, thus putting a stress on ourselves that should be put on the council. We were refused an increase in our grant this year on the grounds that we were too small and didn't cater for enough children to make it worthwhile for the council to spend more. However, people at the centre argue that our size is responsible for the informality and friendliness and is what enables us to avoid the institutionalisation of many nurseries. This is true, but how does it relate to need and to the economics of solving the nursery short-age and infant schools with 30-40 in a class?

Struggle is something which is built into the CCC and the defining factor is 'voluntary labour'; from this spring all the contradictions. The selection of a percentage of children is conditional on at least one of the parents work-ing at the centre and the labour of these parents is used to provide free day care for a number of children whose parents have full time jobs. Because the division between parents who work at the centre and those who don't is defined by the job they do and the hours they work, it is, loosely, a class division and it's no accident that the majority of parents who work easily at the centre are part time or ex-teachers, because this provides both the time and the know-how. But having said that, it would be wrong to assume that these parents are without their problems, especially the women, many of whom are single parents. In many cases, women in this group can ill afford to work voluntarily, and having their labour used to subs-dise 'working' parents, who sometimes because of their work are better off, can and does breed resentment.

We have always considered ourselves to be a parent - controlled nursery and this has been one of the centre's most highly valued features but it becomes clearer and clearer that the parents who take the most active part in decision-making remain those who work at the centre, in other words, the more professional parents. And let me say I'm not being critical, because it is this group of parents who are responsible for the centre being so well run. I do, however, think some very confusing situations have been set up, not least, for parents who are less involved and have less control. For example, there's a lot of talk at the centre about breaking down professional barriers, and these exist not only between paid workers and parents but between parents and parents. But I think there's a danger of using benevolence and patronage to mystify and disguise the barriers when the fact of the matter is that control is inevitably in the hands of professionals, (which raises the question of how different is that to any other nursery?).

We realised a year ago that we needed a learning workshop where people with no teaching experience could learn the skills, but, again because of pressures on everyone, it could only be one evening a fortnight and it wasn't enough to make a serious impact on the situation. Yet the fact remains that it is unrealistic to expect people to work with young children without the support of either past experiences or some sort of parallel training scheme.

Over the past two years there have been many attempts to set up nurseries similar to ours but, to my knowledge, at this time the centre still exists in splendid isolation. Now, if this means that the combination of factors which allowed it to happen was a unique combination, i.e. a liberal council, women in women's liberation who were teachers, a particular locality etc., then it doesn't say much for its value as a repeatable model. But it is interesting that it may have taken exceptional circumstances to create a situation where a lot of ideas could be made real and therefore tested. For example, I now think we have to find ways of establishing parents' control of nurseries and schools which is not linked to voluntary labour, for if it is we are asking for trouble. Apart from the way it defines and limits which parents have control, the use of voluntary labour must undermine trade union struggles for better pay and conditions for nursery nurses and teachers, and where does that leave us?

Even if the centre can't easily be repeated, it is there to be examined and used as reference in all sorts of ways and it still continues to serve a vital function for those involved. We are, however, left with the problem of how to get more nurseries which satisfy the needs of women as well as children.

Valerie Charlton
August 1974

Sexism, Capitalism

& the Family

THE FAMILY UNDER CAPITALISM ******

The Conditions of Illusion

Wherever we look the image of the happy Western nuclear family greets us; from advertisement hoardings, television advertisements, women's magazines and television programmes. The education system still streams boys towards the world of work and breadwinnerdom and girls towards the fulfilment of their putative primary roles as wives and mothers. Marriage and the family appear to be thriving. And on the surface the institution may appear to offer many rewards, especially to women; security (both emotional and economic), a devotion to personal relationships and the creation and care of new human beings, as opposed to the often tedious and impersonal world of 'work'.

However, the Sunday supplement dream not only bears no relationship to reality whatsoever, it positively belies what I believe most of us know to be the truth: that the consequences of the isolation of the nuclear family are destructive to all its members, and particularly so to the women and children. The question is not whether we think there is something wrong with 'the family'. but whether we have the confidence to admit what we know, in the belief that alternative ways of living and working together are possible. Ultimately this involves a historical and theoretical understanding of the nature and function of the family unit in past and present society. But for many women it may mean initially building up and understanding that all the so-called minor irritants and discontents they experience in their day-to-day lives as wives and mothers are an inevitable consequence of the objective situation they are in, not simply personal neurosis, to be cured by an afternoon out, or by pills or therapy.

The ideological pressure to see themselves as primarily wives and mothers affects all women; it is part of the fabric of our society. For women who work and have families it becomes a double burden, in which their work, whether it is financially necessary or done because of their individual interests, is secondary. While they may take their place in the world of paid work, there is no-one to take their place as a mother. For women who work and who have made the conscious decision not to have children, there is often a sense of emptiness, a sense that there is something else they could be doing as well. For women who, because they can afford to, have accepted the notion of wife and motherhood as full time life and career rolled into one, the pressures of the dream are at their most intense. They have committed everything and thus have, apparently, most to lose.

Part One

Although I went to university, and thus, in theory, had more opportunities open to me than to most women, I always assumed I would get married and have children. It was a question of 'when', not 'if'. When I tried to get a job after I got my degree, I discovered, like many other graduate women, that potential employers were more interested in whether I was prepared to take a shorthand and typing course than in my education. The world of work was a hostile and frightening place. By contrast, the prospect of getting married was a tremendous affirmation of my self-identity, of my ability to make decisions which were meaningful to other people. Secretly, it was also a relief - I no longer had to worry about whether I would meet 'Mr. Right'; marriage proved that I had. My existence as a woman was publicly justified and everyone was happy. I no longer needed to worry about work as such; the new partnership was far more important.

We planned our family with love, creativity and excitement. From the moment of conception to how we would tell them about sex and religion honestly, whether we would mind if they called us by our names instead of 'Mummy' and 'Daddy'. We were convinced that we would avoid all the mistakes our parents had made; we were different, we were going to share everything, we were equal. We were in love.

Things went well at first; I got pregnant when we decided, the first child was a boy - also what we wanted. The occasional physical discomforts of pregnancy, my self-consciousness at the way I looked (none of my friends had children yet), the condescension of the maternity hospital staff - all these were minor irritants.

Reality crashes in as soon as you get home with your new baby. Mother and father sharing? Well, as much as possible, of course. But if he's the one who's got to go out to work, he's not there during the day when there's most to be done. Suddenly you are alone with a tiny creature who is totally dependent on you. I used to check that the baby was still breathing every couple of hours; for the first few weeks you search everywhere for this maternal instinct which is supposed to materialise along with the baby. After minimal instruction in the maternity hospital, you are on your own. Babies are, in fact, extremely resilient, but the elaborate mystique of mothercare is such that you inevitably end up feeling paranoid and inadequate.

While child care books and pamphlets stress that each child is 'different', at the welfare clinic babies are weighed and measured every week, minute details about their progress being recorded. A dog being groomed for Crufts couldn't have more attention than a first child; and, while health and welfare are obviously important, the standard is always the mythical 'average' child, with the mother as genius if her child is developing faster, and moron if her child is developing slower. As soon as you become a mother, you enter a new community of other women. In the street at the clinic, each mother eyes the other babies to make sure that hers is cleverer and more beautiful than the others. The world of mothers is one of tacit but cut-throat competition in which each mother is convinced that her bundle is best. It so appalled me that I soon decided to have nothing to do with it. After all, mine was better than any of theirs, anyway.

The social world of parents is that of outcasts. While theoretically exalting the states of motherhood and childhood, in practice both are treated as excrescences on the smooth surface of society:

The mother with prams and push-chairs isn't at the forefront of planners' minds when they design every new building with flights of narrow steps. Even in what is regarded as the woman's domain, like department stores, high rise flats etc., women with young children are simply not catered for. In fact, every aspect of our environment is designed with one thing in mind, the adult healthy male; mothers, along with the physically disabled and the very old, are ignored. (Lee Comer)

In addition, children aren't yet allowed into pubs, are not welcomed in cinemas and theatres (unless there is a 'special' separate children's show on), are shouted off flower beds, and are generally desirable only when in the background as garnish, seen and not heard, but, more often than that, not even seen at all in the adult social world. A child's place is in the home, with its mother. And we are not simply expected to grin and bear it, but to welcome the isolation with starry-eyed gratitude:

Children keep parents from parties, trips, theatres, meetings, games, friends. The fact that you prefer having children, wouldn't trade places with a childless couple for anything, doesn't alter the fact that you still miss your freedom.

Of course, parents don't have children because they want to be martyrs, or at least they shouldn't. They have them because they love children and want some of their very own ...Taking care of their children, seeing them grow and develop into fine people gives most parents - despite the hard work - their greatest satisfaction in life. This is creation. This is our visible immortality. Pride in other worldly accomplishments is usually weak in comparison.   (Dr. B. Spock).

The popularisers of the ideas of Dr. Spock and John Bowlby have a lot to answer for. In fact, the quotation above implies that the effect of having a child is the same for both parents; it isn't. By stating (with variations here and there) that a child is best off with its mother for virtually the whole time for the first few years of its life, Spock and Bowlby place the whole of the day-to-day responsibility on the shoulders of the mother, and create an ideological wall which keeps other people out. People who make decisions not to have children themselves are also making the decision to steer clear of the mess and clutter (and rewards) of other people's children. After all, if they wanted some they would, as Dr. Spock says, have some of their 'very own'.

When you have children and take them to visit friends, you have the effect of bringing wild animals into a flower shop. Even friends who claim to like children are reticent, afraid to interfere. Children belong to their parents, and in the case of small children, mother always knows best.

In fact, mother *does* know best. But the famous maternal instict, female intuition, that telepathic communication between mother and baby, is born of the

190

circumstances and the necessity to learn, rather than some inbuilt genetic trait peculiar to women. Through the intimate and continuous contact with a baby, one learns a whole non-verbal language. Cries which to other people sound like noise can, to a mother, because of this contact, communicate happiness, hunger, wind, pain - with a clarity as great as if the baby could speak. It is like the telepathy between twins, lovers or even very close friends, where an intimate knowledge of the other person enables one to pick up clues which may be totally invisible to strangers. Because of the close contact between the biological mother and her baby, it is she, rather than the father, who learns these signs; by contrast he is heavy and unsubtle in his understanding of what the small baby's emotional and physical needs are.

The subtlety of communication between mother and child should be something to extend to other kinds of relationships, but in the context of the family it has a confining backlash. You understand your child best because you want to and have to; so the rest of the world thankfully leaves you to get on with it. If you are ill, depressed or just plain bored, no-one can simply take over. The job isn't simply functional, it is emotional too. The child senses when someone less sensitive to its needs is looking after it. If you are ill, you find yourself instructing your husband or friends to look after the child in exactly the way you do. Because the child inevitably becomes insecure, having been deprived of the full attention of its mother, you then have to cope with feeling guilty because you are responsible for the child's unhappiness.

The combination of this total and perpetual emotional responsibility with the sheer physical work involved in looking after a home and a child (or children) means that often there are long periods when anxiety, guilt, keeping the house going take up most of one's emotional and physical energy. The idea that you are doing the whole thing out of 'love' becomes so much part of the landscape that you forget about it. You begin to identify that vague, nebulous, seductive feeling of pure romantic love with all the drudgery and worry; the dream doesn't hold up too well against such a background.

The problem is compounded with the birth of a second child. We planned our second child, like our first. We rationalised the age difference between them as follows: 'If they're only one year apart they'll be competitive. If they're three years apart, the gap will be too wide for them to make friends. Two and a half years is the ideal gap. One child will get lonely, three children means too many years coping with babies, two children is just right. Two children will replace us on the planet; ideally they should be a boy and a girl'. The plan worked perfectly, except in the last detail: the child was another boy. The illusion of free choice in the way we were planning our lives was still so strong that we felt a sense of failure at not having managed a girl. We had just missed being the perfect family.

Two children are more than twice as much work as one. A toddler and a baby demand totally different kinds of care and attention. They eat different food, have different routines, wear different kinds of clothes. Above all, they demand different emotional responses. No longer being the centre of attention, the first child is justifiably affected by her/his displacement.Another human being is demanding half his precious emotional share. The situation makes it inevitable that the child is jealous.As a mother you have to compensate for this displacement, while, at the same time, trying to give the new baby everything you gave the first child. Inevitably, you fail.

The work is more than doubled, the emotional strain is more than doubled. You have to be mother and psychologist at the same time. And all the time you have been trying to remain a wife, the adult companion of the man you married. The impossibility of maintaining a cool, smiling control in the face of the contradictory demands from children and husband means that one's sense of purpose as a wife and mother begin to blur increasingly. For me, until the point at which my second child was a few months old, all doubts and discontents were assimilable. But now the family I wanted was a living reality and what could I see? Isolation, a sense of never being able to keep up with the constant mess and chaos, an inability to respond adequately (according to my high ideals) to the children. Guilt at my inability to be calm and coping, maintaining an orderly house in the face of an apparently ordered world. A profound sense of bewilderment and guilt, that I wasn't what I could describe as 'happy' looking after the children and being a housewife. Loving the children, and, after the first two hours of the day, longing for the moment when they both slept in the afternoon so that I could be alone. Even now, I am hurled awake in the morning by the happy sounds of children arguing or playing loudly; the apparently crucial dream time just before waking is always interrupted if you are a mother. Almost every day, for the last few years, for me, has begun with a violent awakening. In those very early days there was no-one who really understood the dilemma; although I complained to and with other mothers, it was always half-jokingly. No-one ever admitted they didn't like being full time mothers. Perhaps some did. But since every woman's loyalty was primarily to her husband, none of us could really be honest with each other. For one of us to explode at the impossibility of the situation would have been too threatening for the others; we were all vulnerable to being thought failures.

It is too easy for women, unhappy in their roles as wives and mothers, to see themselves as individual failures. By nature you *should* be happy. Therefore if you are not you're unnatural. Your children and husband depend on you. You can't walk out or go on strike. There are no apparent wages or conditions of work to argue about. And to whom can you take your complaints? You have no boss. You made the choice, the free and natural choice. You got married and had children out of love. Romantic love is an ideological mask for many other truths. The security of the home and its deceptive freedom from the immediate control operative in any work situation have their own backlash. You lose contact with any sense of the 'real' world, and you think in frames of reference and a language which are looked down on by most people - 'womens's talk'. After a while you come to relish the misery of this isolation as a frying-pan alternative to the fire of exposure as a possible failure; after years of being used to living in a home alone with your children, you become terrified of confronting the world of work and other people outside your family. The isolation is both the cause and the consolation, and every detail in it becomes grossly exaggerated. A child accidentally spilling orange juice on a just-cleaned floor can spill you into a morass of hysteria. I've said nothing about my recurring feelings of resentment and violence towards everything, including the children - perhaps because I have most guilt and fear about these feelings. The emotional maze has no way out.

What actually happens is that you go mad. But nobody notices, not even you. I use the word 'mad' to describe a state of dislocation in which you don't know where or who you are. You are a kind of bewildered prize in the tug of war between children and husband. Your life should be heaven but it feels like punishment and prison. There is no time or space to worry about yourself; you are constantly at the mercy of the demands of those around you. No woman can emerge from this situation totally undamaged, and many women are damaged severely. It's just that the signs are dismissed; they're 'neurotic' or 'hysterical' or 'unnatural'. On the surface women cope, children grow up physically healthy, the family facade is maintained. But, for the woman, her sense of herself has been pushed into the background, in favour of a series of different, and often contradictory, masks which she is required to put on, to play all the roles demanded of her in her function as wife and mother.

194

Part Two

Economic

The majority of women are either totally economically dependent on their husbands, or substantially so; if they work, they either earn a lower rate, work at less well-paid jobs, or part time. Within the family, where the wife does not work at all, and thus has no visible earning power, the situation is not seen as *dependence*, but rather as *sharing*. You could say it was a fair distribution of labour. But his work is defined by another place and by set hours. Above all, his jobs is defined, and he is paid for it. Your work is never done because the place you work in is also your home, and there is always something to do. No-one pays you; no-one defines the limits of your job; it is defined by negatives; the only thing you don't do is earn the money and go outside the home to work. The fact that money, and with it the means for survival, comes into his hands first means that there is an embargo on demands by the woman for him to share the housework. He can refuse to get up in the middle of the night to look after the baby, to do his own washing, to cook or clean, on the grounds that he needs to conserve all his energy for his own 'work', because that's what earns the money to keep you all going. On the one hand, a woman's work is not defined as work because it is the only necessary job in society not given a money value, on the other hand it is defined as work for the husband only when he doesn't want to do it, and places his own work as a priority. If he does 'help' with the housework it is as a favour to his wife, out of love for her, not out of responsibility towards his share of it.

The woman's relationship to money is indirect; she is responsible for spending it - on necessaries and luxuries - but not for directly earning it. Thus she can never buy anything as an autonomous individual, she has to ask her husband for the money (even with a joint bank account this is the basis for the different relationships husband and wife have towards money which is just earned by the husband). If her ambitions are for a bigger and better house, she becomes a power behind the throne, needing to manipulate her man, or 'encourage' or 'advise' him to get on in the world so that the family can have what she decides it needs. It is the fact that she is screened, and that basically most husbands prefer it that way, that turns her into a wielder of psychological power.

The economics of marriage are hidden; it is only when a marriage breaks down that men and women have to cope with the fact that marriage is as much an explicit economic contract as an emotional one. For the woman, this screening from a direct earning relationship means that she is only of value to her immediate family. They are the only ones who depend on what you do in the house. You therefore face the contradiction of being totally needed at home, and totally ignored outside it. In public you are painfully aware that everyone sees you as his wife, not as yourself (whoever that might be). You accept society's definitions of wives; they're only needed in the home. On the one hand you dismiss yourself with 'Oh, I'm only a housewife', on the other you are seething, because you know that the hours you spend working are extremely long; on the one hand you see yourself as not understanding the world of money, wages and prices, on the other you know that you run a complex organisation, doing all the work, and managing intricate budgets in your head. The idea of women's work at home being done for love is so deeply rooted that many men find it personally insulting to suggest that what their wives do can be seen as 'work'. This implies that they have bought their wives in some way. That there is a market where women are bought and sold. Well, there is. The survival of a woman who is not economically independent is as dependent on her husband's feelings for her as that of a slave is on his master's estimate of how useful the slave is to him. In both cases the husband/master has the ultimate power. Often it is not one he welcomes, but the fact remains that society places the power in his hands and then punishes his wife if he won't behave in the way he ought - support her till death do them part. It is virtually impossible for a woman to earn enough to support herself and her children if her husband leaves, or they separate and he either will not, or cannot afford to, support two households.

Unconsciously, I believe most couples have some awareness of this fact. It is hard to see how such a power-conflict situation can avoid affecting whatever relationship a man and woman have before they get married. Many couples have interminable arguments about money; others, thinking themselves more fastidious, perhaps, have tussles of will, psychological battles. These are attempts of the individuals to transcend the crippling unity into which their economic situation forces them. However, the independence is a question both of economics and of fighting for a totally different living situation from that of the family; within its structure the illusion of independence is gained either through a permanent situation of conflict, or one in which the two protagonists mark out different areas of power.

Control in the home

The world is mediated to the wife through her husband. Money comes to her via his work; psychologically her experience of the world is also at second hand. When they go out together he probably handles the money, and the process of transaction. Because his life is broadly divided between two places - home and work - he is better equipped to cope with relationships with other people. Work outside the home is social, you see and have relationships with other people. Men represent 'the world' with good reason; they own it and run much of it.

The helplessness which a woman experiences outside the security of her own home serves to increase the intensity with which she then knows and controls her home. Generally it is the woman who decides how the house is to be organised, where everything - clothes, cutlery, dishes etc. - will go. A man may not be in political control of his work, but he is in control of his working function. By contrast, when he comes home he is in his wife's world; he is helpless. It is necessary for him to be helpless so that she can at least maintain control of the area she's got; it also gives him another excuse not to get involved with the house and the messier parts of caring for children. The woman is subconsciously aware of the precariousness of her control and the game takes on a hectic collusive quality: she complains about his helplessness, while encouraging it by implying he can never do anything properly about the house ('couldn't even boil an egg'). He is allowed to perform structural jobs, make bookshelves, wash the car (work outside the house, even when he's at home) but none of the intimate, personal functions which are a woman's domain. If he could do them as well as she, he would be a threat to the small bit of autonomy she's got. And then she would be redundant. While he may occasionally cook a perfect meal, or look after the children if she's ill, just to prove he could if it were his 'job', he too steers clear of a real sharing; both need to keep the roles and the power areas in them delicately balanced.

Motherhood and roles

The responsibilities of a mother are multiple; you not only have to feed a child, keep it clean and healthy, but you also give it love, help it to learn to live in the world, transmit the values and ideas you believe to be important. At first you have to do practically everything for the baby; dress it, change it, wash its clothes, hold its head up, create a protective environment in which it can be warm, fed, comfortable and happy.

Because a woman's work takes place at home, and is presumed to be motivated by love, she performs many functions for her husband which are similar to those she performs for the child. She cleans the house, washes
198

his clothes, empties his ashtray, makes his bed, buys and prepares his food, looks after him when he's ill. She creates for him a protective environment in which he can relax when he comes home from a hard day's work, in which he can be warm, fed, comfortable and happy. As soon as there is a baby in the house, most of the day is taken up doing these things as mother-functions. But as she does the same for her husband, the distinction between mother-and lover-functions becomes blurred. She becomes mother to both husband and child. He is no longer simply a helpless man, but a helpless child.

However, while her role may become blurred to herself, it is less so for her husband. He still expects the mother to be the woman he married, to maintain the uncluttered sexual relationship (before children imposed restrictions on their autonomous relationship), to throw off the new harrassed Mum-image and compete favourably with all the single, sexy women out in the world. The woman's problem is that the nature of her work is such that she has to be whatever is demanded of her at the time, and most often those demands are contradictory and impossible to meet. She is everyone's emotional cushion; one minute she may be nurse to baby, the next minute she is required (and often requires herself) to play intelligent, sexy companion to husband. She has to please children and husband, and take the emotional consequences of failure if she doesn't.

Mother as teacher and child

A full time mother is with her child or children for almost 24 hours a day. This is because you are acutely conscious of the child all the time, even when it and you are sleeping. From birth until the age of five, the mother is the chief socialiser, teaching the child ideas and values as well as purely mechanical things like how to eat with cutlery, use the potty, walk and talk. A child's first ideas about the world come from its mother. It is a ludicrous situation; cut off from most social and work situations, a mother is supposed to be able to train her child to take part in them. While investing most of her own emotional energy in the child, and inevitably causing the child to be similarly dependent on her, a mother is at the same time expected to bring up a child who will not be frightened when separated from her at school, to bring up her child to be friendly and outgoing, responsible and co-operative, and a whole range of other liberal qualities. A mother is expected to be the perfect teacher and to produce the perfect object: the clean, charming, curious but not obstreperous child. The burden of ideas about 'creative' motherhood is especially strong if you believe in some form of progressive education; you are supposed to allow the child freedom to turn the house upside down in the interests of free development, knowing that you are the one left with the mess when play is over. It is no wonder that most children feel deeply threatened and insecure when their mothers are not with them. They have never learned to trust anyone else; indeed, why should they, unless other people show they are to be trusted, that they take the same kind of responsibility as the child's mother.

There are advantages in the closeness of the relationship; as well as the subtleties of the communication system you develop between you, continuous contact with a child means that as well as teaching, you also re-learn. Emotional spontaneity in play; you giggle at apparent trivialities, the threshold of your emotions resembles that of the child; from fury to bliss in three seconds flat. Contact with small children is liberating in many ways for adults. It puts us back in touch with our basic, more naive responses to things. When children begin to ask questions we have to reassess our world from the way it may appear to a child, we have to find simple and clear ways of expressing complex ideas and explaining situations. In answering a child's questions we become more aware of the way in which we see the world ourselves. You can mess around with paints, make noises, roll around on the floor, and learn to play again. As a child learns to speak it explores language; you also explore language, imitating the child as it makes efforts to imitate you. The process of learning becomes in itself a private language; you use baby talk which is only clear to your own child. You may draw your husband into the private language, and behave towards each other as though you were both children again.

However, the liberating effect of this relationship is again defined by the isolated situation in which it occurs. It is a clandestine activity. If you talk baby talk in the street people will think you're mad. If you persist, they'll think you are regressing. You have to switch on different languages at different times. This is immensely confusing for the child; at home he may experience you as a friend, free and equal in some situations, controlling in others, but in the world he sees you as a more authoritarian mediator. It is a while before you can explain to a child why it is you encourage him to ask questions about everything at home, but if he asks a questions about race or sex on the bus in a very loud voice, it is less easy to answer honestly, and more often than not you evade answering without explaining why.

While some of the emotional freedom may extend to your husband, that too has its limits. If you have an argument and burst into tears he is likely to accuse you of being hysterical, whereas if his child reacted in the same way he would have accepted it as a response. In some situations being free to respond emotionally is seen as retrogressive, while in others it is charming and desirable. As a mother you have to learn to switch being a child on and off according to who you are with, and often this involves a betrayal of your relationship with your child. Within the home, the child feels your loyalty is to him, outside it, to other adults. The emotional power you have over your child is immense. You are his central source of emotional security. This means that until the child is old enough (often not till well into the teens) you can not only express affection and happiness towards him, but also take out on the child all the frustrations and angers you feel about other people and situations.

Mother as sex subject and object

Women are taught that their sexual role is basically the submissive one in the complementary game to men's aggressive role. Women's sexual power takes a more insidious form than men's; while appearing passive and docile and pretty they must also develop ways of being sexually competitive with other women and psychologically making sure their desired man notices that they're there. The game is an unpleasant and elaborate one, of different forms of power play, and in most relationships this pattern dominates sexuality as much as other areas.

Our prevailing sexual morality is a repressive one, and it is naive to assume that two individuals, subject to the moral pressures and ideas of society, suddenly develop a liberated sexual relationship just because their decision to marry means they have the moral and legal sanctions of society. Women's economic and psychological dependence on men is also a sexual dependence. Husbands still want their wives to be sexy (so many women's magazines feature short-cuts to how a housewife can suddenly whip off her work mask and put on her dolly mask when her husband comes home from work), women still want to be reassured that they are still desirable.

To a certain extent the rules of the game do not apply in the physical relationship between mother and child, which is close and profoundly sensual. At first, you *have* to handle a child; you touch every part of its body intimately, you are in contact with all its bodily functions: you feed it, clean its vomit, change nappies, powder its body, caress its softness. Of course the contact is maternal but it is also sensually pleasurable for both of you: skin on skin. Feeding a small warm baby in the middle of the
202

night is one of the most serene and sensual experiences possible.

This contact, sensual but rarely consciously seen as such because of the powerful incest taboos that still prevail, is predicated on a situation in which the mother is in control. She initiates the contact, and then has to restrain this response in relation to other children and adults. The sensual freedom between mother and child contrasts with her relationship with her husband in which she is once more the child, waiting for his initiative, his approval. Her passivity exaggerates the need she has for control over her child, and the control she has highlights the passive role she has to play with her husband and other people.

Coda - noise and tyranny

In the maternity hospital I took great pride in being able to distinguish my baby's cry from all the others. Somewhere in the first Act of Edward Bond's play 'Saved', a baby wakes up and cries. Its mother is watching television and doesn't feel like responding. The baby wakes properly and cries louder. The mother again ignores it. The baby really gets going, settling on a pitch of emotional stridency which is exactly the right frequency to hit the threshold of noise tolerance. By the end of five minutes I was squirming in my seat.

The baby's cry expresses need; other sounds express happiness. At first, with a new baby, one is constantly alert to try and understand the meanings of different sounds. You learn. And the baby also learns that you, as mother, are the most likely person to respond and be able to satisfy its needs - you are the only person there. However, the emotional demand is a one-way system; the child demands and you respond. After a while, constantly available for any emotional demand at any time, you are screaming inwardly too, for your right to be heard, to be allowed to make a demand. The availability is physical too. The power you have to take out your frustrations on the child is returned. The child makes physical demands on your body too. Tugs at you, climbs all over you; your feelings, your mind, your body are not your own. They belong to something you created yourself. The word you awaited most eagerly from your child, 'Mummy', becomes a signal for inner panic - 'What now?' Often, the only time you can be alone in the house is when you lock yourself in the lavatory, and even then the child is likely to come and bang on the door.

Anything you do is a threat to your child's security; the child knows that it's totally dependent on you and, in self defence, becomes a tyrant making petty compulsive demands to be reassured. Children are sensitive; they are right to be insecure. If one of their parents goes, half their emotional world disappears. We have no right to expect them to feel secure. It is not their fault, and yet, battered by demands, often one wishes violently to be completely rid of them in order to get some sense of one's self. Ironically, even when you can go out alone, it merely takes another strange child in the street to shout 'Mummy' to evoke the reflex response 'What now?' The condition of motherhood is always with you.

Answers

The home is a place of refuge and shelter from the rest of the world. It is a defensive oasis: the front door isn't just a plank of wood, designed to keep out the rain and the prying eyes of neighbours, but a symbol of the division between two worlds - the outside, public world, and the inside, private world. We are told that, as women, we belong to the private inner world, caring for children, free to organise our time, unfettered by tedious jobs. We should be grateful. But caring for children in isolation is a nonstarter; we produce isolated children. We are free to organise our time to do housework which becomes meaningless, to be isolated and unstimulated, cut off from all contact with other activities. What began as a dream of love and security, a challenge, the building of a home and family, becomes a nightmare.

I've said little about the way men and children are specifically opppressed by the nuclear family structure. This is partly because children have still got their lives in front of them (if they survive their family horrors) and men have some compensations denied to women. At the very least they can get out of the house and see there is a world outside the four walls. They have more structures within which to organise change if that is what they think is necessary. It is also because I believe that the impetus to change the organisation of the family must come from women. After all, we know more about it than men, and have more power than children.

The work women do in the home is socially necessary; people must eat, have somewhere to live, clothes to wear, be looked after when they are ill. Children must be looked after, loved and taught about the world. The nuclear family structure is the worst possible structure within which to perform these tasks, and within which to build our closest relationships. There are many good reasons why Western society so manically defends the family. As Margaret Benston points out in a pamphlet called *The Political Economy of Women's Liberation:*

...the amount of unpaid labour performed by women is very large and very profitable for those who own the means of production. To pay women for their work, even at minimum wage scales, would imply a massive redistribution of wealth. At present, the support of a family is a hidden tax on the wage earner - his wage buys the labour power of two people.

When women have been, needed in production, the State has hastily provided nurseries (as during World War II); but even nurseries, or the argument as to whether the answer is to acknowledge women's role in the home by paying them a wage, do not touch on the central idea, which is the surface motivating force behind women's 'choice' to become wives and mothers; and that is, that women are naturally more suited to those roles than men. It is nonsense; any human being (including many children) can care for another, can do housework, can love and look after babies.

It is also an insufficient argument to say that child rearing only occupies five or ten years of a woman's life.

Once a mother, always a mother; the emotional responsibility goes on until the children are totally independent (often never). Besides, the only job which makes allowances for school holidays is teaching. Which means that any woman who wants to work and look after her children must become a teacher - an ideological and professional extension of her maternal role. The middle class answer of an au pair system is one of the most hypocritical and exploitative solutions; not only are many of the girls exploited with no way to protect themselves, but the situation is such that the only way women with jobs can solve the problem of who is to look after their children is by taking a total stranger from another culture into the sanctuary of their private homes, as a 'substitute' mother who has no real committment to the situation; it amounts often to a betrayal of the child's needs.

The answers will not come from simply juggling around with the existing elements of the present family structure; a tiny minority of couples can share the responsibilities of work and home between them. Most jobs are full time, and the opportunities for women to earn as much as men are still limited. Attempts like this, plus campaigns for community controlled nurseries will undoubtedly help. Campaigns for more jobs to be open to women, for equal pay, will all help. But the aim must be to transform the basis of the family structure, and those of our personal relationships. And while there is a great deal we can do now, we cannot achieve a complete transformation within the present political system.

Once we begin to realise that there is nothing wrong with thinking that there's a great deal wrong with the family, we are on the way to working for change. Ultimately this must apply to men as well as women. Unless men can also see the way they oppress women in the home, and what they themselves are losing by not taking responsibility for the care of children, we will not be able to push for any substantial change in the family structure - now or in any future system. We must also break down the ideology of possession which makes us consider our children as objects we own. People without children must want to care for children as such, if we are to break out of the confinement of parental responsibility. Those of us who have children have to fight those elements in ourselves; we will have to learn to allow our children to develop close relationships with other adults. There is no natural law that says parents and children *must* like each other. At the very least we need a structure flexible enough for men, women and children to explore relationships and autonomy within a secure context, with as much responsibility and as little dependence as possible.

At the moment it is up to women to stop rocking the cradle and start rocking the boat. We cannot any longer accept our passive role. If we have never before accepted responsibility for what happens in our society, then now's the time to start.

The call to abandon their illusions about their conditions is a call to abandon a condition which requires illusions.

(Marx)

Michelene Wandor
1972

PRESTON.

Functions of the family

The pressure of the family ideal is so pervasive that people outside it - spinsters, bachelors, unmarried mothers, the divorced and gay people - symbolise either deviancy, personal failure or abnormality. It is because the family is the only sanctioned unit for living that everything which in any way threatens it takes on the proportions of a serious 'social problem' - that is, free contraception, 'promiscuity', abortion, illegitimacy, 'broken homes' and homosexuality. All these things threaten the stability and, indeed, the inflexibility of family life.

It's vitally important to capitalism that we should all be hooked on the dream of happy families. It is, actually, a visual dream, projected in the adverts and in children's story books, giving everyone an instant, composite, packaged dream of the 'average' (ideal) family. It's a handsome, briefcase-carrying man, a smiling, ap-roned woman (usually pictured serving food), a bright boy of about 8 and a sweet girl of 6, all living together with an assortment of consumer aids to easy living. There are no old people, no cross words, no illness, no poverty and no rain and no-one ever grows any older. It's a static dream to cherish which is never quite fantasy because it's always around the corner or somebody else has it.

We live in two families - the one we are born into and the one we make. The period when the second family is together is the shortest period in the whole family cycle, but it is the one by which the rest is measured. If we see the whole cycle as a film with a beginning, a middle and an end, we can see that the time when parents and children are living together has been caught in a static frame and blown up out of all proportion, and is so projected as to de-signify the rest of the film. So it is that the family unit is the peak of the pyramid of the social hierarchy against which individual lives appear as one long 'before and after'. It is against this that the following startling facts fit into place. Less than one quarter of the country's households contain dependent children and 40% of the next generation are growing up in only 9% of all households. To put it another way, in one individual life span of 70 years, less than half of those years will be spent in an intact family unit.

On the face of it, the organisation of people on a mass scale into small, privatized units appears natural, inevitable, convenient and desirable. It also seems as though we are not pressured into the family but that, like measles or flu, families just happen to people. So we use terms like 'fall in love' and then, like night after day, children 'come along'. In fact, one chooses to live within the sanctioned unit as adults, because one would otherwise have to make what appears to be a negative choice - that is, not to fall in love, not to marry, not to try and buy a house and not to have children. What this means is that we do not choose the family; we are taken by the hand and firmly led into it. Because the nuclear family per-forms essential functions for capitalism which other social groupings would not do, it's imperative that we remain hooked on the dream and ignorant or sus-picious of its alternatives.

If the family is the backbone of society (capitalism), as its defenders so fondly tell us, then institutionalised monogamy is the spinal cord. Instead of women and men relating freely together - and women with women and men with men - we have the one woman/one man principle which pressures two people into marriage at the first inkling of affection and later persuades them to breed and to love each other through thick and thin and, if not, then at least to carry on living together - so that one woman and one man come to symbolise not two autonomous people but a joint institution. This institution is a fundamental form of *social control.* Admissions that marriage is a form of social control are hard to come by but John Ekalaar, writing a book on family law, let one slip:

The family is a social organism which arises to fulfil certain needs of society and of individuals and which is subject to natural processes of decay and ultimate dissolution. Society cannot eradicate these processes, yet it can, by social pressure and by law, *so channel them as to lessen the risk of family disruption. To this end it employs the purely legal concept of marriage to confer special recognition upon certain family groups* in order to enable them better to perform the functions required of them in society. *(my emphasis)*

In other words, marriage makes men into breadwinners and women into wives and mothers. It imposes on women and men functions which are in no sense natural to them but which act entirely in the interests of the system.

It is clear that marriage is the first and basic model of the division of labour and of power between the sexes, the legalised sanction whereby society justifies the public separation of men from women by throwing them together in private. Marriage contains the gross economic, social and sexual inequalities between men and women. It removes the struggle that women perpetually wage against male authority to an apparently safe and insignificant place - the home. This struggle has always been assumed not to exist merely because it takes place without spectators, and doesn't trouble the outside world. But it's there wherever we care to look - in the 'domestic' row, in the woman's silent hurts, the wells of resentment at male privilege and economic control, the bitterness at the loss of female autonomy, the slammed door and the not uncommon fear of violence. These are the cracks in every marriage structure which romantic love merely papers over.

The bridge that marriage constructs across the sexes is an illusion which most of us are constrained to enact as reality. By disguising the division between the sexes which this society perpetrates and profits from, (e.g. the degradation of women as sexual objects), it reinforces the apartheid of public life and removes the battleground from the public to the private domain. Our personal lives may be disrupted by it, and in many cases, utterly destroyed, but all the while the wheels of capitalism turn smoothly, and indifferently. As long as men and women quarrel in private or submerge their differences in silence, while maintaining a married face to the outside world, the chasm between women and men will continue to serve the society that created it.

The family hinges on monogamy as capitalism hinges on the family. In fact, throughout the world, the growth of capitalism has ushered in the nuclear family, leaving in its wake devastated tribal and clan systems. A sociologist of the family noted, in a cross-cultural study, that:

in all parts of the world and for the first time in world history all social systems are moving fast or slowly toward some form of the conjugal family system and also toward industrialisation.

It is no accident. One of the first requirements of a capitalist economy is a mobile, docile workforce - that is, men and women who are willing to learn skills and sell their labour wherever they are needed, and this they cannot do if they are tied, either emotionally or physically, to a larger family or community network. That the extended family is now nothing more than a quaint anachronism, surviving in a few depressed pockets of industrial society (e.g. Glasgow, South West) is an indication of how effective capitalism is when it invades what we regard as the personal domain.

The arrangements most suited to serve the interests of the system are those most people are forced to make, so that what a worker travels with is that which will keep him happy, fed, clothed, rewarded for his labours, work-fixated, satisfied and perpetuated, i.e. wife and children. (Too many single men and women, without the much valued stabilising influence of a home and family, who are free to go on strike more easily, are an obvious threat to the economic system. So also are the shifting, light travelling brigade of building workers and other lump workers.) So the best arrangement a man can make, regardless of his class or education, is to:

1. take a wife who will care for him and see to all his needs and bear and rear his children

2. live with them in a small, isolated group, preferably away from his first family, with whom his links must be only nominal (aged parents are a liability)

3. be intent on maintaining or improving his standard of living, thereby committing himself to overtime or professional ladder climbing, both of which require long hours away from home and a patient, uncomplaining wife

4. be prepared to move house from time to time (in pursuit of higher paid work, or to move from areas of unemployment to industrial areas) but not to strike

5. support a wife and growing family.

The woman's arrangements must parallel her husband's. But, as well as applying herself to long, unpaid hours of work in the home, seeing to her husband's and children's needs, she must also be prepared to work outside the home for 'pin' money (low pay), but not to identify with her work role. She must only see her job as significant insofar as it adds to the family spending power and gives her something to do when the children grow up. Her work must not give her privileges or independence, because her husband's mobility, which is so vital, depends on her dependence on him. Where he goes, so must she. So that, if she is laid off at work or subjected to terrible working conditions and pay, it will not affect her docility. Thus, two basic needs of capitalism are met. The family gives it a mobile, docile workforce and a secondary, casual workforce.

Most of the functions of the nuclear family hinge directly on the woman's role. We are told, for instance, that the family serves to contain the worker's discontents and alienation. In simple terms, it means that the industrial worker can punch his wife but not his boss. The sociologists have been busy documenting the problem of the industrial worker's alienation for a very long time. Here, for instance, is one typical statement:

At lower job levels the worker experiences little intrinsic job satisfaction; at higher levels he obtains more job satisfaction but is also subject to rather greater demands. At any level, the enterprise has no responsibility for the emotional input-output balance of the individual; this is solely the responsibility of the family, in the sense that there is nowhere else for it to go. The small family, then, deals with the problem which the industrial system cannot handle.

It's not the family which deals with the 'problem'; it's the woman in the family. But there is a gross over-sight. It is assumed that only men work and only men experience work alientation. What is conveniently forgotten is that two thirds of married women go out to work and most of them work in conditions equally as appalling as men's and for far less pay, but who is there to siphon off their work discontents? Who is there to cook the woman's meals, clean her house, put her children to bed, wash her clothes and smoothe her brow? Who tries to get home before she does so that the place will be warm and welcoming for her?

It is *women* who represent the refuge from work, who attend to the worker's - i.e. the husband's - psychological, sexual and physical well-being and who recharge his batteries so that he can continue to be exploited at work.

The function of the family which remains dominant in the ideology is its child rearing function. I don't have to point out that, here again, it is not the family's function but the woman's. If her husband helps, that is his choice but, with the way our lives are structured, even the best intentioned man will find it hard to take a constructive hand in child rearing when he must be away from the home for upwards of 40 hours a week. Whether women work outside the home or not, they take responsibility for and, in most cases, the bulk of the physical work of child care. What I want to stress here is that the child rearing function of the family has given rise to the notion that the family is nothing more nor less than a vehicle for love and nurturance - a tiny enclave of love and caring in a sea of materialism. What is forgotten is that the old, like children, also need loving care and attention. But the nuclear family, being tailored to suit the needs of a capitalist economy, has no space or time for those whose productive usefulness is exhausted. Where once the family was a defensive unit, with the able-bodied men and women working to support the dependent young, old and sick, it is now a unit wholly concerned with consumption and repro- duction. The old are rejected because they cannot make economic contributions to society; the family must be pared down to include only those whom society can use. Knowing this, we are still shocked by the con- ditions in which many old people live - when star- vation drives them to choke to death trying to eat cardboard, or when they've been left to die alone in their homes and their bodies are not discovered for weeks. And the judges at their inquests say that such things shouldn't happen in a 'civilised' society. What we must remember is that such things *only* happen in so- called civilised societies.

It was found that a hundred years ago, when capitalism was still struggling to co-exist with traditional family patterns, 80% of old people lived with their kin. Now the figure is nearer 10% and the remaining 90% are left to live out their days in poverty, in institutions and in geriatric wards of hospitals. Many are also vegetating in mental homes, though it is known that their only complaint is age and 'uselessness'.

While the dependent old represent a burden, the dependent young are an asset. They represent the future labour force, so that time, money and effort spent on them is not wasted as it would be on the old. I would maintain that children are not only reared in the family, they are, to a large extent, processed. They are stamped, labelled, educated and graded, first by reference to their genitals, then by reference to their class and then by reference to their 'intelligence'. To keep the economic system going (and the profits flowing), we need businessmen, bankers, scientists, technologists and academics and, to keep them in business, we need an army of men to mine their coal, assemble cars, build roads, forge steel and, to keep *them* going, we need an auxiliary army of women to work the service industries and, to support the whole unwieldy edifice, we need those same women to care for the children, shop, cook, wash, sweep floors and make beds. The family is capitalism's appointed agent for producing the kind of adults the system needs.

It is within the family that the child learns what has been described as its 'role obligations', and where, also, inappropriate values, expectations and behaviour will be screened out. The young girl who wants to be a vet, ballet dancer or doctor will be discouraged by her parents who, though they do not like it, must nevertheless *act on behalf of the capitalist system.* Society only needs a handful of vets and ballet dancers but it needs an awful lot of women whose life work is caring for men and children, with only the odd stop-gap job inbetween.

Perhaps the most vital function of the family under

capitalism is its economic one. The family consumes.
It is, at one and the same time, the dumping
ground for over-production and the pivot of the capitalist machine. The system demands that each family
barricades itself in, in a small house or flat, in order
to fill it with consumer goods. We have only to look
at a tower block of flats with 80 homes, each one of
which will have its washing machine, hoover, television
set, radio, iron, private kitchen with assorted gadgets
etc. Now we have the technology to collectivise and
eradicate most of the menial tasks which each woman
in each flat performs in isolation from every other.
We have the technology for a shute in each flat which
would carry everyone's dirty washing to a central
automated area in the basement which would wash,
dry, air and iron those clothes and return them. But
the market for 80 washing machines, dryers, irons and
ironing boards is eliminated at one blow, and so also
is the alienated labour of the woman, standing mind-
lessly over the machine which is supposed to ease her
labour. The profit system guarantees that 80 families
will buy a washing machine in order for each one to
stand idle for 90% of its time.

And, here again, it is the woman who is the prime
target of advertising and consumer bombardment and
who is asked to try and resolve the impossible contradictions in her role within the family by succumbing
to commercial pressure. The family acts, then, as a
multiplicity of isolated consumption units and provides
capitalism with an almost inexhaustible market, guaran-
teeing wasteful production, alienated labour and profits.

It is women, more than men, who are both the
victims and the casualties of this, because they are
locked at the base of every family, upholding it and
exploited and oppressed because of it.

Lee Comer
April 1973

*Paper given at the Leeds Conference on The Family
in April 1973. Subsequently published in RED RAG*

The Family, Social Work & the Welfare State

Social work is woman's work in a double sense. Most social workers are women and most of their clients are women. This situation arises, I believe, out of the structural similarities between the nature of social work and the role of women as wives and mothers. Both social work and women's domestic labour within the family are concerned with ensuring the efficient reproduction of labour power. As they are both engaged in similar types of labour, women as social workers and women as wives and mothers share some similar attitudes to their labour and experience some similar contradictions. Professional women in teaching or social work are often considered to be very distinct from the 'ordinary housewife'. However, I want to suggest that there is a real unity of interests between these two groups of women (after all we're sometimes the same person), and that there are many issues on which we can fight together, not just on the basis of sisterhood, but out of the realities of our different situations.

The reproduction of labour power

Obviously any society has to have some mechanism for ensuring its own reproduction if it wishes to continue for any length of time. This means that capitalism, like any other society, has to reproduce its own relations of production, that is to say, it has to reproduce the class system. In particular, there has to be some method which will ensure that the working class (in capitalism the working man), gets up every day, suitably fed and clothed, with the requisite skills and attitudes to sell his labour power in the market, and which will ensure that there are children to carry on the great tradition. In advanced capitalism there are a number of structures which carry out this function, but one of the most significant is the family and women's domestic labour within it.

In other historical epochs the family was more or less co-determinous with the unit of production, although women were still subjugated within it. Under capitalism the family ceased to have a direct relationship with production and women and children were gradually excluded from the factories, mines and workshops. The change in the means and relations of production and the exclusion of women had, I believe, a profound effect on the family and women's labour within it. Women began to labour in the home to reproduce male labour power for the market.

This development had two further consequences. Only labour in the production of commodities for exchange were socially valued and paid a wage. Therefore women's labour in the home was systematically under-valued or not seen as labour at all. Instead, women's domestic labour was submerged in her 'womanhood' and under-written by a number of ideologies, ranging from crude biological determinism to the most sophisticated types of family casework.

In fact, the actual work involved in reproducing labour is complex and varied. As it has been elaborated at greater length elsewhere (1), suffice it to say here that it includes reproducing the means of subsistence, shopping, cooking, cleaning, irnoning, the reproduction, care and socialisation of children and the reproduction of interpersonal relationships, 'tension management' in all its bewildering psycho-sexual forms.

The Welfare State and the reproduction of labour power

The gradual exclusion of women and children from production under capitalism was also paralleled by increasing

218

State intervention in areas of life which had previously been the province of other institutions like the Church or the inalienable right of every man to do what he wished with his own. Indeed, the early factory legislation was opposed by many industrialists for this reason. There is only space here to indicate some of the developments in this process, so it is impossible to go into the contradictions and class conflict which led to the creation of a welfare system. It was out of these, however, that the Welfare State did arise and I in no way wish to suggest that it was just a devilish plot on the part of the ruling class.

The creation of an industrialised proletariat gave rise in the 19th century to several problems. On the one hand, capital was getting through nine generations of its workers in the span of three generations and epidemics were rife, often even carrying off members of the ruling class. Prince Albert died of cholera in 1865. On the other hand, the workforce was by turn and place both profligate and militant. As Tennyson's northern farmer remarked, 'Taake my word for it Sammy, the poor in a loomp is bad'.

To deal with both these situations and in response to working class demand, legislation was introduced throughout the century to improve the health and welfare of the working class and to create a State apparatus in local government and the civil service to administer this legislation. The two most crucial periods of reform were those that occurred under the Liberal Government prior to the 1914-18 war and the legislation of the Labour Government after the second world war. Lloyd George's government created the basic framework of a Welfare State with the introduction of insurance for maternity, health and unemployment, old age pensions and school meals and medical service. These reforms were consolidated by Atlee's government with the introduction of Beveridge's National Insurance Scheme, the 1944 Education Act and the National Health Act 1946. In the period after the war the principle of subsidised council housing was also generally accepted and local councils undertook massive housing schemes to replenish the homes lost during the blitz.

I believe that one of the effects of these reforms, even though they were paid for largely through working class taxation and insurance contributions, was to provide the material basis for working class family life. It meant that the working class adopted patterns of familial relations which had hitherto been exclusive to the upper middle classes. In short, they created a more efficient structure for the reproduction of labour power based on the family unit and women's labour as wives and mothers. Lord Beveridge remarked succinctly:

Taken as a whole the plan for social security put a premium on marriage in place of penalising it. In the next 30 years housewives as mothers have vital work to do in ensuring the adequate continuation of the British race and British ideals in the world.

The role of women

The glorification of motherhood and nationalism will someday deserve its own thesis. Beveridge's conception of motherhood represents an ideology of motherhood which was increasingly elaborated during the 19th century.

In a society where the productivity of labour is low, it is necessary for everyone, including women and children, to work. In these situations, marriage tends to be a working partnership if not an equal one. One piece of advice to servant maids in 1743 reflects this.

You cannot expect to marry in such a manner as neither of you shall have occasion to work, and none but a fool would take a wife whose bread must be earned solely by his labour and who will contribute nothing towards it herself. (2)

One characteristic feature of capitalism is the inbuilt tendency to increase productivity per head and as capitalism developed the necessity for women and children to work decreased. Marriage became instead the husband's sanctuary and retreat from the world of labour. In this 'sanctuary' the wife's task was to service the husband. A wife must have:

.,. the grace to bear even warmth and peevishness, she

must learn and adopt his tastes, study his disposition and submit in short to all his desires. (3)

As a mother, 'the consummation of the world's joys to a true woman', she was to 'generate beings who as women, may tread the footsteps of their mothers, or, as men, may excel in the higher virtues which these, to them softer and sweeter occupations, render it impossible that they themselves should attain.' Many feminists even used these arguments to support better training and education for women, arguing that well educated women would make better wives and mothers.

Certainly all these idologies took some time to bite into the working class. The 1851 Census noted, for instance, that one in four women with husbands had 'extraneous occupations' and one out of every three widows. They also noted with some dismay that 'the districts where women are much employed (away from home), the children and parents perish in great numbers'. However, with the increased productivity of capital and State organised welfare, at least modified versions of these notions of femininity also took on a reality for working class women.

The role of social work

The history of social work has always paralleled the concern of the State for the indigent and feckless working class and in particular the domestic organisation of their lives.

The early origins of social case work can most conveniently be traced back to the Charity Organisation Society founded in 1869 to co-ordinate the charitable organisations in London and formulate some guiding principles. These guiding principles are quite clear. Firstly, case work was seen as a method of sedating the discontents of the working class. In 1872 a COS leaflet warned its readers, 'every household in Belgravia and Pimlico is in danger from a wide bordering hem of poor population'. In 1927 it was describing case work as, 'the only real antidote to Bolshevism'. Secondly, the function of case work was to distinguish between the deserving the undeserving poor. To ensure that only those persons received charity, 'who are doing all that they can to help themselves and to whom temporary assistance is likely to prove of lasting benefit'. Thirdly, case work was to be 'morally regenerative'.

Although the class origins of case work are clear in these early writings there is little emphasis on the working class family per se. Indeed the material conditions of the casual poor in London were such as to make organised working class family life almost impossible. Octavia Hill takes up this point in an interesting way. In a lecture given to District Visitors and Clergymen in 1877, she said:

Depend upon it if we thought of the poor primarily as husbands, wives, sons and daughters, members of households as we ourselves are, instead of contemplating them a as a different class, we should recognise better how the housetraining and high ideal of home duty was our best preparation for work amongst them.

Octavia Hill played a prominent part in the training of social workers. Her case work principles emerged from her housing schemes. The essence of these schemes was that poor and overcrowded courts were taken over and tenants were then 'trained' in 'punctuality', 'thrift' and 'respectability' through the case work skills of the landlord or lady rent collector.

Specialised case work and the psychiatric model

Octavia Hill's conception of social work as housetraining for the wives and husbands of the working class gradually became accepted. By 1912 training courses for social workers had become institutionalised in the Department of Science and Administration at the London School of Economics. A study by S. Clement Brown on *The Methods of Social Case Workers* which compared 80 case records made in 1904 with 80 records made in 1934 found that while the earlier reports were concerned with 'material conditions' and certain types of behaviour such as 'cleanliness, honesty and sobriety', the later records dwelt in far more detail on different aspects of personality and familial relationships. Generally though, specialised case work dealing with discrete aspects of familial life, child guidance, mental health, medical social work etc, with a quasi-Freudian theory of personality, had to wait till after the second world war.

The reasons for this are, I think, clear. Firstly, of course, it was difficult for the specialised functions to develop within the context of the old Poor Laws. Until there was specialised legislation which gave social workers statutory obligation, specialised case work could not emerge. Secondly this legislation was part of a generalised intervention of the State to ensure a guaranteed minimum standard of living for the working class and thus to create the possibility of working class family life. When poverty could be considered a residual category, as it was during the fifties, before the social reformers rediscovered it, and the nuclear family was a dominant form of organisation in the working class, then it was possible for the problems 'clients' presented to be viewed as individual and psychological in origin. An interesting example of this process is given in the preface of a book issued by The Family Discussion Bureau, which was a 'new type of case work agency' set up by the Family Welfare Association in 1948. They say,

The setting up of State Welfare Services, in particular the implementation of the National Health Act and the National Insurance Acts, had taken over many of the functions hitherto carried out by voluntary welfare agencies, and had freed the Association sufficiently to make the quality of family and the personal happiness of its clients its primary concern.

The case histories quoted in the book are filled with success stories, achieved through psychotherapeutic case work, with women 'making astonishing moves towards femininity' and learning to become good mothers, and men rapidly overcoming their effeminacy and homosexual tendencies, achieving new status at work and doubling their earning capacity. Social work in this period, in supporting the current definition of sex roles, strove to lock women more tightly in domestic labour and thus played a part in ensuring the efficient reproduction of a striving and deradicalised working class. It is interesting to note that in this period the changing pattern of working class life was often used by sociologists to argue the bourgeoisification of the working class and the end of all class ideology.

The Seebohm Report, family case work and community case work

By the end of the sixties, however, these arguments looked a lot less convincing. In 1968 the Seebohm Report recommended a major reorganisation of the social services, suggesting that the family and indeed the community should become the primary focus for case work. William Jordan in a book called *The Social Case Worker in Family Situations* welcomes this change and criticises the previous 'narrow definition of the social worker which often led misleadingly to nominate one member of the family as the client'. It could be argued that he is saying that whereas previously there might have been a few wobbly members within the family, now we must realise that, in a number of cases, the family itself is a wobbly institution. The wobbles, to continue the analogy, seem to come from two directions. Firstly, the working class family has been less 'successful' in socialising its children suitably and in creating a fit and adaptable workforce than might have been predicted. Secondly, and particularly in the present period, working class standards of living are dropping or only keeping apace of rising costs. One of the reasons for this is the deterioration and even the withdrawal of certain welfare services and the attempt to exact an even greater relative working class contribution to pay for such benefits as do exist.

The debate about the present state of the family will no doubt continue loud and long. It is only possible to note a few points here:

1.   The rise in juvenile delinquency. The spectre of the mob which haunted the 19th century seems to have been replaced by that of the rabid hordes of the juvenile delinquents. Interestingly the Seebohm Report takes the White Paper 1965 *The Child, the Family and Young Offendors*, which analyses the causes and

cures of juvenile delinquency in terms of familial control, as a major referrant for its proposals. (The Plowden Report takes the same line).

2. The rise in mental illness actually diagnosed, not to say the incidence of 'nerves' amongst women. R.D. Laing et al have also introduced a body of theory which lays this at the door of the family. Women, it seems, not only turn their kids delinquent and make them educational failures, they also send them mad.

3. The rise in marital breakdowns. There are also increasing numbers of young people, albeit a minority, who are chosing not to get married or not to live in a nuclear family type situation.

The changes in the Welfare State and the deleterious consequences for the working class are less problematic. The full scale introduction of a means-tested Welfare State (prescription charges, dental charges, loss of milk for school children, high school meal costs) means not only real deprivation for the working class, but it also means that the Welfare State is a much better instrument for manipulating wage demands.

Generic case work

The 'failure' of the family in many areas, the changing nature of the Welfare State and the rediscovery of poverty has made it increasingly impossible for social work to use the model of individual personality malfunctioning to either explain or solve problems. Especially in urban areas, the 'multi problem syndrome' is so large that it is difficult for even the most blinkered case worker to ignore it. This situation has led, I believe, to the introduction of generic case work; doing a bit of everything, case work, welfare rights, perhaps even a little collective action. Generic case work is potentially progressive in that it does seem to involve some putative understanding of the interlocking nature of social, economic and personal problems. It may mean that more social workers will begin to understand the need for what Seebohm calls the other basic requirements, 'better housing, adequate social security benefits and good health services'. However, as Seebohm also notes:

An effective family service cannot be provided without additional resources and it would be naive to think that any massive additional resources will be made available in the near future.

So, in effect, the generic method applied to the family will involve social workers using women to provide more and more of the services which should properly be undertaken by the Welfare State, like caring for the sick, and the old and forcing families to stay together whatever the cost to the individual women, in order to keep down the demand for housing. No doubt, in order to ahieve this, social workers will exert a good deal of ideological pressure on woman and support her endlessly in the drudgery of her domestic labour.

Conclusions

I have argued that social work is one facet of capitalism's attempts to secure the efficient reproduction of labour. The primary mechanism for this was the exclusion of women from the workforce. This in itself was not enough to secure the domestication of working class life and it was only possible for the working class nuclear family to emerge when the State actively intervened in the organisation of the reproduction of labour power. The creation of the social work profession was part of this process, but the nature and method of social work were always affected by the developing nature of both the working class family and the Welfare State. Finally, I would like to suggest that the present crises in the family and the Welfare State reveal the role of women as reproducers of labour power quite clearly and that in this situation there are a number of strategies which radical women social workers can adopt. We must start from the position that capitalism must pay for the reproduction of its labour power. This means a universal, complete and free welfare service, secondly we must oppose all the forces, legal, ideological and material, which lock women in domestic labour. In practice this means we should concentrate on the following areas:

1. We must expose and oppose all elements of anti-feminist case work ideology. It seems to me that it will be very important, as well as rather difficult to do this at an individual day to day level, in dealing with one's clients, discussing other cases and general office relationships.

2. There is a mass of legislation, particularly in the welfare field, ranging from the cohabitation ruling to unequal national insurance benefits, which keep women in a dependent state. I think that it would be particularly appropriate for women social workers to campaign on these issues.

3 More and more women are going out to work. Some through choice and some because high rents, high taxation and national insurance claw back their husbands' wage packets. Whatever the reason, I believe that women at work should be supported by social workers. This means campaigning for and getting more free full time nurseries and also concerning ourselves with the conditions of women at work, from the size of their pay packet to the length of their breaks. The conditions of working women can be part of our 'community work' brief. We could also support our 'clients' by campaigning for more systematic educational and training opportunities for women. It is disgraceful, for instance, that nearly all government training schemes are closed to women. Such a campaign has great relevance in the light of some Councils' attempts to interpret their community work brief as the setting up of special sheltered workshops where unsupported mothers, unemployed men and truanting kids will be paid supplementary benefit rates and   used as scab labour.

4. Women will never free themselves from the exclusivity of domestic labour until they can control their own fertility. We must campaign for the free availability of contraception and abortion. We must also oppose all attempts to treat sterilisation as the 'solution' for 'problem families'.

5. Finally, none of this will be possible unless we can organise successfully in the Union. The Union is important on two levels. Firstly, it must be forced to take up and

argue for general policies like the ending of the cohabitation ruling. Secondly, the Union is the only protection against the backlash which will certainly occur when women social workers start raising their voices.

Angela Weir
Spring 1974

References

1. See - Women and Labour *Radical America No. 7* and Wally Secombe Housework under Capitalism *New Left Review No. 83*
2. Dorothy George *London Life in the 18th century* 1925
3. J.A. & Olive Banks *Feminism and Family Planning in Victorian England* Liverpool University Press 1964
4. Katherine Woodroofe *From Charity to Social Work* Routledge & Kegan Paul 1962
I would also like to acknowledge Elizabeth Wilson's pamphlet *Women and the Welfare State* Red Rag 1974, and articles which appeared in *RED RAG` No. 2.*

This is a revised version of an article which first appeared in the Women's Issue of CASE CON, Spring 1974.

Sexism, Capitalism & the family

At this conference, we are attempting to discuss, as a feminist movement, the relation between sexism and capitalism. Often this relation is expressed as an opposition: is it a sexist society *or* a capitalist society? Are we interested in feminism or socialism? We see socialist women denouncing feminism as 'bourgeois' and feminists criticising socialism as being 'male dominated'. In my view the present society is both capitalist and sexist. I can't pretend to be offering here a 'theory' of the interrelationship of these two structures but I hope to show that one fruitful *preliminary* way of approaching the problem is to analyse sexism as the structure which dominates the world of reproduction of the species and capitalism as the structure which dominates the world of production. Further, that these two worlds are divided along a sex axis: the world of production is the world of men, the world of reproduction is the world of women, and the male domination of the world of production is an instrument for the economic oppression of women. At the centre of the world of reproduction lies the patriarchal family, within which male domination and female oppression are constantly reproduced. This family system, as we know only too well, is generally thought of as a 'natural' human structure. In fact it is an extremely artificial unit, depending on a high level of economic development to maintain it.

Our objective as a feminist movement should be the abolition of the sexist structure and of the patriarchal form of the family. This is not exactly the same as a struggle to abolish capitalism. The history of socialist revolutions has shown that socialism can coexist with the patriarchal family. If the object of socialism is to make *men* more equal, women can not be expected to have a great interest in it.

As a focal point of this account of the relationship of the patriarchal family to capitalsim, I want to take the working class family and try to analyse the situation of the woman there. For the sake of simplicity of exposition, I assume initially a family within which a classic sexual division of labour exists: the man is the wage earner (breadwinner), the woman a housewife and mother.

Sexism, capitalism and the housewife

The worker's weekly wages are usually divided into two parts - one part the man keeps for his own private use, the rest goes to the woman to provide the means of maintaining the whole family. She is responsible for budgeting, shopping, cooking, cleaning, mending and so on. It is her 'job' to ensure that, insofar as it depends on her household management, the husband will be able to continue in work. In repayment she receives board and lodging: she is in the situation typical of an economic dependent. The man's work is important to her because this supports the whole family. He is a wage slave, she resembles much more a real slave. Tied to her husband economically and legally, bearing his name, often living in a house which is under his control, and isolated within the home, looking after their children, the housewife is tied to her particular man by much stronger links than those which bind worker to a given factory. The ideal which this economic reality produces is that of good service. Many women have spent their adult lives in an attempt to achieve this ideal, dedicating their existence to performing menial tasks for their husbands and children.

It is against this perspective that we should look at the demand that·women be paid for the housework they perform. Does this do any more than demand that instead of being an unpaid servant a woman should be a paid servant? What right does it encapsulate other than the right to have

-a paid servant? Is the right to a paid servant the kind of demand that we as a women's liberation movement should be making? That anyone who calls themselves a revolutionary should make? Surely one of our tasks is to work out ways in which housework, domestic labour in the home, as a task performed by one person for others, can be abolished. If the modern household can only survive by reducing one of its members to being the servant of the others, then that modern household must be abolished and replaced by different forms of communal living and a different form of family. Paying housewives (and that is what the demand concretely means) would serve merely as a new buttress to the patriarchal family.

Economically, the patriarchal family is of great assistance to capitalism. First, it is within the family that labour power is maintained and reproduced, at a relatively low cost. Secondly, the family has become a unit of consumption for the products of capitalism. Advanced monopoly capitalism has opened up the working class as a market for consumption - the 'consumer society'. This policy was determined by the capitalist experience of over-production crises. Hire purchase schemes - which mean that you pay more over a longer period of time, live out your life in semi-permanent debt - took care of the worker's inability to produce lump sums of money.

The pressures to buy are directed mainly at women, and are expressed through an ideology which reinforces the home and the individual household. What is being hawked is not so much a product as a whole life-style. The individual family, with its individual kitchen, its individual TV, washing machine, is an excellent environment for capitalist marketing, which aims at getting the maximum of its products sold. The women who are held captive within those kitchens hate and resent them. But that doesn't prevent them from being held out as living an ideal which other women can only aspire to. In capitalism's fantasy of itself as an 'affluent' society woman remains in her 'proper' place - chained between the kitchen and the bedroom.

It is at the point of consumption that the housewife

has her only direct contact with the capitalist process. During shopping she exchanges wages in the form of money for wages in the form of commodities (wage goods). It is one of the mystifications of capitalism that somehow the process of consumption and the process of production are separate from each other, rather than inter-connected aspects of the same process. Politically this mystification has been expressed as a division between the worker and the 'consumer', whose interests are supposed to be antagonistic to each other. It is similar to the distinction made about the workers and 'the public'. In the portrayal of the consumer, the housewife is often picked out as the one who 'suffers' as a result of the selfish actions of the workers. What is, of course, missing from this schema of housewives versus workers is the intervention of the capitalist interest, and the selfishness of the profit motive. This conservative government has already commissioned reports on the attitudes of housewives to strikes. The implications of such studies are clear - they assess the potentiality of the housewife as strike breaker. Capitalist ideology is always prepared to represent the cause of capitalist crises as the importunate demands of the working class. In the present economic crisis the standard of living of the worker is forced down, and is meeting with resistance both at the level of wages and at the level of prices. The only way in which the situation can be turned to its own advantage is if the housewife-as-consumer can be turned against the husband-as-producer.

It is because, given the present sexual division of labour, the shopper is almost always a woman, that housewives play such a central part in price campaigns. Popular agitation against the rising cost of living has always been an aspect of rebellion against capitalism. But we must treat price campaigns very carefully, if only because in the recent past this agitation has been treated as the limit of women's political potential. This last election was partly fought over the issue of rising prices, with open appeals being made by the conservatives to the housewife. I'm not suggesting for one moment that because price campaigns are instrumentalised with such hypocrisy by political parties that this means that women in women's liberation should play no part in them. But we must be quite clear about the limitations of such campaigns, which are campaigns for an improvement in the conditions of existence within capitalism and do not, important as that aspect of struggle is, necessarily challenge either the capitalist system or the sexual division of labour. Price campaigns are to the working class woman what wage demands are to the working class man. Neither are intrinsically revolutionary.

A further complication lies in the fact that historically the only periods in which the capitalist state has been at all able to intervene to control prices (and even then not with outstanding success) have been periods of war and periods of fascism. And in both situations crippling limitations have been put on the political and economic freedom of the working class - strikes are illegal both under wartime regimes and in fascist regimes, and civil liberties curtailed. The captitalists are in these situations prepared to accept some restriction of their own 'freedom' to maximise profits, but only in return for increased repression of the working class. For the capitalist class has basically only one answer to rising prices, which is to keep wages down. Restrictions on the economic activity of the working class is one way of doing this, and both in the present government's terms of office and those of the Labour government's, attempts were made to introduce and practise State regulation of strikes, wage restraint and so on. These attempts have met with vigorous opposition within the workers' movement.

We must be clear that it is inconceivable that the capitalist market will transform itself into a rational distribution system, mass-producing the material conditions of existence cheaply and at uniform prices, with the aim, eventually, of providing them free. The capitalist system is based on competition, not on co-operation; the aim of the capitalist is to make a profit, not to perform a useful service. Once we start talking about socialised distribution in an economy based on co-operation we are involved in a discussion about the need to destroy the capitalist system and to create a socialist society in its place. It seems unnecessarily devious to express the need for the revolutionary transformation of capitalism into socialism behind a slogan of 'no more rising prices'. To accomplish this task we need to develop a revolutionary politics which raises the question of State power. This is a demand which revolutionary movements make of themselves, not of the capitalist class. Capitalist power will be suppressed as the result of mass political struggle, not as the result of a withering away of capitalist market relations, which is what Selma James' pamphlet *Women, the Unions and Work* would seem to suggest.

I have tried to show why I think it is important to maintain our critical analysis of the divisions of labour between workers and housewife, and would stress the significance, for example, of the refusal of housework expressed in the paper from the Peckham Women's Liberation group at the first Oxford Women's Conference. (published under the title *Women and the Family* in *The Body Politic*, edited by Michelene Wandor, Stage One Publications). We must take a hard look at the conditions which make housework a full time job. Bad housing conditions turn the housewife's day into a constant battle against dirt and demoralisation. Price fluctuations as a result of competition make shopping a time consuming business when we have to shop around for the cheapest buy. The long working hours of the man exhaust him daily. Remember that demands for a shorter working week are often concealed wage demands; they are demands for longer overtime. But by far the most important factor is maternity, and the mother's constant care of small children.

Sexism, capitalism and the mother

Ideologically this society seems to see pregnancy and maternity as mysterious, natural processes which only women are really capable of understanding and knowing about, linked as they are to the vagaries of female psychology. This is the case even though in practice women are often denied real knowledge or control over their own bodies.

There is nothing intrinsically mysterious about pregnancy. It is a biological process through which, given the right conditions, most women can go. But it is a biological process which is overburdened by a heavy ideological weight. Female biology is only 'mysterious' to the extent that it is ignored; the contempt shown by male doctors for 'women's illness' bears witness to the lack of care and seriousness a male dominated society has for women's bodies. It is treated as worthy of attention only to the extent that female psychology is: as a deviation from the male norms. Through an analysis of maternity we can see the twin aspects of the present system - the patriarchy and capitalism.

The most striking feature of biological reproduction in the present system is that the woman, whose part is the longest, the most arduous and involves most responsibility, does not have control over her own reproductive capacities, individually or socially. Decisions which affect reproduction are made by an agency of the male dominated State: the National Health Service. It is significant that medicine is a profession which is proud of the exclusion it exercises against women - only 10% of medical students are women, because it operates a quota system. The main function of women in medicine is to service the doctor and protect him from the patients. These are the men who make the decisions about whether we're to have children, what contraceptive we should use, whether or not we can have an abortion (answer at a price) and if and when we should be sterilised. The birth rate has been a State concern in France for generations. In countries in the grip of neo-colonialist exploitation (like India) 'population control' (i.e. the regulation of the breeding capacities of a whole nation) is not merely the problem of national agencies, but of international agencies. At the other end are States whose problems are not overpopulation, but a fall in the rate of reproduction - i.e. girl children are not being born at a sufficient rate to replace the generation of mothers. Thus Rumania, faced with this problem, has repealed the provision of free abortion and contraception on demand and introduced new and stringent requirements to qualify for abortions. The problem of biological reproduction is clearly a matter of State policy and certainly not a question of the individual woman and whether or not she herself feels in a position to bear that particular child. Pregnancy itself is a traumatic experience for many women. Inadequate ante-natal care, births taking place in over-crowded and under-staffed maternity wards of authoritarian hospitals, where the woman is treated like one object producing another object. No wonder so many women suffer from post-natal depression. This male medical system has to be challenged.

After hospital, the woman returns home with her child. What is the situation of the mother in the present patriarchal family? Early capitalist development in England created a vast new army of the property-less, who were forced to travel to new areas in search of work. Geographical mobility in search of work has been joined recently by the search for a house. The family has remained a biological unit, but pared down to its minimum. Only in ghetto areas can the old extended family be still seen to exist. The extended family is still a biological unit, still, in most cases, patriarchal, but had one immediate advantage for the woman which was a system of support and aid. One of the curious taboos within present society is that against intervening between mother and child unless one is a biological relation. The mystic biological link which is supposed to exist between the two is almost universally respected in practice. There is no other family system which forces women into such a close relationship with her children, creating a pattern of emotional interdependence and jealous mutual possession within which the struggle for domination and submission are carried out. Within the family the child goes through its first socialisation into the rules of survival in a patriarchal and capitalist society. It is within the family, in those early years, that the child learns about authority, power, control, competition, and inferior and superior beings. It is the early experience within the family which structures the individual's emotional development, and the present patriarchal family is a breeding-ground of neurosis. Some women seem to think that the working class family is somehow different, but this is not the case. The working class may not have very many material goods, but in the present patriarchy individuals are regarded as property, the marriage and family system is a system of mutual possession. Neurosis is a mass phenomenon, and not the problem of a few tortured members of the bourgeoisie.

Female neurosis is so widespread that it is taken for granted. The modern patriarchal family drives women to the point of madness. Total responsibility for the child is hers. Not only is the woman supposed to ensure that her child is socially integrable, she is also supposed to teach learning skills in order to equip the child for school - fashionable educationalists no longer talk about the 'unsuccessful children', they talk about 'unsuccessful mothers' instead. The modern mother lives with an intolerable burden of guilt and anxiety. Can we really accept that paying her is any solution to the problem at all?

If the situation of the mother within the family is bad enough, that of the woman outside the family is even worse. Locked between the difficulty of finding a job because she has a child, and the difficulty of finding adequate care for her child if she finds a job, often the only alternative is Social Security, like all the appurtenances of the 'welfare state' which are paid out of working class taxation, are represented as the charitable benevolence of a a paternal State, in a final turn of the hypocritical screw.

The capitalist and patriarchal State undeniably prefers making individual payments like family allowances to social provision of adequate creche facilities. The emphasis is on the individual making 'private arrangements' such as finding a trustworthy private baby-minder rather than the socialisation of child care. Our tasks as a women's liberation movement in this area seem to me to be two-fold. First we must continue our work in creating alternatives to the patriarchal family for women and children to live within: women's living collectives and communes are of inestimable importance. Second, we must continue our campaign for adequate and freely available creche facilities. The lived reality of the patriarchal family point to the need for its abolition as a unit of social organisation. We must organise and press for alternatives.

So far in this analysis of women and the family I have described two ways in which women are in a situation of economic dependence - within the family on an individual man, outside the family on the male-dominated State. I now want to examine the alternative which allows women the possibility of some economic independence - work outside the home.

Sexism, capitalism and women workers

When women work outside the home, this work is an addition to housework and child care: this is what is sometimes described as 'women's double oppression'. Once women *do* work outside the home for the same hours as men, it is difficult to find any semblance of rational argument to justify her doing the housework and child care as well. Appeals to biology don't work. There is nothing 'biologically inherent' about doing the washing up or changing nappies; as for the 'biological link' between mother and child, isn't the father a biological parent too? The only appeal that can be made is to a 'natural' division of labour. It is certainly possible to see some remnant of an artisanal division of labour within the family - men still tend to do occasional repairs or potter around the garden. if they have one. But here the man's work is sporadic, the woman's constant. And there is nothing 'natural' about this division - it is determinedly social. The very process of 'humanisation' which takes place in the patriarchal family trains women to expect to have to serve men, and trains men to expect to be waited on by women.

The spectre of the independent working woman who neglected her household duties and left her children to run wild terrified early capitalism. The advent of factory production destroyed the domestic economy which preceded it. In the domestic economy not only were women legally tied to their husbands, but the husband also controlled the labour of the family as a productive unit. It was the husband who organised and supervised the work and who mediated the relationship between the family and the small capitalist who gave outwork to them. In industrialised capitalism women continued to spin, but in a factory, no longer in the home. Capitalism raised the possibility of mass female employment for the first time: this was the advance which it represented over the economic mode which it replaced. Of course, work in a capitalist economy liberates no-one, men or women, but woman's economic independence from men is one of the conditions of her liberation. Factory women were paid less than males, there was never any golden age of economic equality in early capitalism. Dr. Ure, writing in 1834, celebrated this with all the pompous complacency of the male chauvinist:

Factory females have in general much lower wages than males, and they have been pitied on that account with perhaps an injudicious sympathy, since the low price of their labour makes household duties their most profitable as well as agreeable occupation, and prevents them from being tempted by the mill to abandon their offspring at home. Thus Providence effects its purpose with a wisdom and efficacy which should repress the short-sighted presumption of human devices.

In early capitalism women were in competition with men for factory employment; their already existing inferiority was translated into an economic inferiority - they were seized upon as a source of cheap labour and used to undercut male wages. The mill girl, with her immorality and vulgar freeness horrified bourgeois society. Women, when given the chance to turn the tables on men, took it, and male reformers shook their heads over the sad reversal of the natural order. Engels noted, in his *Condition of the Working Class in England,* that:

very often the fact that a married woman is working does not lead to the complete disruption of the home, but to a reversal of the normal division of labour within the family. The wife is the bread-winner while her husband stays at home to look after the children and do the cleaning and cooking ...One may well imagine the righteous indignation of the workers at being virtually turned into eunuchs.

239

And later on:
We shall have to accept the fact that so complete a reversal of the role of the two sexes can be due only to some radical error in the original relationship between men and women. If the rule of the wife over the husband - a natural consequence of the factory system - is unnatural, then the former rule of the husband over the wife must a also have been unnatural. Today, the wife - as-in former times the husband - justifies her sway because she is the major or even sole bread-winner of the family. In either case one partner is able to boast that he or she makes the greatest contribution to the upkeep of the family.

Factory legislation restricted the work of both women and children within the new factories, and industrial production became a sector dominated by male labour, their interests protected by male trades unions, from which in the 19th century women were often openly excluded. By the end of the 19th century a movement was in train to teach domestic economy to working class women. The other main alternative to factory employment - domestic service - conveyed to women working there the 'proper' management of a patriarchal family. In this century the teaching of domestic science has increased rather than diminished, with women's magazines and courses in school supplementing the training they are supposed to receive in the home. The patriarchal family, which constructs woman as wife and mother through a process which blocks women's psychological, intellectual and sexual development, is deeply rooted within the human personality produced by the sexist system: this family is internalised, we carry it around with us.

Economic necessity still drives women out to work: in present day Britain most working class women do some work outside the home, in a situation of economic inferiority: the average wage of a woman worker is £13, that of a male worker £26. Working women still sell their labour at a cheaper rate than do men. The so-called equal pay act will hardly change anything, since only a minority of women workers can be proved to do the same jobs as men. Even

240

those women affected will probably not get their increase, since the employers have decided that wage increases for equal pay should be restricted by a £2 wage restraint.

The exclusion of women from industrial production effected by early capitalism continues. To find employment women have to go to the servicing sector of the economy, a sector which is itself dependent on the point of production. The sexual division of labour within the economy mirrors with startling clarity the division within the family. The mass-rpoduction of clothing employs female labour overwhelmingly, similarly food packaging and preparation, canteen work and cleaning. Nursing is almost wholly women's work and teaching is gradually becoming a woman's profession (with a consequent diminution in teachers' salaries) and the social services which prop up the family are staffed by women. Both the consumption and service sector and socialisation are maintained by women. Their relationship to the situation of women in the home, which I described earlier, are amazingly clear. Apart from that, women still work in textiles (traditionally a female occupation), in light industry (usually producing goods for the consumer market) and as clerical workers servicing the needs of male administrators. Here the patriarchal family and capitalism mutually reinforce each other. In the home and outside women's work bears a heavy ideological weight. The term itself can be used to attribute a kind of femininity to the work itself as much as to the worker.

It would be a mistake for us to underestimate either the importance of the economic base or the importance of the sexual division of labour. We should insist that women's 'right to work' means not the right to work inside the home, or the right to work outside the home at jobs determined by the patriarchal system, but the right of women and men to perform the same work, at the same rate of pay, and to control their conditions of work in a society based on co-operation. Women's liberation must develop a strategy aimed both at the patriarchal family and at the sexual division of labour in the economy, Both of these conditions of the oppression of women are built into the capitalist system. The situation of women in the Soviet Union indicates that they can be built into a socialist system too - the patriarchy can survive changes in the mode of production.

The conditions of employment for women are usually worse than for working class men. In 'normal times' female unemployment is much greater than male unemployment, and is one of the forces which keeps women in the home. Women usually compete for jobs with other women in a low-paid sector with appalling work conditions and a low level of unionisation. The struggle of women for unionisation rights - which mean the same rights to mutual protection which male workers have, bring women up against male working class privilege, just as do demands for equal pay and equal job opportunity. A generalised struggle means to me that our movement should be able to articulate all the levels at which women are combating male privilege, in the home, in the State, in the factory.

The possibility of marriage and the family is constantly held out to women as the only attractive alternative to full time employment. And it does have its attractions: at least you're involved in relationships with other human beings rather than with machines. Moreover, through the childhood experience of the family, women have been conditioned to regard marriage and the family as their natural destiny. Represented as the way of fulfilling and channelling female creativity, the questions often only begin after women discover what the real conditions of family life are.

Nineteenth century reformers were quite straightforward about their determination to preserve the patriarchal family as at least one place in capitalist society where 'human values' could still be expressed. This has created a deeply-rooted fear that the abolition of the patriarchal family would mean the destruction of 'human values' themselves. To preserve these 'human values' women are coerced into putting the home and family first, almost to save men the trouble of having to think about them, and live with the burden of this imbalance. So great is the power of the ideology of the family that many unmarried women, faced with bad work conditions, chose marriage rather than organise against them. The sexual competition, compulsive heterosexuality and repression of female sexuality which this entails are too large a subject to go into here. But passive female acceptance of the roles of wife and mother contribute to the continuation of women's oppression as much as the workers' acceptance of capitalism as the only economic system possible contributes to their continued exploitation. Feminism - the political movement of women to abolish their oppression - is a precondition, the main condition, of a women's revolution. To construct a feminist movement means developing a new form of female creativity, in solidarity and sisterhood with all women, against their day-to-day oppression and the structures which determine it.

Rosalind Delmar

Postscript

This was written as a paper for the Acton Women's Liberation Conference in 1972, when the movement was discussing the issue of wages for housework. Reading it through now, two years later, I'm aware that there are certain points in it which I would not now agree with, or would not necessarily put in the same way. However, I am still convinced that we are oppressed by social structures at once capitalist and patriarchal, that we need to develop an approach at once feminist and marxist. And I still feel that wages for housework is a regressive demand. Whatever its limitations I hope that this paper will still be of some use in the ongoing debates of the women's movement.

November 1974

TRYING TO STAY HUMAN ✳✳✳✳✳✳

Women's Work in the Industrial Revolution

The women's liberation movement has become increasingly concerned with the problem of analysing how capitalist and male domination are interlocked in the oppression of women. What follows is an attempt to look at this question for the period in which British industrial capitalism emerged at the end of the 18th century and first half of the 19th century. Even though the forms of women's subordination have altered very much since that period, they represent a case study of the ways in which both capitalist and patriarchal domination of women are interconnected and can be modified in a period of major social change.

The rise of industrial capitalism did not, as assumed by Engels, abolish patriarchal relations between working men and women but re-established them in a new form. This process was very uneven, having different implications for different groups of workers and so,as well as trying to trace the general changes in the nature of sexism, it is also necessary to see how these changes reinforced divisions within the male working class. As feminists and socialists, we have not really looked at the ways in which sexism divides male workers, as well as dividing men and women.

The rise of capitalism in Britain was a very long process entailing two major stages - on the one hand the transformation of the majority of working people into wage workers and on the other the transformation of productive processes into those of large-scale industry. (1)The first stage dominated the period from the 16th century to mid 18th century whilst the second characterised the next 100 years. During the first phase, the domestic family economy of the mass of producers, based on access to land or a trade, ceased to be self-sufficient; dependence on wage employment resulted from the loss of independent means of production through the enclosure of land and industrial changes like the development of the putting-out system in the textile trades (2). The majority of men and women came of necessity to work for wages, employed either as individuals or on a family basis, with women's wages generally lower than men's from an early stage (3). In the second phase, industrial production was transferred at a highly uneven rate out of homes and small workshops into large-scale steam-powered units of production - factories and mills - and traditional skills were superseded.

Engels, writing at that period, drew the conclusions that women's position relative to men's would be affected for the better by these changes for two reasons (4). Firstly, he held that patriarchy in pre-capitalist families was based on the private productive property vested in male heads of household and the power this gave men over women's labour and fertility. From this he concluded that capitalism, by depriving workers' families of their productive property and independence, would undermine patriarchy and create the basis for sexual equality in the working class. Conversly, bourgeois men in whom the private productive property of the society was now vested were able to maintain male supremacy and the bourgeois family came to represent an extreme example of the patriarchal family. Secondly, as women workers were drawn into the factories they would be employed as individuals on an equal basis with men and gain independence from the family.

Engels failed to perceive that although the rise of capitalism made the domestic economy of workers' families no longer self-sufficient, it by no means eliminated the role of women's domestic labour. Dependence on wage employment has never meant that all of workers' needs are in fact satisfied through the purchase of commodities which a wage makes possible. Women's domestic labour has continued in changing ways to contribute to satisfying these needs at the same time as women have, in varying degrees, also shared the upkeep of themselves and their families through working for wages. In fact, with the development of capitalism, working men were deprived of all productive property except their direct rights over women's (and in the early stages to some extent children's) labour. Thus, patriarchy as a system of property relations between men and women was not abolished within the working class, but transformed to create a new form of inequality between working men and women.

Women's domestic labour, in fact, came to assume a quite different significance for men and women. On the one hand their rights over women's labour represented for men the only property rights which capitalism had left to them, their last remaining area of economic independence, in a sense, which they would therefore fight to preserve.(5) On the other hand, domestic labour, because it became totally dependent on incoming wages, either earned by the woman or by men in their families, was not a source of independence for women - in fact, the contrary, although superficially the work women did in their homes might appear independent, being outside direct capitalist control.

In addition, Engels overestimated the extent to which married women would derive economic independence through factory employment, since the majority of women factory workers in the first half of the 19th century were young and single and women's wages scarecely rose at all with age to allow for children's subsistence. (See Table I)

These are points to which I shall return by examining in greater details the changes that occurred in the industrial revolution, which was concentrated in cotton manufacture during the period we are considering.

It seems one can characterise the evolution of working class family economy, before the development of the factory system in the latter third of the 18th century, in the following way. All members of families depending on wages (the vast majority of families by this stage), from small children upwards, were able to contribute to family earnings, but men were already considered as the major breadwinners because of the relatively higher adult male wages. Married women earned wages either through some form of domestic employment like spinning or through (predominantly seasonal) agricultural labour. Neither form of employment precluded women from also taking the major responsibility for care of home and children.

TABLE 1

Wage returns from Lancashire cotton mills 1833

Age	No. women employed	Average weekly wage	Men's wage
Under 11	155	2/4¾	2/3½
11 - 16	1123	4/3	4/1¾
16 - 21	1240	7/3½	10/2½
21 - 26	780	8/5	17/2½
26 - 31	295	8/7¾	20/4½
31 - 36	100	8/9½	22/8½
36 - 41	81	9/8¼	21/7¼
41 - 46	38	9/3½	20/3½
46 - 51	23	8/10	16/7¼
51 - 56	4	8/4½	16/4
56 - 61	3	6/4	13/6½
61 - 66	1	6/-	13/7
66 - 71	1	6/-	10/10
Total	3844		

Source: Factory Commission 1834 quoted in Ivy Pinchbeck Women Workers and the Industrial Revolution.

The changes that took place over the subsequent 70 year period affected the working class family and economic relations between men and women in fundamental ways. To understand these changes it is necessary to look at factors such as the breakdown of traditional skills and transfer of industrial production from homes to factories; capitalist attempts to minimise labour costs and reduce the bargaining power of employees; conservative ideologists representing politically powerful groups; attitudes of old and new labour aristocracies.

The implications of Engels' statements concerning the effects of the industrial revolution on women's economic position are that increasing opportunities for factory employment would be available to married women and that such employment would be a source of economic independence for them from the family. A rather different conclusion appears to emerge from evidence discussed by Marx concerning the employment of married women. He refers for example, to a cotton manufacturer who:

employed females exclusively at his power-looms ...gives a decided preference to married females, especially those who have families at home dependent on them for support; they are attentive, docile, more so than unmarried females, and are compelled to use their utmost exertions to procure the necessaries of life. (6).

Such evidence throws doubt on the argument that waged work represented a desirable alternative for married women to economic dependence on the family.

In the first half of the 19th century, married women's factory employment appears to have been uncommon except in Lancashire. In the Scottish cotton mills for example, there is evidence that married women were not generally employed. (7) In Lancashire,moreoever, married women appear to have been in minority of female operatives, for example, only 18% of about 60,000 female workers employed in selected Manchester factories in 1844. (8) In addition those married women who were employed in factories were mostly younger married women with few or no children. (See Table II) From Anderson's study of Preston

TABLE 2

Employment and type of employment of wives co-residing with husbands by life-cycle stage: Preston sample 1851

Life-cycle stage	Percentage of all wives working	Of working wives percentage in factory jobs*
Wife under 45, no children	44	
Wife under 45, 1 child under 1	38	72
Children at home, none in employment	28	
Children at home, under ½ in employment	23	52
Children at home, ½ or more in employment	15	
Wife 45 and over, no children at home	16	19
All with children	23	52
All	26	52

* These figures are minima as they exclude weavers who made up 11% of working wives in life-cycle stages 1 and 2 2, 13% in 3 and 4, 25% in 5 and 6. Only some of these and almost certainly a smaller proportion in the later life-cycle stage would have been factory weavers.

Source: M Anderson, Family structure in 19th century Lancashire.

it appears that poverty was the major reason for mothers working and, where a family was well clear of the poverty line, wives appear to have worked only if they had no children needing care. (9) There is evidence from the study quoted above of Manchester factories in 1844 on the occupations of husbands of married women factory workers which indicate that a majority had husbands who were also factory operatives, probably in the lower paid categories, and a higher than average number were married to unemployed men. (10).

From Table II it is possible to conclude that, if Preston was typical of the Lancashire cotton towns in the middle of the 19th century, about a third of wives were working in factories before they had their second child, the proportion falling to ten or fifteen percent as more children were born but before many were old enough to contribute to family income themselves. When most children were able to get employment, the proportion of married women working in factories fell to a very low level. Thus, women's factory employment appears to have been important in many male-headed families in the early years of marriage and childbirth, but diminished to insignificance as children's earnings became a viable substitute.

To illustrate the economic pressures operating on working class families during this period, it is helpful to look at information on the wages paid to different workers and the amount required to keep a family at subsistence level. (11) If one accepts Anderson's assumptions on minimum subsistence needs towards the middle years of the 19th century, a family with two adults and four children would have required at least 26 shillings weekly income. The range of earnings of male workers was very great with skilled factory workers being paid over 20 shillings, rising to about £2.00 for mule spinners on the finest work, and unskilled factory workers earning 15 shillings or less. The desperate male hand weavers, still fighting for survival in their cottages if they worked alone, seemed to have been earning as little as 5 to 6 shillings by 1833 and their position continued to deteriorate thereafter. Amongst women, the best paid were the power loom weavers who were earning on average about 10 shillings by the 1840's. Women working in spinning departments as piecers or throstle-spinners might be earning as little as 7 shillings, about the minimum subsistence for a single adult. There does not appear to have been any work by which women could earn sufficient to support adequately both themselves and several children (the minimum required for each child being about 3 shillings). Also, as can be seen from Table I, those men who were actually able to retain factory employment beyond the age of 21, mainly the minority of skilled workers, were able to increase their earnings substantially up to the age of 36. Women's earnings, on the other hand, at no age rose substantially above the level of individual adult subsistence. Finally, children under 15 appear to have been able to earn up to 6 or 7 shillings in factory work, nearly as much, in fact, as adult women.

What emerges from these figures is that whilst factory employment is no doubt a source of economic independence for many, young single women in this period, it does not appear to have provided a viable alternative to dependence on a husband and family for older women with children. In addition, families of unskilled male factory workers, low paid hand-workers and unemployed labourers were highly dependent on wives' earnings for periods when children's earnings were limited. In a relatively small number of working class families, those of the highest paid skilled male factory operatives, husbands were earning sufficient to eliminate for the first time their dependence on wives' earnings.

Although it is difficult to piece together the evidence, there does appear to have been a major change in attitudes to women's work on the part of the new factory based, skilled male labour aristocracy, exemplified by the cotton mule spinners in the period we are examining. In the early years of factory spinning in the 1790's, all mule spinners appear to have been men who were previously craftsmen such as hand weavers or millwrights. (12) During that period, the spinners' unions were also open to women who at that time were employed on some of the preparatory processes. (13) The male spinners established a very strong bargaining position vis-a-vis employers at this time, having essential skills which could not be superseded owing to the very slow pace of mechanisation and their own ability to limit entry into the occupation, largely restricting it to sons and brothers. It also seems to be the case that these men still expected their wives to work and contribute to family income. As late as 1818 one finds a highly class conscious spinner lamenting the reduction in wives earnings arising from industrialisation. He refers back to the period when male spinners worked on large jennies and mules in small workshops and factories:

The cotton was then always given out in its raw state from the bale to the wives of the spinners at home, when they heat and cleansed it ready for the spinners in the factory. By this they could earn 8 shillings, 10 shillings or 12 shillings a week, and cook and attend to their families. But none are thus employed now; for all the cotton is broken up by a machine, turned by the steam engine, called a devil: so that the spinners wives have no employment, except they go to work in the factory all day at what can be done by children for a few shillings, 4 or 5 shillings per week.

This spinner's hostility to the way in which factory employment was then developing indicates both regret at the loss or reduction of wives' earnings, (this was before the somewhat better paid women's factory occupation of power loom weaving was introduced) and resistance to women's work removing them from the home and domestic duties. At the same time, there is growing evidence of male spinners feeling increasingly threatened in their work situation from female competition. Again in 1818 they are found expressing indignation at masters' attempts to employ wome spinners, probably on the smaller mules, and at half the wages. (15) In 1824 the same process triggered a strike in Manchester. On this occasion a union official wrote in the *Manchester Guardian* that most of the women had only themselves to support whilst men had families, and thus the women were willing to accept less than the men. It is evident that resistance to employment of women and girls arose from a whole complex of attitudes, and not just fear of their wages being undercut; this union official went on to add that girls from 14 to 20 were:

rendered independent of their natural guardians, who in many cases, indeed, become in consequence of this very employment, dependent upon their children.

There is no doubt however that the skilled men's fear of competition from women workers was very real and that, in addition, by the 1820's they were under pressure from a number of other factors, like the improved productivity resulting from the larger mules being introduced and the development of self-actor mules in place of manually operated ones. These changes were likely both to reduce the employers' demand for mule spinners and to undermine the bargaining position of those remaining in employment as their traditional skills were increasingly superseded. Thus the spinners adopted more and more defensive positions, one of which being the exclusion of women from their unions. By 1829 there were no women in the Manchester Spinners' Union and in the same year when an attempt was made to form a spinners' Grand Union, women spinners were deliberately excluded.

By the 1830's and 1840's the ideology of women's place outside the wage system and in the home was becoming a trend in the factory based male labour aristocracy. The skilled tailor, Francis Place, in a letter to a cotton spinner in 1835, wrote that the men who had been thrown out of employment in cotton were to blame for their own misery:

If then the men refuse to work in mills and factories with girls, as they ought to do, as other males have done, in workshops, and for those masters who employ women and girls, the young women who will otherwise be degraded by factory labour will become all that can be desired as companionable wives, and the whole condition of factory workers would soon be improved, the men will obtain competent wages for their mainenance. (16)

In the 1840's, during the agitation for a ten hour day, some of the short time committees representing male oper-

atives included in their demands one for the gradual withdrawal of all females from factories; this was based both
on the fear of women's competition and on a desire to
keep women at home to perform their domestic duties:
'home, its cares and its employment is woman's true sphere'
... women brought up in factories could not 'make a shirt,
darn a stocking, cook a dinner or clean a house'. (17)

Whilst such arguments were made in part to express the
ruling class to whom the workers' demands were addressed,
there seems little doubt that this ideology was also increasingly adopted by the workers themselves. By the latter
part of the 19th century, it appears to have become firmly
entrenched in the organised sections of the working class,
judging by statements such as the following, made the by
secretary of the Trades Union Congress in 1875: he declared the purpose of unions to be:

*To bring about a condition ... where their wives should
be in their proper sphere - at home - instead of being
dragged into competition for livelihood against the great
and strong men of the world. (18)*

The sharp decline in wages of the men who formed the
old labour aristocracy of domestic craftsmen, exemplified
here by the hand loom weavers, (in the first half of the
19th century) was caused firstly by the excessive numbers
of workers who flooded into the occupation when their
traditional sources of livelihood had been disrupted by the
combined effects of enclosures and the industrial revolution.
They also included wives and families of the hand loom
weavers themselves, who were drawn into stem the declin-
ing wages but overall helped to intensify that decline. The
second cause, which came into operation from the 1820's
onwards, was competition with the power loom, which
provided employment mainly for girls and women, and in
many cases for the daughters and wives of hand weavers
themselves. This was for two reasons. On the one hand,
employers preferred to chose power loom weavers from
those who already had some experience of hand loom
weaving, and on the other hand by the 1830's and 40's,
the weavers' families were in such a distressed state on

account of the low wages that in areas within easy reach of a mill, they were forced to seek factory employment (19).

It seems that for the hand weavers, who were men who had prided themselves both in their economic independence and in their craft, to see their wives and children becoming the major breadwinners and moreover, being taken out of the home where all the family had worked together, was the ultimate degradation. In 1835 some weavers protested against:

the unrestricted use (or rather abuse) of improved and continually improved machinery ... the neglect of providing for the employment and maintainance of the Irish poor, who are compelled to crowd the English labour market for a piece of bread. ...... the adaption of machines, in every improvement, to children, and youth and women, to the exclusion of those who ought to labour - THE MEN. (20)

As they accepted the inevitability of power loom weaving, they put forward various proposals including the restriction of hours in power loom factories and the employment of adult male power loom weavers in place of women and children.

Evidence on the attitude of working class women themselves to these changes is very limited and does not give a clear picture. The expansion of factory employment for women certainly appears to have increased the economic independence of single women and widows, and to have provided a basis for women's participation both in radical politics and in independent trade union action (21) But there is also evidence of women regretting the loss of their traditional domestic role, which enabled them to earn their living around the homes and families. There is evidence too that what we refer to now as women's double shift was already becoming established for married women factory workers. In Preston at least they did their shopping and housework at weekends whilst men and single women took a holiday. (22)

It seems reasonable to argue therefore that the economic conditions of married women actually changed for the worse during this period. Those who worked in factories maintained their role as important contributors to family earning, albeit by exhausting and debilitating work, but were no longer able to combine their paid work easily with domestic responsibilities. As a result of this they were on the one hand subjected to attacks from State officials, politicians and working men along the lines they were neglecting families and ignorant of domestic skills. (23) On the other hand, they were forced to work longer hours than those of the factory to comply with domestic committments.

Conversely, the married women in families where husbands husbands, or husbands plus children, earned sufficient to enable wives not to seek factory work were able to concentrate their efforts upon homes and families; but again their domestic role had been totally transformed into one of total economic dependence.

The notion that male workers should strive to a situation in which their earnings were adequate to support a wife and family was a very new idea, produced by the changes outlined above in the first half of the 19th century. There is no doubt that many women also came to accept this, perceiving it as preferable for them to the doubly burdensome and low paid alternative of most factory employment available to them. But this cannot be taken to mean that those women perceived these overall changes as an improvement. In addition, throughout the 19th century, it is unlikely that more than a small minority of working class families had earnings consistently high enough to make wives' earnings at no time necessary. Thus, the new sexist ideology, which degraded men who depended on wives' earnings, reinforced the division existing between the relatively high paid, skilled male workers and the men who were low paid, unskilled and unemployed.

Jean Gardiner
1974

References

1. See K. Marx, Capital Vol. 1 for a very detailed account of this.
2. Alice Clark: Working Life of Women in the 17th Century.
3. Alice Clark gives a very thorough account of women's wages and some of the likely reasons for the male/female differential.
4. F. Engels: Origins of the Family
5. For a discussion of marriage as a property relationship see Sheila Rowbotham: Woman's Consciousness, Man's World p. 64 Penguin.
6. K. Marx: Capital Vol. 1. Moscow 1961 p. 402
7. W. Neff: Victorian Working Women p. 40
8. N.J. Smelser: Social Change in the Industrial Revolution p. 203
9. M. Anderson: Family Structure in 19th century Lancashire.
10. As note 8.
11. The figures for wages are taken from Smelser (p.213), Anderson and B.L. Hutchins: Women in Modern Industry (p. 37)
12. For detailed accounts of the evolution of occupations, technical processes and workers' organisations in the industrialisation of cotton manufacture see:
   H. Turner: Trade Union Growth, Structure and Policy.
   J. & B. Hammond: The Skilled Labourer 1760-1832
   N.J. Snelser: as above
   Ivy Pinchbeck: as above
13. See Smelser p. 236
14. Address to the public of strike bound Manchester by 'A Journeyman Cotton Spinner' quoted by E.P. Thompson: The Making of the English Working Class Penguin, p. 218
15. See Smelser ch. X for evidence on this and what follows.
16. Neff. p.31
17. Pinchbeck p. 200

18. From the TUC Congress 1875 quoted by Turner p. 185
19. Pinchbeck p. 184
20. Thompson p. 335. Subsequent evidence on the weavers is taken from the same source.
21. Thompson p. 454
22. Anderson p. 77
23. For a critical discussion of these debates see Margaret Hewitt: Wives and Mothers in Victorian Industry.

Women's Work

The term 'women's work' in industry, has one indisputable meaning - *low pay*, and the term 'women workers' signifies *double exploitation*, that is exploitation as women and as workers. Unfortunately both terms are surrounded by many myths which often obscure these basic facts. First it is necessary to dispel some myths before going on to look at the particular forms the exploitation of workers take.

Attitudes towards women working in Britain not only alter from class to class but also appear to be a reflection of the economic fluctuations of the capitalist system. In the war women were encouraged to work, they were praised for their work and even middle class ladies worked for the war effort. Then came the fifties, the era of economic boom, the expanding economy which required the housewife to be a consumer whilst the husband's wages were rising faster than any time before. This was the era of the 'latch key' kids, the era when the press and sociologists railed against women who were 'selfish' and went out to work for 'pin money' and 'neglected' their children. Meanwhile the true wife and mother was at home consuming, and producing babies for the expanding economy. The late sixties saw rising unemployment, the increasing realisation that the boom was over, concern over the 'population explosion' mounted and consequently a change in attitude towards women working. It was recognised that many women needed to work to support their families or that many families could not survive on one income. This coincided with a feeling that the country needed less babies as the economy can't cope with such expansion. None of these changes have been concerned with the actual needs - psychological, material or physical - of women. By the 1980's, it is predicted that women will form 40% of the workforce and it is hoped that some radical change in attitudes towards women working will happen, and not one which just reflects the whims of the capitalist system.

The employment of women in particular industries is more a case of economics, prejudice, training and availability than anything to do with inherent difference between the sexes. There are many examples throughout history to illustrate this. Women were traditionally 'spinners' until the advent of machines when men took over the jobs, jealously guarded them and even appealed to MP's and employers to help them protect them. In both world wars women have done most industrial jobs but the real thanks they got for their war effort was to be booted out of the skilled jobs and knocked off promotion ladders. Work is known to become 'women's work' when employers can't get men to do the job at the pay offered.

The picture now of where women work gives a very clear indication of the discrimination against women in employment and in training for employment. In the professional grades, women predominate as nurses and as teachers, both forming the wide, lowest paid base of their professional hierarchies. They form the bulk of skilled women workers; however, over half the women workers in this country are in semi-skilled and unskilled jobs. One third of all women work in industry, mainly in the distributive trade, electrical, tobacco and textiles. It is these women who have least access to any form of training. Apprenticeships are still almost exclusively a male preserve and women have only a little more access to day-release schemes. Clerical and office workers form the other main area of female employment.

******

Many reasons, mainly spurious, are used by employers and male workers to justify creating areas of so-called 'women's work'. One most frequently used is that women have a high absentee and turnover rate. It's about time this myth was finally busted. Low paid, unskilled workers have, understandably, a high absentee rate, a large number of women are unskilled therefore the average absentee rate for women workers is higher than that for men. There is no evidence to suggest that women in skilled grades have a higher absentee rate than men in the same jobs. Turnover follows roughly a similar pattern, although the statistics show that married women, who form 64% of the female workforce, when they return to work after having children, have a *lower* turnover rate than men.

Another reason used is that women can't work 'night work' and aren't prepared to work overtime. This is particularly used in evading the equal pay act. A woman shop steward neatly summarised the duality of attitude towards women and night work

You've got women you know, who can't work nights in most industries ...But in some jobs it's not only allowed but we clap them for doing it like nurses, we're human, we want our cake and eat it.... (imitating men). *Our women must not work night shifts but if we go into hospital we want women to nurse us on nights.*

In fact, factories can get dispensation to employ women on nights but as the same woman went on to point out

I personally don't think a man should have to work night shifts and I feel very strong on that as well because I think of the family life. I don't think they start to do it because they want to, they're probably made to. There's a night shift allowance and a lot of men get used to being paid that allowance and if they haven't got it, they've got a short week.

Surely unions should be fighting for a situation where any employer has to get dispensation from the State to employ people on night work and not trying to expose more people to a vicious system of working. The same goes for other legislation which protects women and ought to be applied to protect all workers.

Not only are women in industry discriminated against because of their lack of training - which was never offered them in the first place - the skills which they do have usually go unrecognised and unrewarded. Ernie Bevin once commented that if men had nimble fingers they would demand a bonus.

Most systems of job evaluation and grading give muscle mass more value than manual dexterity; the former merely a fluke of birth, the second a product of upbringing and training. If there were any logic in the way we evaluate jobs, the women with manual dexterity should be given more than men with mere muscle mass.

At a GEC telecommunications factory in Coventry the women are asked in an interview for a job there whether they can knit or sew or are good with their hands. If the answer is 'yes' they are much more likely to get the job but are not likely to get recognition and financial remuneration for their skills. Here's how one worker describes the 'work at GEC and the skill involved.

I worked at GEC as a young kid, you know, and I went back. You have a spell inbetween because you're having children and that, and I started back because my husband was on short time and the two eldest boys, they were going like to the comprehensive school and it's rather expensive school uniform, books and everything else and I started back - well I was a coil winder and once you've done coil winding you never lose it. The product could be different but you never lose the skill.

The skill of coil winding? It would be the dexterity, the swiftness of the hands, the ability to read and understand prints and although your prints can be different they're still alike. The colours for wiring, you

*never forget them. The touch with the machine it's
all important. When I say touch, the type of machine
I work on is a Swiss machine. It's very delicate the
touch of it. You get your own tension on the wire,
these wires are very fine that you use, and you learn
your machine and you can have, we have had, six or
seven identical machines, brand new and each one
different.*

It's about time they demanded a bonus but they're
still struggling to get equal pay. The story is the same
in many industries and reflects the singular failure of
the union movement to negotiate recognition for women's
skills. It's something for which women in unions should
be pushing hard now.

The equal pay act leaves much to be desired, both
for the way it was drafted and for what was left out.
Many women workers don't come into the scope of the
act and will have to rely on industrial strength to improve their wages. Even those who do manage to get
some form of equal pay will find that what they
take home at the end of the week will be significantly
less than their male counterparts, the differential being
made up by payments for such things as long service,
merit, willingness to work overtime etc. For all the
Act states that its aim is to eliminate discrimination
between men and women in pay and other *terms* and
conditions, it doesn't include sick pay and occupational
pension schemes, which are important financially to the
workers and make a substantial difference to the terms
and conditions of the job. These schemes should obviously be equally available to all men and women
workers on equal terms. However, the picture is very
different from what it should be. *Only* 19% of women
manual workers compared with 50% of men get occupational pension schemes; 48% of women are covered
by sick pay schemes and 65% of men. The situation
overall is, not surprisingly, much better for non-manual
workers; 50% of women get occupational pensions
schemes and 78% of men; 90% of women and 93%

of men get sick pay. The most disgraceful figure is for women manual workers. Like the non recognition of women's skills, this is another area where the unions have failed to negotiate decent schemes for their members.

In a survey done about eight years ago on the reasons why women went out to work, the four most frequently names reasons were:

- financial reasons   80.8%
- for company   39.5%
- to dispel boredom   29.5%
- for independence   11.5%

It is quite obvious that most women who work need the money.   The second two main reasons are interesting and lead to another myth. No doubt if a survey was done with men, the middle two reasons would hardly appear in their ratings as they would not imagine themselves bored and isolated in their homes and therefore would not think of that as a reason for working. Faced with the choice of doing a boring, repetitive job isolated at home and a boring repetitive job with company for an independent source of income, many would chose the latter. However, many employers still argue that women only go out to work to gossip and that they are quite happy doing boring, repetitive jobs because they are then able to gossip, listen to Jimmy Young, worry about their families and not care about their jobs. For most women it is the other way round. They gossip in order to cope with their boring repetitive job which don't involve them in any way. It's a case of humanising a totally de-humanised situation. Workers have learnt it over the ages. In a factory in Nottingham at the beginning of this century a group of workers appointed one person each day to read to them. They listened to Dickens and Jane Austen whilst they worked. Women weavers learn to lip read in order to communicate over the deafening noise of the looms. One woman describes the art;

They seem to have this ability to concentrate on the job and they're going like the clappers, they're really working like mad and they're holding a really good conversation and I mean I've done it and you have a conversation with one of the machinists and she doesn't turn round and she's yakking away.'

Boredom, or rather isolation, is often compensated for when assessing jobs (housewives take note), i.e. a woman working on her own for instance, in a stores room, will, because of the isolation, get slightly more money than her shop floor mates. On the other hand, repetitiveness can be a bargaining disadvantage as one shop steward explained:

When you're talking of the piecework value, you can talk of the boredom and the repetitive part of it. Sometimes because it's repetitive, you might not get such a good value.

Where women, as workers, are most vulnerable and therefore most open to exploitation is as mothers. Women as a group are exploited because they are the child bearers but it is those women with children who suffer the most. There are obvious changes which would help women greatly, like proper maternity leave, jobs being retained for women to return to after having a child and also State run creche and nursery facilities for all. Women must learn to demand and expect these things, as of right, and not as a privilege. At the moment not only do many women, particularly with small children (who are discriminated against by employers) feel the employer is doing them a service by employing them, if they are then given a small amount of flexibility they feel positively grateful. One good, tough shop steward with children of her own thought her factory very good;

They're sympathetic to a married woman who has to take her children to a nursery, you know they'll allow them to come in at certain times, later and things like this and they're very good if you're sent

for. Say your child is off colour, they're very good
that way.

Besides part time work some factories have changed
from an eight hour shift system to a four hour system for their women workers. They put out a lot of
PR about how it suits women, particularly with children. What they don't say is, productivity is considerably increased by having two separate four hour
shifts but they still only pay out the equivalent as
for the eight hour shift. Part time workers are notoriously exploited and vulnerable because of their responsibilities to their children.

Another shop steward, a clerical worker and a
woman, alone with a child, said of her employers;
They're quite reasonable, I'm allowed to vary my
hours, for instance if I get into work half an hour
late in the morning I have to make it up in the
afternoon or I'm allowed to work through the lunch
hour which also lets me leave a little earlier.
Obviously reasonable employers are better than unreas-
onable ones but people shouldn't have to work through
the lunch hour because they have a child. It's about
time that society recognised that child producing is an
important function and that women or men who care
for children shouldn't have to be thankful for the fact
that their employers allow them some leeway to fit
in children with their other productive life. The latter
steward did suggest how workers could set about changing this;
If working women could get together and ask their
employers if they could reduce hours for instance, they
could enlist the support of the whole union, making
it a collective issue - this would involve working fath-
ers too - and ask them to be a little more realistic
about hours where necessary and not just think along
the lines of pay increases but the thing is that women
must get in a union in order to introduce these de-
mands.

The hopeful sign is that more and more women are joining unions and let's hope they make their presence felt. Women clerical workers have certainly been making their presence felt in their strike for equal pay at GEC SEI Salford. They're proving that women are having a hard fight to get what is allowed by law, let alone anything better. The most recent survey on the progress towards equal pay published by Incomes Data Study in July 1973 just confirms all the evidence available so far. They found that not only is progress towards equal pay slow, it was slower in 72/73 than in 71/72. It is clear that many industries will not reach 100% by the end of 1975. It also found that in some industries the differential between men and women's basic rates has increased. For instance, in Flour Milling the differential between the male and female rate has widened by 2% from 85% to 83%. It's going to be a long hard struggle to get even minimal equal pay for women workers, let alone any more recognition for their skills. Obviously, the whole question of women workers is inextricably tied up with the way society sees women's role, first as mother and housewife, secondly as worker, however much that contradicts both the facts and their needs. For men, the role is worker first and father second. Undoubtedly, the role women play as workers in the home, producers of children, of meals, clean clothes etc. for the male worker goes unremunerated by this society. This, has led some women to suggest that women should be paid for child rearing and housework on the grounds that it is a form of labour which helps to produce profit. This would have two dangerous implications; one, it would tend to reaffirm women's role as child rearer and house worker even though men would be paid if they opted for that role, and secondly they would just form another group of exploited workers. An independent wage for women at home would be an improvement on the present state of affairs but it doesn't solve the basic problems of women at home or out at work. Personally I would like to see some system of sharing, between couples or groups, the roles of child rearing and working. This would involve the recognition by society that child rearing is important and should be paid for. Any such system should have flexibility to suit the needs of the people instead of people being moulded to suit the system.

In thinking about how these roles and attitudes can be radically changed, one is led inevitably into considering how society can fundamentally be changed. Whilst we we are caught up in a system which is guided by the profit motive, women can only improve their situation from being doubly exploited to being merely exploited and possibly they may do that at the expense of another group. The capitalist system operates on using pools of cheap labour and if women cease to provide that in this country, the employers will move to using other pools of cheap labour, like people from the Third World countries. We do not want our liberation on the backs of others.

Workers will only be able to control their lives, their work patterns, their family responsibilities and their roles when they control the means of production, that is when they own and control where they work and live. So the struggle for women workers must not just be a struggle to level up to men workers, but it should be, to quote August Bebel, a struggle for the *removal of all impediments that make man dependent on man and consequently one sex upon the other.*

Accordingly, this solution to the Woman Question coincides completely with the solution of the Social Question. It follows that he who aims at the solution of the Woman Question to its full extent, is necessarily bound to go hand in hand with those who have inscribed upon their banner the solution of the Social Question as a question of civilisation for the human race.

Sarah Boston
1973

First published in SPARE RIB, No. 16 1973.

The Independence Demand

At the Oxford Women and Socialism Conference in March 1974 on the demands and campaigns of the women's movement, it was proposed that we should adopt a new demand, one relating to women's status as dependent persons. Since then, a group of us in Oxford have been investigating the possibilities of such a demand. Unfortunately, we haven't had time to discuss the issues fully, indeed many questions about the family have arisen which we haven't been able to explore in this paper. Our ideas are only tentative, and we don't necessarily agree on all of them. We have tried to formulate the demand concisely as:

Legal and financial independence

We want to attack the State:
- for its role in upholding the family in its present form
- for forcing women into a position of dependence on their husbands
- for leaving single women with inadequate means of support

Immediate campaigns would centre around National Insurance, pensions, supplementary benefits etc. But our long term aim is that women should no longer be regarded by others, nor by themselves, as dependent people, but should have legal and financial independence and moral autonomy.

We want to add this further demand as it deals with serious problems, affecting all women, neglected by the four demands. It concerns the relationship between the State and the family, and consequently the relationship between men and women.

This paper is a discussion of the demand, why it is important and what areas it can cover. The details relate to the summer of 1974, but the underlying problems are more enduring. First we try and place the demand in the context of the women's movement, and then we consider practical campaigns and examine in in particular National Insurance and Supplementary Benefit.

Theory

Before discussing the issues involved in the demand itself, we want to place it in the context of the women's movement's struggle against oppression.

The demand covers two broad areas:

a. The way marriage creates and reinforces the economic and legal dependence of women on men, and consequently hinders the development of our economic and social independence;

b. The way the State underpins the marriage relationship in order to preserve the existing social structure, and so hinders the development of new social and sexual relations.

We do not wish merely to attack individual laws which deny women their independence, but rather to attack the way women's dependence is assumed by the State, especially in social and financial legislation. This assumption is not an unhappy historical accident: it is an integral part of the way society operates. This assumption of dependence has been institutionalized, and so in challenging laws we are also challenging the ideas on which they operate.

This kind of demand, however, has serious problems as it could fail to develop beyond a simple fight for equal rights within the existing social structure. This is a danger it shares with the other demands, i.e. that we demand from the State things which can be granted, but which can never be enough. If the demand became locked at this level, its potential to challenge the family and the State would be diverted into a struggle for legal changes as an end in themselves. It is precisely to avoid being trapped like this that we must attempt to examine from the outset what the long term applications and implications are. Careful discussion and consideration must take place when campaigns are being organized and we must never lose sight of the inter-relation between short-term campaigns and long-term ends.

In its curiously haphazard way, thinking in the women's movement does move forward. Thinking about the family is certainly now much deeper than can be sufficiently expressed in the demands for abortion and contraception or in the nursery campaigns alone. The connection between the family and inequalities in work and education are now much clearer. It is also clear that the inequalities under the 'welfare state' are based on the assumption that wives will be dependent on their husbands, and are designed in such a way as to preserve that system of dependence (tempered by the need to prevent people, especially children, from starving when the system slips up). Motherhood makes us especially dependent on husbands, but the existence of widows' pensions and of tax allowance in respect of childless wives makes it clear that the dependence is a way of ensuring the provision of housekeepers (if only part-time ones) for men, as well as housemothers for children. This demand, then, highlights the links between the State and the family, and the way the State systematically bolsters the dependent-woman family.

This demand touches those areas in which women are treated as a special category as the result of a State-recognised relationship with a man. And we are affected when we aren't in such a relationship as well as when we are. For the recognition by the State of certain kinds of relationship hinders the development of alternatives which are seen as aberrant - for example, single and divorced people, those experimenting in communal living, gay people. Discrimination against social groupings outside the family is surely no accident. We will not be able to develop alternatives to the nuclear family unless and until we understand the ways in which marriage functions to perpetuate women's subservience in sexual and reproductive relations, and thus in society as a whole. In marriage a woman sells not only her domestic services, but her sexuality, in exchange for economic support. This demand can act to raise our consciousness in this area, as will become obvious when we examine women's relationship to the 'welfare state'.

It is hard for women to choose to have children outside marriage, for in the eyes of the State other kinds of households have no existence, and in the eyes of most employers, women need only be paid as subsidiary earners. The majority of women, therefore, have their children within marriage, with all the disadvantages of dependence while the marriage lasts, and the disadvantage of chasing husbands for support, should it 'fail'. It is impossible for our individual attitudes and behaviour to change fundamentally while the social context remains this way. All we can involve ourselves in is life-style politics, which, though important, have limited partial results.

This demand, therefore, is a most challenging one, because it calls for a rejection of one of the few compensations for our position of inferiority: the right to be supported by a man. The demand challenges us to think of the evils of the system as a whole, rather than the individual benefits.

Practice

This demand brings together the following main campaign areas:

Pensions and National Insurance contributions
Supplementary Benefit (e.g. Cohabitation)
Taxation

Separation and Maintenance Orders

Student Grants

Mortgages and Hire Purchase Agreements

Tenancies

Pensions and National Insurance contributions and the 'cohabitation rule' will be discussed later in this paper.

The issue of taxation should be taken up since the present system, based on the assumption that marriage is the norm, penalises those who are unmarried, whether they be sharing, 'cohabiting' or living alone. It gives the married man an allowance enabling him to 'keep' his wife at home while compensating for loss of her potential earnings. The whole system assumes that the husband is the main wage-earner. Also, there is only an allowance for mortgage repayments and not for rent, and rented accommodation is the kind usually occupied by unmarried mothers and single people.

Separation and maintenance orders are difficult to enforce. In a large number of cases women are left with an inadequate income. Women should not be forced to depend on their ex-husbands for financial support; nor should ex-husbands be expected to support them (except where young children are involved).

The main difficulty with regard to the student grants system arises out of the fact that a married woman is expected to be supported by her husband and her dependence upon him is assumed. This does not apply to married male students whose wives are working.

It is very hard (though getting easier) for women to complete hire purchase and mortgage agreements without the signature of a male guarantor, even if in all other respects they are 'credit-worthy'.

Finally, all women should be able to rent property without difficulty, and all tenancies where two or more people are living together, including husbands and wives, should be automatically registered in their joint names thus safeguarding all the tenants.

273

These issues are so diverse that no one law could cover them all. Some stem directly from the law, some are discretionary aspects of the Welfare State and some result from what is regarded as 'good' business practice.

An example

The Social Security scheme starts with the assumption that women are dependents of men. Because of this expectation, it almost forces them to be so.

For example, when trying to get supplementary benefits (i.e. support which hasn't been insured for by payment of stamps), a married woman must rely on her husband and not directly on the state for support (and if neither she nor her husband can support themselves it is he who must make the claim and collect the money). Whenever possible, the Supplementary Benefits Commission tries ·to force women who are not married into dependence upon men. If a woman can be shown to be living with a man then she is not allowed to apply for supplementary benefit herself but must rely on him for support. This is described as the cohabitation rule. Criteria for deciding whether or not a couple are living together as man and wife are complex, and give the Social Security people the right to investigate your life closely. This rule works reciprocally for men living with women, but does not effect so many of them, partly because they need supplementary benefit less often.

The form of discrimination encountered directly by *every* woman in this country is, however, the National Insurance scheme. Most benefits based upon it are unequal - but that is justified in the eyes of the bureaucracy because contributions are unequal. It is this seemingly rational 'fairness' in the relation of benefits to contributions which is so dangerous in perpetuating woman's secondary role, for behind it is the acceptance of the pattern of man as the breadwinner. The man is expected to make contributions 'on behalf of himself and his wife as for a team' (Social Insurance and Allied Services: a report by William Beveridge). And in consequence, over

274

a quarter of a century later, the statement by an official of the Department of Health and Social Security that 'married women...can generally look to their husbands' contribution record to provide them with a retirement pension' betrays the unchanged economic status of women. Lack of provision in the scheme for the apparently atypical turns such descriptive statements into prescriptive ones. Thus women are denied the exercise of full responsibility for their own well-being.

For example, a single woman cannot choose to pay more in order to get more, even in the (still rare) cases where her wage would allow her to. Her contributions are less than those of a single man, as are her benefits - at least until retirement age when single persons of whatever sex are belatedly acknowledged as being equally in need. But at least the single woman has individual rights: married women, whose ranks she is pected to join, still bear the full brunt of economic chatteldom. Occasionally there is a seeming recognition of the possible detrimental consequences of dependence: a divorced woman (if she does not marry again before the age of sixty) can adopt her former husband's National Insurance record to help qualify for a single person's pension, for presumably had she not married she would have had that work record as her own. But in general the system works to worsen the syndrome.

Even if she continues to pay insurance contributions in her own right, a married woman will receive less than three-quarters of the amount of unemployment benefit due to a single woman, despite the fact that she needs the same number of stamps to qualify. The sickness benefit scheme operates a similar differential. The judgment is evidently being made that married women suffer less hardship in these circumstances because they can depend on their husbands. The result is that they have little choice.

This assumption is explicit in the case of women who 'opt out' of the insurance scheme after marriage.

This is a tempting alternative for women who in any case get low wages and small benefits, but they then are made totally reliant on their husbands' stamps. The woman is not eligible for unemployment benefit, irrespective of how great a contribution her earnings have made to the family's living standard. And only when her husband retires will she be entitled to any form of pension - a married woman's pension, the full rate of which (payable only if her husband has a yearly average of 50 stamps over the 49 years between the ages of 16 and 65) is less than 70% of a single woman's pension.

To earn this same princely sum under current arrangements, a man or single woman would need to have collected 50 stamps a year for about 28 years. But even if a married woman has *bettered* this average, she cannot claim an increase. Unless, that is, she can pass the iniquitous 'half-test'. At present, to qualify for a flat-rate pension in her own right, a married woman needs contributions for half the number of weeks between the date of her marriage and her 60th birthday (unless married after her 57th one). If this condition is not satisfied, no retirement pension *at all* is payable on her own contributions, whenever they were made. Women who marry late, having perhaps 20 or 30 years of stamp payment behind them, find their own claims wiped out: those who happen as well to be older than their husbands have the situation compounded by the need to wait until the man staggers to the age of 65, at which point a married woman's pension can be drawn. It would seem that individual rights are not inalienable.

This particular manifestation is to continue, probably, under the new pensions scheme, which is still in a state of flux. Others would have been introduced under the Tory Government's Social Security Act. In addition to differential benefits during working life, *all* women of whatever marital status, have been threatened with the introduction of a lower pension rate, in both occupational and state reserve schemes. This was justified on the actuarial basis that women need a pension for longer. Therefore the money, on this rationalisation, is eked out in smaller portions per week. But one parameter, at least, of this cold calculation could be altered: the age of retirement. Fix it at 60 for everyone, or float it between the ages of 60 and 70 for everyone - and part of the 'logical' basis of this argument collapses. On humanitarian grounds, it should not even have been contemplated.

Women should press for equal benefit rights with men, regardless of marital status. Specific campaigns might be:

- abolition of the cohabitation rule
- equal pension rights and equal minimum requirements in occupational pension schemes
- stamps to be credited for all people caring for small children, the sick and old people

One thing that is very clear is that none of these campaigns can be seen in isolation. Women's dependence on men and women's low wages go hand in hand: so must our struggles against them.

Katherine Gieve, Lesley Gilbert, Mary McIntosh, Liam Morton, Lucy Robinson, Margaret Wheatley and Leonora Wilson.

Amended version of a paper first given at the National Women's Liberation Conference held in Edinburgh in June 1974.

Trying to Stay Human

It's quite right to think that there is very deep rooted male domination in every aspect of our society. This permeates absolutely everything, every social grouping, every organization. Women are defined in terms of men and the working class is defined as male. The Trade Unionist is defined as the Trade Unionist with his *wife and family*. Well there are two and a quarter, at least, million women Trade Unionists and it's pretty self evident that they have no wives! So this stereotype that comes on of the Trade Unionist with his wife and family is clearly deriving from this picture of society as male. We are all some sort of sub-species and never more than when we join a Union, but you see two and a quarter million of us *have* joined Unions. The trouble is that we've made very little impact on those Unions so far.

Now it's true that *workers organise Unions and not Unions workers.* This, in a nutshell, is why I am a Trade Unionist. I am a Trade Unionist first and foremost as a declaration of class solidarity; I am not willing you see to have the class defined in terms of men. Because Trade Unions are run as if they are male working class clubs, that's no reason for me to let them get away with it is it? It seems to me that if we say that women are an integral part of the working class then we have to behave like this and so to me joining a Union is a declaration of class solidarity. I want women not only to join Unions but to participate, *to take them away from male domination.*

Now I think it's not a simple crude question of either you join a Trade Union or you participate in an autonomous women's movement because I think both these things are necessary. You see if you look at the question of why aren't women participating, straight away you're up against social questions .. the structure of Unions, the rules and regulations, having to talk at meetings and the fact that meetings are at night when women are supposed to be washing up and putting *their* children to bed. *Their* children, the children of all these females here. Well I tell you my children were not my own product and have not been brought up as though they are my own product and when women are made responsible for children, part of the job of women's liberation and of women in Unions and of women in general is to make men realise that children are the children of both sexes.

The revolution therefore that we need in women's consciousness cannot be strictly defined in terms of work nor can it be strictly defined in terms of home. These things interact and the woman who is at home now without wages - she probably was out at work earning wages; she probably intends to go out to work in the future. There simply isn't a division between the woman at work and the woman at home. She is the same woman at different stages in her life.

Low level of consciousness

It's perfectly true that Trade Unions behave as if it's only those who are actually in employment that have any right to speak for the working class, but that is no reason why we should accept this. It is no reason why we should therefore believe that we have no place in the organization of class solidarity. Trade Unions are, or should be (some of them are, some of them aren't, but they all should be), defensive organizations for the workers. They're not really revolutionary organizations in their intention although some of them do include revolutionary aims - even my own Union does intend to take over the distributive trades but it's forgotten about that, that bit's not very often read! But they are defensive organizations and *women workers do need defending* and there isn't really any reason at all why we should accept the definition that the Trade Unions are the man's business.

Part of fighting the boss is fighting for control of our own organisation. It's difficult, of course it's difficult. Look

279

at the number who can really be called the ruling class at the moment and look at the rest of us, who work in one way or another, who sell our labour - there is a considerable disparity in numbers isn't there? So why does the majority put up with this minority rule? Because men and women *alike* are at a very low level of consciousness and of course it's difficult. It's difficult to help women understand that they are people, that they shouldn't always be defined in terms of their family or husband and so on. It's difficult to get all workers, men and women, to realise that they don't really need the boss and it doesn't seem to me that we make this difficult job any easier by behaving as though we lived in a strictly sex segregated world.

Effects of the women's movement

I believe that a woman's movement has a very important place. I didn't always believe this but I've learnt. I've kept my mind open and observed and the women's liberation movement *works*. You have meetings like this where women can come and take part and you have it spilling over.

Now I think that the job of raising consciousness, raising people's awareness, getting them questioning things is very subtle and it doesn't always show in membership figures or meetings but it can show in attitudes. It seems to me that in its short life the women's liberation movement can look around and see definite changes in consciousness. Of course the capitalist class try to cash in on this - look at all the adverts ..... the new way to freedom which is some sort of product ... but it's interesting that advertising uses such methods - it shows that they think women are thinking in terms of freedom, liberty etc.

There's a tremendous film called *The Salt of the Earth* which has many lessons for workers in general and especially for women. You see it's about Mexican American miners who have the most oppressed conditions - *worse* than the non Mexican American miners so that in the surrounding pits all the non Mexican Americans can look at *this* pit and say well at least we're better off than them. And this, of course, is a well known bosses trick, it helps to keep people happy if they can look and see someone beneath them. They feel that much elevated. We're taught in our society to measure ourselves by how many people there are underneath us and this is the second point of the film. But the essence of the film is that when the strike happened the men are unable to bring it to victory *on their own*. The women have definite demands they want to impose as well, they don't see why it should just be things relating to the men. They want it to be things relating to the home because this is a company town, you see, and everything is ruled by the company.

Now in order for the women to be brought actively into the strike and win it, they had to adjourn the Union meetings and have a meeting of the whole community instead. That's where it's at on a national and international level. The essential pre-requisite for this was the first action that the women took (and these were not employed women, they didn't have the right to join the Union - they weren't themselves miners and it was a miners Union), they *went to the Union meeting*. The Union meeting didn't become a meeting of the whole community just out of the blue. *The women went to the Union and insisted on their right to be there*. It's this development which is so important. If it works for women who are not even employed to insist on being involved in the struggles of the Union, how much more appropriate it is where women are employed. There is no need - there wouldn't be a need to adjourn the meetings of USDAW because it is mostly women. They are in a majority within our present membership and if we recruited our potential membership of two million, the majority would increase to 75%. The fact is they don't act as if they were in the majority any more than they act as if they were in the majority in the adult population at large, but we are. The job is not to adjourn the Union meeting in this sense but to *take it over*, and this is practicable and possible.

Cogs in a machine

I found that a lot of things said about women are quite

untrue. Women are not averse to being in Trade Unions. Women workers are just as interested in their working on conditions as male workers, *but sometimes in differenct aspects* and this is not dealt with by Trade Unions. Women aren't interested just in wages, equal pay is much more than a wage demand. Equal pay is a demand for self respect, it's more than just a demand for equal money, it's hygeine, safety, cold and things like that.

Women are interested, in other words, in their working conditions as much as, or more than, their wages, because women are *trying to stay human*, even while working. Now the male Trade Unionist is too pat to allow himself to become part of his machine - you've got good wages in car factories by my God at what a cost. And all the things like tea breaks on the job.. it's an acceptance of money as the capitalist evaluation of people - they're economic units. Men are taught to value themselves as breadwinners, that's why they get so worried by things like equal pay - they're like the American miners looking at the Mexican miners - they've got to have somebody beneath them. There's no doubt about it that many working men get compensation for being cogs in a machine at work by coming home and being 'head of the household'. And there's no way of breaking it down but battering it. And it's difficult - autonomous women's movement, Trade Unions or both - as I think it should be - it's a difficult job.

So I maintain that women are interested in their working conditions, because they're trying to reamin human. They're interested in *personal relations*. 'Women aren't interested in management', 'women aren't interested in top jobs', 'women haven't got a sufficiently responsible attitude to work'...well, bravo say I. I'm not in women's liberation to get women top jobs - I'm in women's liberation to get top jobs abolished. We get too apologetic. We get too accustomed to accepting the male definition of us - and this applies to all of us, no matter what field of activity we chose.

At sixteen I went to my first Union meeting - it was

all men and they voted in alphabetical order.... I couldn't bear it and I just wasn't confident enough to deal with it. Nowadays I've had young girls come to my branch meetings and they're perfectly happy to talk because they're listened to. They have a perfectly logical, sensible attitude to their work, and they're delighted if things get taken up because of their attendance. But the way to come to political terms - and survive - in the movement is to look around at what is and say well this *is* it, how do I change it? And the way to change it is, you say .... is there any positive feature in the situation, and you will usually, if not always, find that there is a positive feature. The positive feature about men asking for overtime is that they want more money, so you have to build on that ... and show them that's it's not the right way to go about it.

Producers and consumers

Women at work have many positive features - including the fact that they are not so inextricably tangled in the work machine as men are. The fact which we usually regard as a weakness, i.e. that we are conditioned to be mothers, that we are at home and so on - this keeps us at one degree remove from the work situation, just one degree. It doesn't keep us out of it - it gives us the extra dimension. We are producers, we are consumers - there isn't an aspect of life which doesn't touch women at some stage, whereas there are many aspects of life in which men aren't involved. So what we should do is build on this - build on this complexity. So of course it's quite right to campaign on on prices, for instance, but I believe that the essential dividing line between just a movement for a palliative and a movement for a basic change, isn't the issue itself, it's the lessons that you draw from the issue and the way the issue is presented. Such as nurseries ... we can succeed in getting nurseries - we've had them before, for instance during the war when the female labour force was needed. And this shows it isn't for *liberation*, if you get nurseries given to you by the employers, it's for the *employers' benefit*, and of course it's very right to talk about community control of these things. Now it's fraudulent to campaign for price control *as if this can be done in the present system*, because the present system depends on profit, and profits depend on freedom to charge what prices they like and what prices they can get. But it's good if you campaign on prices and show this - and strike at the root of the system.

A different economy

On the question of night shift - one of the best moments I ever had at a meeting was at the Gloucester Trades Council. My position was that in the factory such protection as women workers had got should be retained, that we should not accept a levelling down, so that in return for equal pay women gave away this concession and I was being told by a male Trade Unionist the usual things - 'won't accept responsibility' and 'the economy demands it' and 'what about exports - we'll price ourselves out of the market' - and up got a woman, beautiful creature - and said 'if the economy wants me to work night shift, *THEN I WANT A DIFFERENT ECONOMY!* And it was said in exactly those words. And that is the consciousness we've got to get. We've got to get it, I think, by participating in all the organizations of the working class to *make* them class organizations, and in our own organization as well.

We get used to a picture of society that is almost entirely a male picture, and I believe that - it's my personal rule - we must challenge this at every point. *Don't* let men say that women are backward. When you're talking to a woman, and she says that she doesn't want equal pay, what she usually means in the end is that she doesn't want night work and so on - she doesn't want *conditions negotiated by men* - which often they should never have accepted. So she is saying, when she says 'I don't want equal pay', 'I don't want to worsen my working conditions even for more money'. Far from being *backward*, there is a really progressive voice. If we talk enough, get these conversations going and realise that it *is* a progressive voice, that when male Trade Unionists talk only in money terms they are accepting the system .... I just saw an ad in Euston

Station for National Savings which showed a young lad and he's saying to his mate 'My Dad's better at making money than your Dad - and he's got certificates to prove it'. So you see the *values* - talk about conditions for *women!*

There are all sorts of things about which you can feel resentment. For instance, if you have an injury at work and you are a woman and you get compensation through your employers' insurance (not the Industrial Injury benefit but the lump sum sort of compensation), your husband signs. They do make the cheque out to you, but your husband signs. In fact, I lost the vote in Union elections of a large branch because I had the temerity to object to this and to take it up on behalf of the women in that branch. I discovered that the reason given is that insurance companies are afraid that men will sue for *loss of their wives' services.* Therefore, they have to indicate that they are satisfied with the compensation but it means that women have no privacy. I think it's a pity if they need privacy but often they do and anyway it should be their choice. Taking this up, which seemed to me quite straightforward, that a woman worker who is injured should get compensation for her injury full stop ..... I found a hornet's nest around my head with the men in the branch who all immediately felt threatened by this. And on the question of unfair payment, unfair training opportunities, there is only lip service paid to it, if that, and in the end we come down down to the fact of *the breadwinner* - 'I'm the breadwinner' and frequently they're *not* the breadwinner. They are older men who are putting this point of view and their children have ceased to be dependent and their wives work .... but ipso facto the man's the breadwinner.

And then there's also the deep-rooted male terminology. At one meeting I was at, the chairman used the term 'old women of both sexes', and when I objected to the term old *women* being used in a derisory fashion, I knew I'd be told I had a trivial mind - 'Oh the trivial minds these women have always going off and so on' - and sure enough up got the other speaker and said 'I'm very surprised at

Comrade Wise bringing us down to this trivial level'. But you see it isn't trivial and you have to take a very deep breath to stand up for women as a sex, as people. The kind of attitude expressed by 'You are good *for a woman*' and all that sort of thing can only be broken down in struggle but it can be broken down. We live in a mixed world and we must break it down in all the organizations of the working class.

The demand for a shorter working week is, I believe, an absolutely crucial demand. Now it's a demand which should fit in with the way political things are going - you've got a million unemployed - and the men should be insisting on a shorter working week for themselves. In fact, it's commonplace that they work overtime, never mind a shorter working week. So the reason this demand is crucial for women is that we need not be at work, then at home, then at work; we need not to have our lives in this sort of compartment. We need to be at work and at home *simultaneously*. And in order to get that we need to have men at home and at work simultaneously. So a shorter working week for men and for women gives the grounding for the removing of sex typing in working class homes, in a way that there is no opportunity for at the moment. It is just too much to expect a man who has worked 50 hours perhaps (do you know that lorry drivers' negotiating rate are on 60/70 hours a week - sure they demand a 35 hour week but they negotiate their rates on the basis of 60/70 hours a week) to share the housework. It's imperative that we put our voices behind the demand for a shorter working week for everybody, precisely so that men can take *their rightful place at home* with their children. Of course we want community care, community support, nurseries - there shouldn't be a block of flats built without games rooms and toddlers' rooms and everything - but we don't just want the situation where we free ourselves to go and work the hours that men work. Double exploitation is the danger.

One field that we, women's liberation that is, miss the boat completely on is secretarial work, generally regarded as the office wife type of thing. It's true to some extent that it's a carry over from the home role but in fact it is a skilled job and lots of girls know that they can make a better shot at the boss's work than he could at short-hand and typing! I think we should elevate women's self respect at all times so that instead of saying poor thing, office wife and go and cry in the cloakroom, why not say, skilled worker and what about skilled workers' rates? I think women's liberation often unconsciously slights women as mothers and workers by accepting male evaluation. There's a tremendous amount of skill in the work women do and it just isn't recognised by society nor is it paid for and it's often not recognised by the women themselves. I believe you'd get a better movement among people who have gained some self respect, who are standing on two feet and not just crying, poor little me, I'm badly done to.

I don't think you'll get the overthrow of capitalism, not in a progressive direction that is, without the participation of women. Without women really kicking up, I could see a fascist development being much more likely and people being relegated much more to just bits of machinery. The two things interweave all together. The only way to smooth it a bit is the more that women are asserting themselves in their home, at work and everything, the more they back each other up, they give each other credit and confidence and of course, I believe very firmly that men will realise that this is an improvement for them as well. I mean it isn't a generally anti-men movement, it's a pro people movement, but undoubtedly if you find men who act as blacklegs then you've got to expose them - if they strike because they don't want women working beside them, or women driving buses or whatever, then you've got to treat them as if they were striking because they didn't want to work with black people say. It's often hard to make even progressive men see this but if men act as agents against the class then we have to be quite merciless against them.

Audrey Wise

This article is part of a talk Audrey Wise gave at the Women's Struggle and the Unions workshop *held in London in 1972. It was subsequently published in RED RAG, No. 3.*
She is a member of the Union of Shop, Distributive and Allied Workers (USDAW). She was a branch secretary for nine years and is now Labour MP.

AND THE STRUGGLE GOES ON

******

Equal Pay

In reviewing the situation to date with regard to the implementation of the Equal Pay Act, the outlook is bleak. Knowing what has happened so far is important, not to commiserate, but in order to understand what tactics are being used to deprive women of equal pay. Also, there is some urgency about the matter as the women who find themselves re-graded, segregated or job-evaluated into the same badly paid jobs at the bottom of the wage scale, but called 'D' instead of 'Female rate', will have greater difficulty getting their rights later than now. Whilst employers have to change rates, terms etc., women can push their claims, but once a new 'Equal Pay' agreement has been negotiated it will be much harder for women to re-negotiate to get some real equality of pay.

Two basic shortcomings in the Equal Pay Act have made the struggle even more difficult. First it is a compromise Act full of ambiguities and loopholes, rushed through in 1970 by Barbara Castle with one eye on the elections; second Barbara Castle decided that five years were needed to soften the cost impact of implementing the Act for the employers. The first shortcoming means that the Act applies directly only to women who are engaged in:

 a) 'the same or broadly similar work'
 b) 'on work rated as equivalent with that of any men, if, and only if, her job and their job have been given an equal value'

Therefore, it does not apply, in the main, to the areas of traditional, low paid female work. Also the ambiguity in the wording of the Act leaves it open for the employers to take the narrow interpretation of 'equal pay for equal work', and not the much broader concept of 'equal pay for work of equal value'. The second shortcoming means that the employers have plenty of time, often unopposed by the unions, to re-organise their labour force and re-write agreements in order to minimise costs very substantially.

Besides the shortcomings of the Act, progress towards Equal Pay was undoubtedly hampered by the Tory Government wage restraint policies and its repressive Industrial Relations Act. Although Phase II of the Tory Government Wage Policy made special provision for Equal Pay, it only allowed women to claim one third of their existing differential with men over and above the £1 and 4% allowed on all wage claims. That meant that all women (a substantial number), with an existing differential of 85% or less than the lowest male rate could not and did not achieve 90% of the male rate by the end of 1973 - the date by which the Act hoped most women would have reached the 90% mark. Given that there might be slow progress in achieving Equal Pay, Clause 9 of the Act empowered the Secretary of State to order that women's rates be raised to 90% of the male rate by the end of 1973. Not surprisingly, Maurice Macmillan, then Tory Secretary of State, did not chose to wield the power given to him. Speaking at the 1973 TUC Conference on Equal Pay he said that the government would make no such order, for to do so 'would be to use a crude weapon in the orderly progress towards equal pay'. The Labour government missed the date by only being returned to office in spring 1974; however, it did not see its way to making another interim order.

The Office of Manpower Economics report of 1972 is the the most comprehensive study so far on the implementation of equal pay. It was commissioned by the Tory government to give a solid body of information on which the Secretary of State could make his decision about Clause 9. He obviously ignored the findings of the report which found very little progress and not much order. In fact, they found, out of 169 agreements studied, 24% had made no movement towards equal pay, 57% minimal or negligible progress and only 19% had a phased plan or had eliminated differentials ... and of 200 small companies not covered by collective bargaining or wage council agreements, only four had made plans to introduce equal pay. It also found that some employers were circumventing the Act, some didn't know of its existence and many thought it didn't apply to them. The unions have an equally unimpressive record. The report found that only a quarter of firms visited had experienced agitation by the union for equal pay, and in some places unions had agreed to management plans for circumventing the Act. Recent evidence does not suggest that much has changed since that report; if anything the situation has worsened. The gains made in 1971 were not equalled in 1972 and it would appear that progress is slowing down. Women who idly thought that by 1975 their wage packet would have risen substantially are beginning to learn that they will have to fight for that rise.

The employers

First a look at how the employers are organising themselves. In fact they began organising when the Act was but a Bill. A document circulated by the Engineering Employers Federation to its members after the first reading of the Bill indicates how the Federation with other members of the CBI intended to pressurise parliament into minimising the scope of the proposed Act. Fortunately some of their suggestions were not accepted, for instance, *The five year period of implementation is irresponsibly short.* With regard to the '90% end of 1973' clause, they, in fact, have finally got their way... *It is hoped that any attempt to use this so-called 'intermediate stage' as a means of implementing in full some or all of the clauses of the Bill (in the light of Trade Union demands for full implementation in 2-3 years) will be strongly opposed in parliament.*

The other clause which caused them great distress is the

one which relates to claims from *her employer or any associated employer at the same stablishment or at establishments in Great Britain*. The Federation were terrified that a woman employed in one member firm in the North East (low paid area) could claim comparability with a man doing the same job in a member firm in the midlands (high paid area). The Federation won in the interpretation of the Act. The DEP pamphlet interprets two companies as being associated when they are under the same financial control.

Since the passing of the Act one main message is being proselytised by employers' organisations. The message is - organise now, evaluate, adjust, re-write, move, whatever, but sort it all out before December 1975. *You can do anything now to eliminate the cost - so act quickly* they advise, *Because after December 1975 you may be caught by the Courts and have to pay out.* The CBI, in a letter, advises its members that before 1975 .... *it is open to the parties to negotiate any methods of eliminating discrimination which may appear appropriate* and in their pamphlet on the matter they warn ....*if action is not taken before the end of 1975, the legislation could have the effect of raising the pay of many women to the level of the minimum rate laid down in collective agreement for men* ..
Specific Employers' Federations have similar advice to offer, act now and *determine the least costly and most effective method.* Anne Mackie (Unilever), speaking to a conference recently organised by the Institute of Personnel Management, re-iterated the point by advising them to settle equal pay disputes before December 1975 so that they might get a less costly settlement than that which might be imposed by the Industrial Arbitration Board.

The other main discernible trend in the employers' approach to equal pay is their determination to keep women as a separate section in the work force, mainly at the bottom of the wages pile. Although it will be illegal to use the terms 'male' and 'female' in agreements etc., grade, areas of work and certain jobs will remain exclusively female. Again Ann Mackie gave the clearest indication of this trend with an illustration of how the employment distribution will look before and after the Act.

As is evident, nothing much has changed and it appears that there is an implicit assumption that the present female rate will be the new trade minimum. This is borne out by the Paper Box Federation who advise their members *Fundamentally the women's existing rate should become, at an agreed date, the minimum rate for each industry*. Anne Mackie also gave a few handy hints as to how employers could re-arrange the work distribution pattern in anticipation of an Anti-Discrimination Act. She advised the employing of *a few women at the top and a few incompetent men at the bottom so that you can defend it legally*. She did concede that it may not be good for the firm's industrial relations to use such tactics.

Employers and unions

The ways and means of keeping women separate and depressed takes different forms. The crudest is to move employees around so that they are physically separated. *Firms, may, as a part of their equal pay policy, consider isolating these individuals, sections or departments, by ensuring that no males are recruited into these fields...*which is what the Engineering Employers' Federation advises and evidence shows that some firms have already acted on this advice. Another technique is one which is being used at a firm in Worcester. There, the women have negotiated a rise which brings them up to the male minimum rate; and Equal Pay situation? Not exactly as none of the men receive the minimum as a basic rate. They all receive as a basic rate about three pounds above the minimum and it is quite obvious that the minimum has been kept static purposely
a) to minimise the women's wage rise and
b) to protect the male differentials.

But the greatest dangers lie in the area of grading schemes, job evaluation schemes and word games called 'job description'. Although Unions are usually represented in such schemes and can object to them, it does appear that the Unions have not been acting with the interest of women in mind and in some instances have collaborated in schemes which have blatant in-built loading against wo-

293

men. From the following it would seem you can call a job what you like and fix rates accordingly, that is if the Unions and the employers agree.

In the Shoefayre agreement, male shop assistants are designated 'Trainee Manager' and paid three pounds more than a female shop assistant who receives £12.50. Shoefayre are based in Leicester and are part of the co-operative union although they negotiate separately with USDAW. (Incomes Data Survey, July 1972)

The most obvious element available for loading schemes against women is the 'heavy' and 'light' work factors. The Paper Box Federation advise re-negotiating agreements with this in mind.

a) Men's rates should be re-written for heavy work, e.g. shifting coal

b) Women's rates should be re-written for light work, e.g. making cardboard boxes.

An agreement which reflects this obvious loading was one negotiated and signed by USDAW and covers workers in the bacon curing industry. This agreement replaced an old grading scheme with a separate women's rate and provided a new four grade structure open to all men and women in accordance with the Act with a plan for the phased reduction of the differential between men and women. On the surface it sounds reasonable until you look at the grades and the sex distribution in those grades. G. Sheridan analysed this agreement in an article for *The Guardian* and found that 80% of the women found themselves in Grade D (bottom) which was defined as 'light work requiring limited training' (no men in this grade), and most of the remaining 20% of women were in Grade C1 defined as 'work involving a considerable degree of manual dexterity', but of light nature. Conveniently any men in Grade C fit into a different category C11 'Heavy work requiring limited training'.

Just in case such factors don't give enough scope for loading things against women or the men employees are demanding that their differentials be preserved once again the Paper Box Federation have the following suggestions

to make 'seriously', not 'cynically':
Discrimination factors available:
Long Service
Merit
Attendance Bonus
Willingness to work overtime to a given number of hours (NB. Extra daywork rates could be paid for those willing to work a given amount of overtime)

The Act provides other loopholes which give scope to the employers to circumvent it. There is the whole area of 'material' difference whereby some small task can be attached to the male job to establish its difference. On this a final bit of employers' advice is:

Jobs should be changed now where areas of conflict are likely to arise, i.e. the lavatory cleaner. NB. In this connection it is suggested that if for any reason it should be impossible to designate this as a woman's job, then outside contractors should be brought in to take care of the situation, and similarly of course with other jobs at present done by both men and women, and where it should prove impossible to change a light job over to women.

If all this fails, there is always automation and the resultant redundancies for women. As yet it is difficult to ascertain how many redundancies are due to Equal Pay negotiations and how many are just a reflection of general economic trends.

The Unions

As is evident, the union position is considerably more equivocal than that of the employers. The employers aim to minimise the costs by one means or another. There is no such clear policy with the unions. in 1888 the TUC passed a resolution demanding that women should receive equal pay for equal work. Since then they have accepted the principle of the ILO Conventionof equal pay for work of equal value. The Tory government, rather quietly, also ratified the Convetion. No doubt it was a concession they had to make for their treasured common market but one which they haven't publicised to the employers who prefer to stick to 'equal pay for equal work' formula. So publicly and in principle the TUC supports a liberal interpretation of equal pay but in practice the picture is very different.

The *New Unionist (G & MWU)* edition on equal pay provides a brief resume of the broad spectrum of opinion amongst its members with regard to women workers and equal pay. Many of the traditional ideas are there, the myths and misinformation, but also there are some good points made too. For instance, a bloke at a cigarette factory maintained that women wouldn't work in bad conditions like heat etc. and a fellow worker quickly replied.. 'Who works in greater heat than the girls in the canteen?' Another thing that emerges is that different traditions are set up in different industries and are governed largely by supply and demand. In the laundry trade, certain heavy jobs were done by men but when they coulnd't get men to do the job for that pay, women took over. The war is the classic example of traditions being broken because of economic necessity. Many statements also reveal the fear amongst many men and women workers that one or other section will be made redundant. *Where will they work, it's inflammatory. Industry won't pay for it, the community will have to pay for it* - the frightened male worker and a female worker in the same factory said *with equal pay management would think twice about putting women on the same job.* Although many saw that equal pay was related to job opportunity, training and educational facilities, there was a sad lack of any radical viewpoint in relation to the role of women.

The official Union attitudes along with that of the Union leaders, so called, is little more encouraging than those expressed by the rank and file. The one day conference on Equal Pay held by the TUC in 1973 gave a good indication of their thoughts. The importance Vic Feather attached to the issue was succinctly shown in the way the Chairman begged us to thank him for having devoted less than an hour of his precious time to attend and address the conference. The conference had a small attendance and a large number of delegates were full time officials of one kind or another. Many were keen to trumpet the achievements and commitment of their Unions in the equal pay matter. It sounded pretty hollow particularly in such cases as USDAW whose record in some agreements leaves a lot to be desired. One other indication of how the TUC pays lip service to the matter but very little active support, is the lack of information they have provided on the subject. The conference had to use the Office of Manpower report as a basis for discussion which, as I have said, is a good enough report but good hard factual information culled from the shop floor would be of great help and that is exactly what is lacking.

No doubt it is lacking for another reason too. The hard facts about grading schemes, about agreements such as one mentioned by a T & GWU delegate, where differentials between men and women in some areas of textiles have increased since a new 'unisex' agreement was introduced, are just the facts the TUC would not want to be publicised. Fortunately there were a few good contributions made, some basic questions asked about 'value' and 'value to whom?' of one's labour; some basic demands made for a rate for the job and a decent living minimum wage and some basic connections made about the struggle for equal pay being related to the struggle of the Trade Unions against the attacks of the Tory Government. One AEU shop steward from Manchester summed up the conference with : *So much for this lot, we'll just have to go back and do what we always do ...fight it on the shop floor.*

If women are going to get any real form of equal pay they are going to have to do just what that shop steward said. First they must join unions (a hopeful sign is that they are doing so in increasing numbers) and secondly they must become active members who assert themselves and make sure they are party to all negotiations, evaluation schemes, whatever. Women must make their Unions work for them and just as men expect support from women Trade Unionists, so women have the right to demand and expect support from men.

Until the Act is fully in force this is the only course open to women but from January 1976 they can take their cases of 'unequal pay' to the Industrial Tribunals. Once again women must make their Unions take up and fight their cases for them. Women workers should not be left as isolated individuals to fight for what is their right by Law. Cases may, and will we hope, be won at Tribunals and a few successful test cases could have a strong influential effect on employers, but Tribunals are no substitute for winning the battle on the shop floor, which means women actively ensuring their Unions work for them.

The following example is an indication of how women flexing a little bit of industrial muscle can make substantials gains. A group of clerical workers (wage clerks etc. 95% women) in APEX threatened to strike for a new equal pay related grading scheme. The management were slightly bemused by this expression of militancy from a recently organised group of workers led by a woman shop steward and didn't believe that they could carry through with a threatened strike. The situation changed very dramatically when the men on the shop floor pledged their support and said they would refuse to accept their wage packets from 'black' labour or in any unproperly calculated form. The management settled up pretty smartly and the clerical workers didn't even have to go on strike.

Sarah Boston
1974.

This is a revised version of an article which first appeared in SPARE RIB May 1973.

Some Facts about Equal Pay

The Equal Pay Act, introduced by Barbara Castle and brought in by the Labour Government in 1970, provides for equal terms and conditions of employment for men and women workers working in the same establishment, or in other establishments owned by the same employer or associated employers, if they are employed on 'like' (the same or broadly similar.) work. The ruling about other establishments does not apply unless the employees have common terms and conditions of employment between establishments, either generally or within each class, e.g. men and women; otherwise women can only claim equal pay with men in the same establishment. 'Equal conditions' doesn't apply to retirement, marriage or death matters. The final decision on whether work is 'broadly similar' is to be taken by an Industrial Tribunal. The Act provides for equal terms and conditions for work rated as 'equivalent' under a job evaluation exercise, but does not enforce job evaluation. (Job evaluation schemes place all jobs at a given place of work, or within a company etc., within a rigid system of grading so that they are paid according to the value of their content, according to 'scientific principles').

The Equal Pay Act is supposed to come into force on 29th December 1975. Under the Act, the Secretary of State was empowered to make an order for women's rates to be raised to 90% or more of men's, if he thought 'orderly progress' was not being made by 31st December 1973. Before doing this, he had to consult 'such bodies appearing to him to represent the interests of employers or of employees as he considers appropriate'.

A report published by the Office of Manpower Economics in August 1972 gave evidence of deliberate circumvention by regrading and the separation of men and women workers - with union agreement - general lack of progress and a widespread attitude among employers that they would wait for the Act to be enforced before doing anything. Only four out of two hundred companies investigated had made any plans at all.

However, the then Tory Secretary for Employment, Maurice Macmillan, reached agreement with the TUC and the CBI that he would not use his powers to enforce progress (owing to the inflationary situation etc.)

The Incomes Data Services Study of 31st May 1974 showed that 36.5% of industries looked at were still paying rates to women of less that 91% of the men's lowest rate, and 79.2% were paying less than 96%. The average women's rate was 92% of the men's lowest rate at that date - an average cash differential of £1.49. (If actual *earnings* are compared, the disparity is much more striking; a New Earnings Survey for April 1973 shows a cash differential of from £18 to £22 between the average gross weekly earnings of adult men and women, a percentage differential of 46% - 48%.)

However, the Labour Secretary of State for employment. Michael Foot, discussed the matter with the TUC in June 1974 and again it was agreed not to push the matter.

As for the European Economic Community, the provisions for 'equal pay for equal work' under the Treaty of Rome of 1957, with special procedures for implementation within three years added in 1961, have not so far led to equal pay for women at any level in any of the EEC member countries. A survey conducted in France in 1970 showed an average 33.6% discrepancy between the pay of men and women. France has had equal pay since 1946.

***

The great upsurge of interest and activity around Equal Pay in 1968-9 lost most of its momentum with Labour's introduction of the Equal Pay Bill in 1969. There is plenty of evidence that the collapse of the movement was not merely due to blind trust by women workers in Parliamentary methods, but also to organised resistance by employers and inertia (if not opposition) from the unions, especially in their traditional strongholds. Apart from noting yet again that the sanctity of the Law is only a matter of the class relationship of forces (and in this case the working class's representatives have been objectively helping business interests), we need to take a closer look at the many and varied kinds of 'equals' that have been dragged in to befog the discussion so far, which have been preventing any effective action from being taken.

Equal pay for equal work

The Equal Pay Act, even if implemented, and even without the numerous loopholes devised by ingenious employers, management advisers and the like to get around the wording, would affect, at best, only about one third of the female workforce, for the simple reason that the majority of women *do not do* 'the same or broadly similar work' to male workers.

Traditional female areas of employment are women-only jobs at the bottom end of the manufacturing industries - over half the female workforce is in either semi-skilled or unskilled manual jobs (and this percentage is increasing), or in the badly organised distribution and service sectors. We saw earlier the huge differentials between men's and women's average pay which the Equal Pay Act, as it stands now, will not touch.

So while we must, of course, fight for the 'rate for the job' for women in all cases, 'equal pay' in this sense, really amounts to little more than smoothing out a particularly glaring anomaly in a rather restricted area of women's employment.

Equal pay for work of equal value

This is a slightly more liberal interpretation of 'equal work'; it is the definition used by the International Labour Organisation and is a possible meaning of the part of the Equal Pay Act which allows for equal pay for *equivalent* work as rated by a Job Evaluation exercise. For this reason it is a more dangerous interpretation, and one that has caused confusion in the labour movement.

To talk of 'value' and 'evaluation' raises the question 'value for whom'? And as we live in a capitalist society where individual workers must sell their labour power to their employers in order to survive, it is the employer who is in a position to answer the question in terms of *value to him* - his profit.

We can argue that job evaluation should take account of value to society as a whole, but in practise any job evaluation exercise is going to be done at company level or even lower, and all within the context of what the 'market' and profit margins will stand.

And since we are only working because we have to - and not for the sake of the company profits - our 'value', in the sense of profitability (or even 'value to society') is of no interest to us, as long as we get our wages. (Though in a socialist society where we would be producing for the benefit of all, we would be very concerned to make a valuable contribution through our work.)

So to argue for pay to be based on 'value of work performed' can only end up in everyone competing to see who can be of most value to the employer - a recipe for low pay all round. It is also particularly irrelevant as a criterion for women, in that it cannot take account of the reason for their inequality on the labour market in the first place - the value of their contribution to society in unpaid domestic responsibilities and child rearing.

A fair wage

In actual fact, of course, as labour power is a commodity for sale like any other, rates of pay are ultimately based on the state of the labour market - taking into account not just local conditions but availability of all kinds of labour power in society as a whole. Broadly, the availability (and therefore price) of a particular kind of labour power will depend both on how easily it can be produced (taking into account necessary training etc.) and on the strength of organisation of the working class in that field. It is the traditional function of trade unions to defend the living standards of the working class by restricting the number of workers willing to work below a certain wage: the greater the unity and solidarity of the working class, the better the price.

But we also have to take account of the many complex factors which determine what the union membership considers a 'fair wage' to hold out for, beyond which the necessary unity cannot be maintained. These will include custom, prestige etc. (for whatever historical reasons) and factors such as unpleasant or dangerous conditions, which again push up the scarcity of the labour power available for a particular job, and therefore its price (though the presence of under-privileged strata such as immigrant workers for whom this is the only work available may complicate the matter). One important idea in negotiating for wage claims is that of comparison with other workers, via parity claims or 'leap-frogging' to re-establish the differential. The workers picked for comparison are not necessarily in the same area or even the same country, so there is an ideological factor involved; it is not just a case of threatening to go to an employer who pays better (and thus adjusting the state of the local labour market).

Many different methods of payment have been peddled by the employers as being more 'just' and 'rational' than each other. Payment by Results was favoured till the 1950s when Measured Day Work began to be introduced; the bourgeois press even discussed a *national* job evaluation scheme on the lines of the one tried unsuccessfully in Holland. The idea, of course, is simply to introduce confusion into the second, subjective factor determining wages, and profit by dividing the interests of the working class. Hence the introduction of grading schemes where each has his bit extra to defend against the one below, merit payments etc.

This is where women workers lose out, as with all the weight of everyday social relationships and pressures, backed up by the media, reinforcing the idea that women's domestic role gives them different interests from those of workers at the point of production, the trade union movement in general (including women workers themselves) cannot see the interests of the working class as a whole and fails to take up seriously the question of equal pay.

The militant AUEW, for example, has repeatedly chosen to drop the 'equal pay' part of its claims both at local and national level, despite its nominal support of the idea at conferences. The April 1974 agreement brought women - whatever their degree of skill - up to only 91% of the unskilled male rate, a level previously reached in 1968 and lost again. (An intermediate increase for women in November 1974 brings their rate to 96% - but still only of the *unskilled* male rate). In addition, divisions may be reinforced inside the unions, with graded membership according to sex and skills.

So the trade unionists who maintain that equal pay can only be achieved through industrial action (and not through legislation, job evaluation etc.), while entirely correct in one sense, rather beg the question of how such industrial action is to come about, since the TUC has been calling for equal pay for the last 80 years or so without noticeable results.

Working class organisation

In fact this problem highlights the basic contradiction in the position of the trade unions in a capitalist society like ours; that they defend the standard of living of the working class against capital - the employing class - but at the same time, by operating within that framework, reflect the basic social structures and ideologies of capitalist society within themselves.

So if we say that the gaining of equal pay is a matter for the unions, we immediately run into the union version of the 'relative value' principle used by the employers. Since the unions defend the working class only as *workers at the point of production*, it is logical that their view of the matter will be similarly limited. The eligibility of women for equal pay, in their eyes, will depend on their 'equal' contribution at the workplace, ignoring women's social role. So we meet arguments that women 'can't lift heavy weights, aren't available for awkward shifts, don't work nights, retire earlier, take days off when their children are sick etc.' In other words, we're all for women's access to equal work *and* equal pay as long as they pretend they're really men.

This opens the door to the favoured few (and should be taken advantage of), but does nothing to improve the situation of the mass of women workers who, because of their social role and family responsibilities - to say nothing of probable lack of training and confidence - are not in this position. What this attitude by the unions really boils down to is an acceptance that the working class itself - via working class women - should take full responsibility for keeping itself going for capitalism.

The union movement (and the left in general) will have to take the problem more seriously than that. The economic crisis is now continually forcing the ruling class and its government (*any* government) a policy of breaking the working class's organised resistance to increased exploitation. So union members must see the choice before them clearly: if the unions don't take up seriously and fight for the needs of the working class *as a whole*, but instead go on upholding sectional privileges and prejudices, then they lay themselves open to the only alternative - division and control by the State.

Equal pay and equal work

So how can we go about turning the unions into real working class organisations? To help to put the principles of equal pay and equal work into practise - and so also increase the confidence of women workers that their demands are justified - there are many issues we must fight on at a very basic level; not only equal pay and job opportunities, but also the right to the training that can make this a reality (in 1970 there were 110 female apprentices to skilled craft occupations, compared with over 112,000 males; 8.9% of young women workers outside national and local government get day-release, compared with 39.7% of young men, and this falls to 2 or 3% in industries with a high female workforce).

The fight for equality shouldn't only go one way, either; if women need protective legislation, restrictions on night work and retirement at 60, then so do men. Women lose out both at work and in taking an active part in union affairs by their home responsibilities; the unions must make sure that marriage or time off for pregnancy does not cost women their jobs. They must also make it *possible* for women to take part in activities by providing creche facilities where needed and by finding out at what time women can attend meetings - if the only time available is in working hours, so much the better.

Reforms of this kind are valuable not only in themselves, but also in changing attitudes of the people involved, so that ingrained ideas and habits can be challenged and changed.

If we take these reforms seriously, we must also fight for the means to bring them about. So we must fight, not only for women's right to equal union membership, but also for their right (and the right of other oppressed groupings) to have their own organisations inside the unions to fight around their particular problems and needs. Such organisations can only be active rank-and-file organisations: we must resist any attempt to substitute token 'Women's Advisory Committees' and the like, as these have no effect and only serve to confuse the issue by taking women's questions *out* of day-to-day activity, rather than ensuring that that is where they are fought.

So the demands we would put forward for women workers inside the unions would include both our long-term goals and immediate demands which will begin to make their achievement possible. For example, while we will always put the demand 'Equal Pay Now', we will also always fight against any increase in the cash differential (as always happens where equal *percentage* increases are agreed to): equal cash increases for all, as a minimum. Other principles would include:

- Equal Training and Job Opportunities
- No inequality of status between union members
- Proper representation of the interests of *all* workers affected over any agreements made in their name
- The right of specifically oppressed sections - women, black workers, youth etc., to organise themselves

Finally, we must recognise that the trade unions themselves, by their very nature in representing the interests of the worker against the boss, cannot solve the basic problems of our society: that will only be done by removing the boss altogether and taking over ourselves. So as it becomes more and more necessary for the unions to go onto the offensive against the capitalist class merely to maintain the living standards and rights they have won so far, it also becomes increasingly obvious that we must extend not only the scope of our ideas, but also our organisations which express them, beyond the relationships of the workplace to take up the questions of the whole of society.

For example, in the case of women workers, it is clear that, although we can help to free women to fight for their rights, nothing will really be solved until the central question of women's responsibility for housekeeping and child rearing is dealt with, and that will take a complete reorganisation of society, calling in far wider forces than the present membership of the unions.

The women's liberation movement has a vital function to perform here, and not just in the long term. It is important that those of us outside the union movement, or in its newer, less male-oriented white-collar sections, both support the efforts of women workers in getting the unions to represent them, and take up the wider issues relating to the oppression of women in the family and society - childcare facilities, maintenance, housing, contraception and abortion rights etc. Given the balance of forces against us, we must find every way in which these essentially inter-related struggles can lend each other strength.

It is a good comment on the nature of our society that it will take a thorough-going social and economic revolution to concede such seemingly basic democratic rights as equal pay and equal work. As a first step, we must start to build the degree of political organisation to achieve this by involving all the different forces concerned in work towards these goals on a day to day practical level.

Felicity Trodd
1974

A revised version of an article which first appeared in SOCIALIST WOMAN November/December 1972.

The Nightcleaners' Campaign

The night cleaners' campaign occupies a special position in the history of the women's liberation movement. It was the first time - in London at least - that the women's movement became actively and publicly involved in a struggle among working women to organise themselves at their place of work.

Several questions arose out of the campaign, some of which remain unresolved within the present practice and development of the women's movement. Firstly, the cleaners' situation highlights the position of women on the labour market; it tells us much about the relationship between the sexual division of labour and class exploitation. Secondly, a whole cluster of questions arise from the contradiction between our aspiration to be a movement which involves all oppressed women and our present predominantly middle class membership. For example, how do we extend our practice beyond its existing constricted boundaries? What is our attitude, as a political movement, to the Trade Union and socialist movements, etc?

This article cannot attempt to resolve these questions, it will simply describe the context in which they arose and offer some hopefully useful observations. But first I must give as concise an account as possible of the campaign. (See also *Nightcleaners Shrew* December 1971; *The Body Politic* edited by M. Wandor, Stage One 1972; May Hobbs' *Born to Struggle* Quartet 1973)

How did the women's movement get involved?

In October 1970 May Hobbs, a night office cleaner who had been trying to organise cleaners for the previous eight years, approached the International Socialist Group. Through them she went to a meeting of the Dalston Women's Liberation Workshop. Almost immediately women from IS and the the Workshop began leafleting cleaners outside their buildings as they went into work. The leaflets explained the purpose of collective action, and urged the women to join the Union. An incident on a Board of Trade building in which two women were sacked gave impetus to the campaign, and an atmosphere of urgency was generated by the wider struggle of the Labour Movement against the Industrial Relations Bill. Despite the unfavourable outcome of the Board of Trade picket, the early months were full of enthusiasm and optimism.

Formation of the Cleaners' Action Group

It soon became clear that helping the cleaners meant more than catching them as they went into work at nine or ten o'clock and persuading them to sign a Union form. In order to unionise cleaners we had to organise ourselves. We formed a collective, the Cleaners' Action Group, which sometimes, early on, fell under the domination of women in the IS and International Marxist Group. This was probably because these women were more articulate than us, self confident in the knowledge that they had a 'line' - from the groups - to push on the Trade Union Movement, whilst we, in the London Workshop, hadn't even got a line to push. But May was always the most vigorous and enthusiastic spokeswoman for the cleaners, the one person who could both encourage and inspire the cleaners, and speak for them as a group. After some months, both IS and IMG withdrew from the campaign, although they contributed valuable support during the 1972 strike. At the same time, a film collective of three men and one woman was formed to document the campaign.

The collective met at regular intervals for several months; lists were kept of which group was leafleting which building; other women stepped in if a leafleter went on holiday or dropped out. Leafleting a building meant visiting it on the same night, and getting to know the cleaners, many of whom were often too nervous to speak to us for fear of victimisation or intimidation. When or if the women joined the Union, we continued to visit the buildings to collect their dues, and to establish a link between them and the Union. This was much more difficult than it sounds. The women work in small groups on separate buildings scattered throughout central London, which makes any contact amongst themselves almost impossible. But also, and even more important, the Union, The Transport and General Workers Union, was extremely reluctant to take cleaning seriously as an area of recruitment. We found, therefore, that we had to put on the pressure at two levels - the women to join the Union and the Union to take the women seriously. Partly because of these difficulties there was a rapid turnover of leafleters in the first one and a half years. But enthusiasm in the Workshop ensured that if one person dropped out, another woman stepped in to take her place.

Strategy

The CAG considered and discarded several different campaign plans. In the beginning we did not seriously question the feasibility of Union organisation for the nightcleaners. Our aim was simply to organise the cleaners into one Union, the T &GWU to set up a cleaners' branch within it and to make May Hobbs branch secretary. In the meantime, however, the nightcleaners would enter the window cleaners' branch.

Next we turned to the problem of recruitment. The first plan was to systematically leaflet every building being night-cleaned in London. Lack of resources made this plan completely impracticable. There were not enough leafleters and too many buildings. Next we decided to concentrate on the buildings of one individual employer. This also proved unsuccessful for several reasons. It was not always possible to discover which contractor worked the building; leafleters also worked better if the building was near their own home. Most important, the contractor would either move, or sack a cleaner he suspected of joining the Union. To be moved on to another building can be an effective form of victimisation. Many cleaners, particularly the ones who have stuck in jobs for several years, have chosen their place of work with some care. Either it is near their home, or on an easy transport route, or the pay and conditions (which vary considerably) are better than most, or they are working with their friends, etc. It is difficult to prove unfair dismissal since the cleaner is always sacked on some pretext, e.g. inefficiency, late attendance, or changing over from night to morning and evening cleaning. May did take a case through the courts in the summer of 1972 but the contractor naturally won it.

Our third and final plan was to unionise one large building which employed lots of cleaners. This group could then form the nucleus of the cleaners' branch. The two Shell buildings in Waterloo, Shell Centre, were selected because May knew that the T & GWU had always been interested in them.

By this time (summer 1971) it was beginning to appear as if the Union's apathy towards the nightcleaners were unsurmountable. May's demands and protestations merely aggravated the Union Officers, while at the same time, they were wary of the publicity she might provoke. The cleaners and ourselves were treated with almost total indifference by the Union Officers. There had been some discussion within the CAG of forming our own Union. But the problems facing Pat Sturdy and her co-workers demonstrated the futility of attempting to build up a strong workers' organisation outside the official Trade Union movement. (She broke away from the AUEW at the end of 1971 in Blackburn and formed the breakaway Industrial Women's Union.) We also considered the possibility of forming a cleaners' co-operative, but this would have meant running a business, which neither women's liberation nor the cleaners themselves wanted to do!

We began to experience the frustration and limitations of Trade Union work, and to recognise the particular resistance male Trade Unionists showed towards women workers, but we decided to have one last attempt at arousing their interest and assistance. Shell Centre was the carrot we hoped to dangle in front of a Union Official's eyes. It almost worked.

Shell Centre and the T & GWU

About half a dozen women from the Pimlico and Chiswick Workshop groups started leafleting Shell. Straight away we made friends with three cleaners, and soon we were visiting every week to collect the dues, bring new forms and liaise between the women and the Union Officers since

most women were not on the phone. Several meetings with the Union Officers were arranged, and each time the women stated their demands firmly and clearly. To start with there were lots of 'small' complaints about working conditions. For instance, in the summer the air conditioning was turned off, the heat was stifling but the cleaners were not allowed to open the windows. In the winter, however, it was the central heating that was turned off so there was the opposite problem. There were no proper facilties for making tea so unless the cleaners brought a thermos they went without. There was one dinner break at 1 a.m. for an hour but no other tea or coffee break. The women were locked in the building at night, and were not allowed to leave their own floor to visit a friend. There were also the usual demands of three weeks holiday with pay, adequate staffing, proper equipment, notice of dismissal etc.

After two meetings between us and some of the cleaners in a cafe near work we drew up a formal list of demands and asked for a meeting with Mr. Ferriman and Mr. Churchouse of the T & GWU. In spite of the Union's insistence that cleaners never turn up for meetings, seven or eight women came, as well as May, the leafleters and the film group. We had the names and addresses of the other 25 or so women on Shell who had joined the Union. Their Union dues were up to date but they were unable to attend because of baby-sitting problems. The Officers did seem impressed by our efficient paper work and thorough record keeping. They must have been grateful that we were doing their work for them. In fact, we wanted to be certain that we would not be dismissed with the usual complaint about

women not joining Unions. On the contrary, having visited
Mr. Fred Sage, the Secretary of the window cleaners'
branch, we discovered that in the previous couple of years
almost a hundred women night cleaners had joined the T
& GWU. Union apathy had led to their eventual falling
behind with their dues.

The two Union Officers assured the cleaners that they
would write to their employers demanding Union recognition. They also explained that when the Union puts in
a wage claim, other conditions necessarily follow, so some
demands were superfluous. The first step anyway for any
Union was to win recognition, then the Union would put
in a wage claim after one from the women themselves had
been turned down. The situation was complicated on Shell
because the two buildings - the upstream and the down-
stream - were contracted to different cleaning firms. To
overcome this sort of problem, Mr. Ferriman explained,
the Union was working to establish a national negotiating
structure with the employers' association, The Cleaning
Contractors Maintenance Asscn., but this of course might
take years.

Perhaps the most urgent demand of the cleaners was for
Union meetings at their place of work. Baby-sitting is a
constant problem, the weekend is spent shopping and catching up with domestic chores. There is no time for women
to go to Union meetings outside working hours. Most important, the cleaners who were too nervous to join openly
the Union would be more reassured by the presence of a
Union Officer at work than by women from women's liberation.

Escalation of the campaign

Several other meetings were held with Mr. Churchhouse,
Mr. Ferriman and other T & GWU Officers. Sometimes we
visited their offices, once we sent a petition to Jack Jones
signed by all the Shell cleaners asking for their own
branch. We, the leafleters, talked to the women regularly
as they went to work or before work in the cafe. We took
as many who could manage it to other meetings and demonstrations relevant to the TU or women's struggle. We
also leafleted the TUC and the T & GWU Womens Confer-

314

ence and attempted to make links with other groups of women workers. We spoke to every Officer in the T & GW GWU who would listen to us. May travelled to different parts of the country where cleaners were organising. The CAG began to build up national contacts and its magazine, *The Cleaners' Voice*, helped to spread news and keep everyone in touch.

In spite of all this activity, however, Mr. Churchouse, the T & GWU Officer responsible for the nightcleaners, was very elusive. He seldom replied to letters or telephone calls, twice he did not turn up for meetings and specific requests for help on issues such as victimisation, unhealthy conditions etc. were ignored. We made two formal complaints. Eventually Mr. Ferriman, a group secretary, agreed to replace him. Both men finally did meet the employers, however, and on the second occasion they took the two shop stewards from one building to negotiate with them. One or two small gains were made. The cleaners were given two rises of 50p within a few months (their first for two and a half years), making their wages up to £13 and the cleaners on the upstream received a bonus for Christmas 1971 and 1972. In 1973 there was another small wage increase. Each time the rise had been given independently of Union negotiation. The contractors' representative did not turn up to the second meeting arranged between them and the women shop stewards, and the Union Officers never took the matter up. Sometimes the Officers' attitude seemed absurd. For instance, the shop stewards were told by Mr. Ferriman, in all seriousness, that the contractors refused the demand for open windows on the grounds that, as it was well known that women are hysterical, they might throw themselves out.

The Fulham cleaners strike

Meanwhile the leafleting on other buildings gradually stopped. Finally in the summer of 1972 when the numbers of leafleters was sadly depleted, and May and the CAG were growing despondent, the cleaners on the Ministry of Defence building came out on strike for more pay and adequ-

315

ate staffing and equipment. Two other government buildings followed suit. These three buildings were in the Civil Service Union which, during that year, had been mounting a campaign to unionise nightcleaners. The CSU made the strikes official and paid ten pounds a week strike pay. Other cleaners, Trade Unionists, and groups of workers came along to support the picket line which had to be maintained day and night. The left groups and women's liberation were also there in force. The atmosphere was one of great excitement, and enthusiasm, as cleaners brought their children and husbands down to the picket line, spoke at workers' meetings, and visited other cleaners as they went to work. The strike received sympathetic media coverage, especially in the liberal press because nightcleaning has always been a potent liberal issue. (In the 1930's for instance, the Women's Co-operative Guild raised the question of nightcleaning in the media whenever they could.) But *The Morning Star* gave the strike the most sympathetic and consistently encouraging support.

Victory was won after two weeks but the cleaners had to stand firm to maintain it. On one building the contractor changed over to morning and evening cleaning and none of the women strikers who applied were given their jobs back. The conditions of the Fulham cleaners have been maintained and improved by the action and solidarity of the women themselves. Their wages were raised at the end of 1973 to £21 a week — not very high but £6 or £7 higher than average.

After the summer of 1972, the CAG concentrated on two issues. First of all, it continued to press for a cleaners' branch in the T & GWU with May as branch secretary. This was promised in Christmas 1972 and we are still waiting. May has become more involved in other issues — housing, women's prisons etc. and has had less time to devote exclusively to the cleaners; so unless the CAG can raise the money to support women other than May to become full time organisers the branch might never materialise.

The second policy of the CAG has been to raise the

question of contract cleaning on government buildings in the House of Commons. Joe Ashton and Lena Jeger head a lobby of sympathetic MP's and they arranged meetings with with the relevant minister. In 1968, Harold Wilson successfully cut down the size of the Civil Service by sacking all direct cleaners and contracting the work out to Office Cleaning firms. This means that the lowest figure receives the job, and since labour is the single biggest cost factor, wages reduced to the absolute minimum. It is hoped that by abolishing contract cleaning on public buildings, something will then be done in the private sector. The abolition of contract cleaning will not unionise nightcleaners, but will raise their wages by removing the middle man between the cleaner and their employer.

The CAG is smaller now than it was a year ago and more diverse. It includes men and women from the Labour Movement and the Communist Party as well as women's liberation. There are no longer weekly meetings and leafleting has stopped. But there is now an office at 66 York Way, Kings Cross London N.1 where May answers enquiries and deals with cleaners' social problems (e.g. rate rebate claims etc.) as well as the question of unionisation. The CAG has applied for money from a Trust which is vitally needed to support more cleaners as full time organisers. May has always emphasised the importance of women organising themselves.

It is still hoped that when the film of the campaign is finally finished it will be used to publicise the cleaners' situation and to recruit more leafleters. Meanwhile, however, there is no doubt that the campaign has encouraged cleaners in different parts of the country to organise themselves. May and the CAG often receive news of cleaners waiting to participate in the campaign or asking for information and support.

Women's liberation and the nightcleaners

Women's liberation first began to work with the nightcleaners because May Hobbs asked for help. Our participation was not a strategic intervention in the working class

317

struggle. In the true spontaneous tradition of the womens movement organisation, politics and strategy developed as we went along. The contrast between the cleaners' lives and our own was one of the initial influences on us.

There are between two and three thousand nightcleaners in England, of which about one thousand eight hundred are working in London. This is probably an underestimate as many women work without cards, moving from job to job. Cleaning workers have always been one of the most exploited groups on the labour market, but the exploitation has dramatically increased with the introduction of contract cleaning in place of direct employment. For more about the contract cleaning industry see *Prices and Incomes Board Report 1971.* Labour is the biggest single cost factor in the industry, so contractors ruthlessly compete · with each other to win contracts by lowering wages.

The cleaners are mostly between the ages of 20 and 60, but there are a substantial number over 60. They nearly all have several children whether, divorced or widowed. Lack of nursery facilities forces women out to work at night. The women are either the sole providers in the family or else their husbands are low paid. Some do two cleaning jobs, one in the day or early evening as well. Others take different part time work during the day. A large percentage of the women are immigrants: West Indian, Asian, Greek, Spanish, Irish. Immigrant women are uncertain of their rights, cannot always speak English very well and are the most easily intimidated. Cleaners work in small groups on different buildings throughout London. This isolation is accentuated by the different nationalities, or rather the attempt of the supervisor or firm's manager to victimise one or two 'troublemakers' and to provoke racial tension. In fact, the women work together very well, but we have never met a black supervisor, although over half the cleaners are black.

Very few supervisors are sympathetic to the Union. They often have their employers' interests at heart. A great deal of fiddling goes on in contract cleaning and sometimes it suits the supervisor to be able to manipulate the women by threatening their jobs. When economic pressures are so great, fear of losing one's job or even a week's pay keeps the cleaners silent. It is important to be on good terms with the supervisor because taking a night off to care for a sick child will depend on her good will, so will 'cover' work, which brings in an extra few shillings a week.

The contractors themselves vary in their attitudes towards the Union. Generally, the larger the firm the more indifferent they are to it. It is the smaller firm which is the most vigilantly anti-Union. Because the small firms are gradually being swallowed up by the larger ones, they desperately undercut to stay in the market. Their survival depends on paying subsistence wages.

These facts, and many more, we learnt as we worked and talked with the women. The dreary round of housework interspersed with a menial job during the day, then more housework all night for a pittance, with no sleep all week, aroused our sympathy and concern and made us do all we could to support the cleaners. Loyalty to the women with whom we had made friends prevented us from dropping out when we felt most inadequate - which we did feel very often.

We leafleteres were mostly young women in our twenties and early thirties: students, teachers, young mothers. (There is a strong tradition of co-operation between middle class feminists and the working class in the history of the labour movement, e.g. Annie Besant and the matchgirls, Eleanor Marx and the gas workers, Sylvia Pankhurst and the East London Federation.) Because of the cleaners' isolation, they need help in maintaining contact with each other. Lack of time prevents them from attending every meeting and keeping up with the bookwork. However, our role could only be limited and we were never sure quite what those limits were.

Criticism and self criticism

The CAG indulged in self criticism on several counts. Perhaps our most serious failing was that we never managed to develop leadership and direction among the cleaners themselves. We should have raised the money to support one or two cleaners while they worked on the campaign for a few months. We could have used the film (or part of it as it is not yet finished) to help raise the money, and at the same time to publicise the nightcleaners' campaign among other groups of workers, men and women. It is possible to leave groups of cleaners on specific buildings to their own devices until they ask for support, but there is no way of spreading this self activity.

Part of the problem has been that as feminists we tend to reject the concept of leadership. We recognise the need for self activity and for direction within a campaign, but we associate leadership with domination, lack of democracy and male politics. We ignored the fact that May, at least, was already providing leadership and that the burden of that responsibility was too much for one person. The women's liberation was also, de facto, providing leadership. In practice we tried to avoid this. We shifted nervously from one foot to the other, explaining the Union to the cleaners, and the cleaners to the Union, feeling unable to identify strongly with either, albeit for different reasons. We could neither urge the women to strike, since the effect of militancy on their lives was so uncertain, nor could we openly attack the Union, since there seemed to be no other way of helping the cleaners.

It was difficult to raise the subject of women's liberation with the cleaners. Most of the women could only spare a couple of minutes outside the door before they rushed into work. Those who arrived earlier were obviously more interested in hearing about the Union than anything else. We were known to the women as 'the Union girls'. Whenever women's liberation was raised, there was initial self consciousness on our part, and probably a joke about bras or man-hating on theirs. The cleaners often talked about their feelings as women, and especially the burden of two jobs, in the home and at work. It is easy to talk to any woman about children, schools, shopping etc. but some of the problems that occupy feminist consciousness raising groups feel awkward in discussion when women's lived experience is so different. Abortion is an obvious example. The difference between a middle class private abortion (unpleasant though that can be) and the abortions of women who have neither the money to pay nor the self confidence and determination to obtain one from the national health, need hardly be emphasised. Class differences were complicated by our own reticence as a movement about ourselves. This was much truer two or three years ago than it is today. Then there was a strong belief that the movement should speak for itself, that we must not proselytise or harangue, women will discover us when they need to. The media will always distort everything we say so say nothing. This is an overstatement, of course, but when that belief - inarticulate though it might be - is accompanied by middle class self awareness of privilege etc. it can be quite an inhibiting force. The women's movement like the rest of the left, still has to learn how to popularise its ideas and politics successfully.

The nightcleaners, trade unions and women's work

Several Unions have nightcleaners in their membership, but cleaners are only effectively organised in factories or firms where there is a strong closed shop already operating, e.g. some engineering works, or government buildings, Otherwise nightcleaners have remained outside the Trade Union movement both because their work is classified as unskilled and casual - the sort of work which historically has always been more difficult to organise - and because most cleaners are women. Low pay inevitably accompanies women's work and casual status. But high wages are determined by the firm's profitability and the collective militancy of the workers, not the degree of skill. So - why aren't the cleaners organised?

When women's liberation first began to help the cleaners we were very conscious of our naivety and ignorance and sought the advice of experienced Trade Unionists. Some women in left groups tended to be combative in their attitude towards the Unions, but we felt tentatively that we might make more progress if we adopted a more conciliatory approach. We listened as male Trade Unionists inside and outside the T & GWU patiently explained the problems of organisation, emphasising the limitations of TU resources. Few were as succinct as the 1971 PIB report on the contract cleaning trade which stated that Trade Unions had not promoted the campaign because *workers are widely dispersed, in isolated small groups and working at inconvenient times for Union organisation.* Some Officials were more helpful than others. Fred Sage, for instance, the window cleaners' branch secretary, emphasised the need to establish a skill. But all that most emphasised was that women are notoriously hard to organise because they are home oriented, women are not interested in Union work, and women are easily intimidated.

Some of these arguments carried more conviction than others. In particular, the problem concerning the organisation of casual workers, and the cleaners' vulnerability to intimidation. Like most women workers, cleaners have interiorised their inferior economic status. They see themselves primarily as wives and mothers, and regard their job outside the home as a necessary but temporary expedient. They feel fatalistic about changing this situation. However, those who do have the courage and energy to start helping themselves and their workmates, quickly generate enthusiasm and optimism. The cleaners are not uninterested inUnion work. But they are sceptical of the effectiveness of Trade Unions. Their scepticism has been nurtured by the Union's neglect. When the Officers fail to reply to letters or phone calls, do not arrive for meetings, ignore their most deeply felt demands, then paying out a shilling or more a week becomes an unnecessary strain on a tight budget.

Male Trade Unionists have always had an ambivalent attitude towards women workers. On the one hand, their wives go out to work, their income is vital for the family, and they recognise the need for working class solidarity. On the other hand, most men believe that woman's place is in the home and that she should stay there. Working class men's support for the sexual division of labour in the family is not just backward ideas which will change
322

when men recognise the source and extent of women's oppression. Its origins are complex, but one of its deepest roots is the very real fear that the entry of women into a trade or industry will reduce wages, lower job status and throw men out of work. Historically, women *have* been used to break strikes and undercut men's pay. From the beginning of capitalism women, restricted by child bearing and discriminated against on the labour market, have been forced to accept the most unpleasant jobs, for the lowest wages. This situation was accentuated by the separation of home and workplace. Women on their own have always been the worst off. Denied proper education, apprenticeship, or training and without nursery facilities or a male wage to prop up the family income, they have had to accept any work available even if it has meant blacking a strike.

But women's exclusion from the Trade Union movement has confirmed and perpetuated their weak and secondary status on the labour market. As Audrey Wise has shown in her pamphlet *Women and the Struggle for Workers Control* (Spokesman) women are at present 38% of the labour force, but concentrated in the lower paid jobs, and the situation is getting worse. Many women work part time and intermiittently throughout their lifetime, and this work is termed 'casual' and given a lower status by employers and Trade Unionists alike. It is no more regarded as *real* work by male Trade Unionists than housework and childcare.

Nightcleaning occupies just such a position. It is described as casual (although the women work a 40 hour week) and 'unskilled', and it is performed by women and immigrants. Nightcleaning has a further claim to secondary status in that it lies outside commodity production in the service sector of the economy (again, like much women's work), that is, it is regarded as 'unproductive' labour, a category which is often ascribed an inferior value by the left. In fact, the service sector is not peripheral to capitalism, it is an expanding sector of the economy and the workers in these sectors are as vital to the British labour movement as the assembly line workers at Fords.

Like many women's jobs nightcleaning is labour intensive, i.e. it could not survive without a large supply of cheap labour. Two demands of the women's movement - nurseries and equal pay and job opportunity - would remove the worst conditions of nightcleaning and other night work, since women would then have an effective choice of employment (within the restrictions of capitalism). But these aims recede into the distance in the present economic climate. Women workers *must* organise themselves at work, both to win better pay and conditions, as well as to effect wider changes in society.

Men workers will have to radically change their attitude towards women. Trade Unions are the backbone of the working class movement in this country, and they are the bastions of male privilege. At every level in the hierarchy of the labour market, women occupy a weaker position than men. The Unions are doing nothing to alleviate this situation. Out of 600 full time Officers in the T & GWU for instance only one is a woman.

Conclusion

By arguing for women to organise at work outside their homes I am not advocating that all women should go out to work, participate in production, and thus ease the road to socialism. Nor am I advocating Trade Unionism as the panacea for women's oppression. Nor am I putting it forward as an alternative to organising around the family or in the community. The struggle against capitalism and sexism must be fought at every level - TU organisation is only the first tentative step towards workers' self consciousness and unity. For this reason alone the women's movement must actively support it.

But the nightcleaners campaign also revealed two other urgent priorities for the women's movement. We vacillated between co-operation with and ineffectual criticism of the Unions because we never resolved the dilemma of being neither the cleaners nor the Union. Strategy is learnt through political practice as well as from theory. As we had no immediate experience of our own to draw on, and as political practice is hard to learn out of books, it is not surprising that we were hesitant. But marxist feminists are needed in the labour movement. We must develop a guideline for action within the trade unions. At the same time, of course, the most effective support for women wage-workers is a strong articulate feminist movement whose ideas and actions penetrate and transform class struggle.

Secondly, the women's movement must produce a historical materialist analysis of the position of women's work in the labour market - i.e. the relationship between women's work (both waged and non-waged domestic labour) and capitalism.

At present, women's secondary status on the labour market is echoed in the class struggle - because they are casual workers, because they are low paid, un- or semi-skilled, because they work part time, because they are wives and mothers. We are not asking simply to participate in the class struggle as it is - by challenging the sexual division of labour the Women's Liberation Movement will necessarily redefine it.

Sally Alexander
Nov. 1974

Revised version of an article which first appeared in RED RAG No. 6

325

Working Women's Charter

A campaign has been launched in over ten towns up and down the country to fight for the demands in the Working Women's Charter. In March 1974, the London Trades Council circulated the Charter throughout the London labour movement and later called a Conference.

At the conference, attended by over 200 women, many of them delegated from their Union branches, there was a split between those who saw the conference as a talk shop to share experiences, and others who wanted to defer discussion on the detailed demands of the Charter in favour of a discussion on how to use the document to initiate action in the labour movement around the problems of women workers.

This disagreement was not resolved by the conference. No clear decision was adopted 'for lack of time'. However, since the conference, it is being resolved in practice by Union branches, Trades Councils, women's groups and individual Trade Unionists which are now promoting the Charter. It is being used as the basis for a campaign among workers, taking up many aspects of women's oppression and exploitation as workers.

First stage

To most women in the women's movement, the actual demands of the Charter will seem unexceptional. Although the sum total of the demands do not equal liberation or an end to oppression, this is an extremely important document. It represents a first stage in bringing together the ideas and analysis of the women's movement - particularly on the relationship between the oppression of women in the family and their exploitation as workers - with the strength and organisation of the labour movement.

The labour movement generally accepts the unwritten rule that there is a definite sphere of influence for the Trade Union: they deal with problems of wages *on the job*. Men see a relatively clear divide between problems of home and problems of work, so this unwritten rule seems to be adequate for them.

Bills, household budgets, baby-sitters, and another baby on the way are all 'individual' problems - not ones to be tacked by the Unions. But for women workers, especially for those with children (whether single or married), that kind of separation is rarely possible. Never before has the. Trade Union movement acknowledged this impossibility in such a clear way as it does in the Charter. Alongside demands for equal pay, opportunity and training, are listed ones for contraception and abortion, for nurseries, for changes in the laws relating to passports and HP agreements.

This is neither a haphazard development nor an isolated one. Only a couple of weeks prior to the London Trades Council conference, the National Council for Civil Liberties held a conference for women Trade Unionists in London - followed up recently with others outside London - on the question of women's rights. Over 500 women attended this conference and again many were Union delegates. The discussion broadened from the strict 'Trade Union' issues to one on the interrelated nature of the problems of women workers. Many women identified themselves as belonging to both a Trade Union branch and a women's liberation group.

After the Fords' Women's strike of 1968

Much has happened since the famous Ford Women's strike in 1968. One of the results of that strike for equal pay and grading was the formation of a national organisation of Trade Union women to campaign for equal rights. Increasingly, the campaign centred on the equal pay demand. This organisation (NJACCWER) attracted women from

327

many unions up and down the country. But with the introduction of the Equal Pay Bill, the campaign lost all impetus. It faded away ..... just as the new women's movement was beginning to emerge. By the time of the first conference of the women's movement, held at Ruskin College, Oxford (Feb/March 1970), the NJACCWER had more or less died. As there was little overlap between the membership in the two groups, the possibility of a structured relationship between them was still born.

Groups within the women's movement wanting to work with working women supported local strikes as they happened, or campaigned with working class women on issues such as nurseries, mainly outside the job situation. But with the death of NJACCWER there was no longer any single focus for this continuing radicalisation among women; it was evident in local struggles but they lacked any national character.

What is happening now bears examination. The women's movement has not grown numerically recently, and has not attracted large numbers of working class women. Instead, there has been a *qualitative* development in the movement: the socialist current has hardened out as is reflected in the increasingly sophisticated debates. Socialists in the movement are seriously considering the relationship between the class struggle and the women's movement. Given this new level of debate, it is no accident that the number of socialist women joining trades unions is on the increase.

In addition to a physical overlap between women trade unionists and the socialist current within the women's movement, there is also the general impact of the women's movement on the consciousness of women (and men) whose experience is strictly trade union. There are cracks emerging which indicate that the very backward ideas towards women within the trade union movement are beginning to give. These ideas could be severely ruptured by systematic work and significant struggles over the coming months.

Maximum gains

The importance of a document like the Charter in this situation is that it can be used *now* as the basis for campaigning among the *entire* labour movement — but specifically aimed at women workers — to lay the groundwork for the maximum possible gains out of any future struggles involving women. The equal pay struggle at Lentheric's perfume factory in North London in April 1974 indicates that women workers are being forced to think of things like equal pay in order to maintain their standard of living against the ravages of inflation.

Although the Equal Pay Act is partially implemented, women still receive only 50% of the male rate, on average. In the months before its full implementation, employers will continue to find ways to escape the Act and women will see attempts to maintain the low rates paid to them. So we can expect Lentheric's factory to be only the first in a long line of such struggles. In many cases, the battle will be more difficult and prolonged.

Women in struggle need all sorts of assistance. The Charter campaign can draw together the trade union movement to provide solidarity for women involved in a difficult dispute. Male workers will not automatically down tools to support a fight to reduce differentials, especially when their own wages won't be increased at the end of the the fight. The Charter campaign can prepare the way for male trade unionists to understand the need for solidarity when such a situation arises.

The campaign could lead to significant developments in the level of struggles involving women, thereby effecting permanent changes in the degree of male chauvinism within the Unions and the degree of involvement of women in working class struggles. Only then can a much more effective and co-ordinated challenge be raised to the present attacks on the working class as a whole. The division between social and economic problems, between home and work, between the responsibility of the individual and the class as a whole, and the division between what is the responsibility of the Unions and those of the politicians, must be broken down. The Charter campaign could begin this process.

Linda Smith
1974
First published in SOCIALIST WOMAN

THE WORKING WOMEN'S CHARTER

We pledge ourselves to agitate and organise to achieve the following aims:

1. The rate for the job, regardless of sex, at rates negotiated by the unions, with a national minimum wage below which no wages should fall.

2. Equal opportunity of entry into occupations and in promotion, regardless of sex or marital status.

3. Equal education and training for all occupations and compulsory day release for all 16-19 year olds in employment.

4. Working conditions to be, without deterioration of previous conditions, the same for women as for men.

5. The removal of all legal and bureaucratic impediments to equality, e.g. with regard to tenancies, mortgages, pension schemes, taxation, passports, control over children, social security payments, hire-purchase agreements etc.

6. Improved provision of local authority day nurseries, free of charge, with extended hours to suit working mothers. Provision of nursery classes in day nurseries. More nursery schools.

7. 18 weeks maternity leave with full net pay before and after the birth of a live child; 7 weeks after birth if the child is still-born. No dismissal during pregnancy or maternity leave. No loss of security, pension, or promotion prospects.

8. Family Planning Clinics supplying free contraception to be extended to cover every locality. Free abortion to be readily available.

9. Family allowances to be increased to £2.50 per child, including the first child.

10. To campaign amongst women to take an active part in the trade unions and in political life so that they may exercise influence commensurate with their numbers and to campaign amongst men trade unionists that they may work to achieve this aim.

Striking Progress

1973

July

H.K. Porter (GB) Sterling

87 men and 13 women strike for one week demanding £18 minimum basic rate for women workers. Settle for rise in the basic of 27p

Civil Service

Women cleaners win an equal instalment of 60p a week backdated to April with the aim of achieving parity.

Chelsea Quilt Factory, Barnstaple, Devon

24 women end two week strike over management attempt to alter differentials and deny Union recognition. The Union and shop stewards are recognised, differentials unaltered and the future regulation of conditions and procedures to be made with Union representatives.

Salford

Over 150 housewives march in protest through the shopping precinct of a large housing estate in protest at the rising prices in the local shops.

August

Salford Electrical Instruments, Heywood & Eccles, Lancs.

11 week strike of clerical workers for equal pay ends in increase of £1.65 for women, £2.00 for men. Manchester Women's Liberation member accused of assaulting a policeman on one of the picket lines.

GEC, Spon Street, Coventry

The strike by 200 women workers is renewed after the

annual two week holiday. Management attempt to intimidate the pickets by calling the police. The AUEW convenor, Albert Beardmore, violently hostile to the women's case has 1) instructed his own Union members to break the picket lines although the women are also members of the same Union in the same factory; 2) attempted to take away the AUEW card from Elsie Noles, the deputy convenor, who is trusted by the women on strike; 3) repeatedly told the strikers that they were acting 'illegally', confusing them and attempting to frighten them out of their rights; 4) has crossed the picket lines, even to work overtime, while his own members on strike.

Wilderspool Sports Leisure Centre, Warrington, Lancs.

Maureen Spiers, women cleaners' shop steward, TGWU, sacked for challenging weekend work rate of 35p per hour (the ordinary rate). Women picket all weekend.

Seiko, Kilburn

8 women and 16 men, recent recruits to TASS,the clerical section of the AUEW, come out on strike when one of them is sacked for 'non-co-operation' with the under-manager at this Japanese watch repair centre.

September

Slumberland Beds, Paisley

29 office and supervisory workers, mainly women, on a 10 week strike for Union recognition (ASTMS)

Crompton Parkinson, Dundee

400 women on strike since August 31 over management pay offer of £1.80 (to men) which would increase differential. Union negotiators say women are entitled to an increase of 1/3 of this as a step to equal pay.

GEC Telecommunications, Stoke, Coventry.

48 hour strike wins women pay parity with men.

British Marco, Grantham, Lincs and Thomas Bolton & Sons, Stoke and W. & T. Avery, Digbeth, Birmingham.

APEX authorise strike action over equal pay

Pilkingtons

16 women representing female staff in every site meet to push forward women's demands in ASTMS regarding pay and and job opportunities since women are in the bottom eight grades.

Tampax, Havant

AUEW fitters on strike for Union recognition are gradually joined by women workers in the factory. The women hold a one day total stoppage in support. Meanwhile, members of the shopworkers union black Tampax supplies at Boots central warehouse in Nottingham.

SEIKO, Kilburn

After 5 week strike for union recognition and reinstatement, 15 men and women barricade themselves in when it's rumoured that the US 'trouble shooter' working for the Japanese firm is about to shut down the factory. They occupy the manager's office with sleeping bags, plenty of food, television and hot and cold water laid on. Since they are now in charge of 5,000 watches and £60,000 worth of equipment, the management can't cause too much trouble in retaliation — they cut off the telephones and lights and lock the fire exits. Members of the strike committee complain that they are treated like 'robots' (they are continually monitored by TV cameras for 'security reasons') and that management had stirred up racial antagonism by demanding that Ugandan Asian workers only talk in English.

At the end of this 24 hour sit-in, all their demands are met - management agree to recognise the Union, reinstate the strikers and pay them for the five weeks they had been on strike.

But three months later: All of them get dismissal notices two days before Christmas and the watch repair centre is closed down.

Hungerford School, N. London

86 teachers in a one day protest outside the school, supported by many parents, in support of Ms. Dorothea McColgan. A teacher for 20 years, she had been victimised for her anti-authoritarian views which she had made public in a magazine. ILEA was 'transferring' her into a supply teachers' pool, though she was a very popular teacher at the school.

GEC Spon Street, Coventry

Factory is completely shut down after lay-offs resulting from 5 week strike of women workers. A mass meeting over-rules convenor Albert Beardmore and votes to continue the strike against management's retiming of jobs and not to hold another meeting for a further two weeks. Beardmore is continuing to work and has organised a kangeroo court of shop stewards which has voted to expel deputy convenor Elsie Noles from the AUEW branch. She is immediately reinstated by the AUEW District Committee.

October

London Transport and Central London

Bus delegates committee starts talks on full job equality for women

Adwest Engineering, Reading

400 men and women occupy in order to prevent closure, winning an important victory after controlling the plant for 6 weeks. Management agree to job guarantees and across the board increase of £2 per week, coupled with bonus increases which would raise earnings between £3 and £6 per week.

Pressed Steel, Cowley

Women office workers strike for a week for equal pay. Men in the office support them with a work to rule and ban on overtime. The swtichboard completely dead and the wages department in chaos. The men hold a one day sit-in when management send out letters to the women threatening sacking if the strike continues.

GEC Stoke Plant, Coventry

60 women workers in strip wiring plant threatened with lock out, after a 2 week work to rule in protest at low piecework rate.

Rotaprint, Queensbury, NW London

450 strike when 2 are suspended for refusing to clock on. In one assembly shop, 21 women are split by the management who pay 9 the male rate for the job, while the other 12 women are being paid the lowest semi-skilled rate, which was supposed to have been abolished in a previous strike 2 years before.

Triumph, Meriden Works

1750 workers occupy this motorcycle factory near Coventry when closure is threatened. Some wives of the Triumph men form an action group which calls on all wives to back the sit in and organise to get payments from the Social Security.

November

Hawker Siddeley, Chadderton & Woodford Factories, Lancs.

Men and women workers on strike for the demand of £1.50 a week increase for women.

Reading

70 women workers are BiroBic in dispute for Union recognition. It began with a petition signed by all the women but one, asking for elementary improvements in conditions, tea breaks for example are not allowed. After two half day walkouts, 60 apply to join the AUEW and elect three shop stewards. The factory is a sweat shop with women working from 7.15 a.m. to 4.15 with one 30 minute lunch break. Take home pay is £15 a week, and if anybody misses a day they are fined £1.75 on top of lost wages.

Hattersley Newman, Henders Valve Manufacturers, Ormskirk, Lancs.

APEX members strike for equal pay. They have a 24 hour picket.

December

Babcock and Wilcox, Renfrew

200 women clerical workers win settlement in move towards equal pay.

Lyons, Greenford

200 maintenance fitters, 300 process workers (women and truck drivers, white and Asian) strike for wage increase of £6.

Oxford

Provincial journalists in NUJ campaign for £15 a week increase. At Oxford, Ann Edwards, Mother of NUJ Chapel was picketing *Oxford Mail* offices; a delivery van accelerated away from her while she tried to talk to the driver - her arm was caught in the window and her shoulder was badly wrenched.

Maclaren Control, Glasgow

300 workers, mainly women, at this subsidiary of ITT strike for 5 weeks for £5 pay rise. When threatened with the sack in 7 days, they occupy the factory. ITT try to break the occupiers' morale by sending them their insurance cards just before Christmas, but the workers collected them up and gave them to the stewards. They hold Christmas and Hogmanay parties inside the factory, and delegations of workers come from nearby factories to help out. The strike is to last 19 weeks, with the occupations lasting 15 weeks. By March, management agrees to meet the full claim, but the number to be taken back is reduced - this agreement follows pledges by shop stewards in the Glasgow area to·step up support and blacking, and the ITT mangement really are frightened when steps are taken to set up an ITT combine committee of shop stewards.

January

Rank Radio International, Camborne, Cornwall

Women shop stewards threaten strike action when working week is re-organised so that women have to work on New Years Day (supposed to be a paid holiday) and stay away another day, thus losing one day's paid holiday. The threat is successful - they get extra pay and another days holiday. There was a rumour that Ranks chairman was planning to send Valentine cards to all his women workers.

Beverley, Yorks.

Jean Jepson, convenor at Armstrong Patents, is sacked for refusing to accept 3 day week. Management have the cheek to announce over the internal loudspeakers 'Your convenor has been dismissed. Anyone who supports her can leave as well'. 80 men and women in the 500 strong workforce walk out. The management has been trying anything to get rid of Jean; on one occasion they offered her £5,000 to leave, another time she was offered a supervisors job so that her militant activities could be restricted. Hull dockers black Armstrong Patents products in the following weeks. A Dept. of Employment enquiry subsequently approves her dismissal, while the local TGWU official fails to give the pickets any support, recommending a return to work. Management blackmail Jean, compiling a dossier of slanderous personal accusations which they send to the Union. The local TGWU officials while mouthing support for Jean and the other women, never recommend any kind of action. Eventually, 100 women leave Armstrongs after picketing into the summer.

February

During the miners strike, many miners wives form action groups to look after children and provide pickets at the collieries with food.

500 delegates attend one day conference on trade unions and women's rights organised by the NCCL. Delegates from

Trade Unions, women's liberation groups and trades councils.

March
London Trades Council
Draws up Working Women's Charter
Coventry
200 women at Raglan Street GEC on strike to defend jobs. Management intend to 're-deploy' women in electronics production unit, moving the work to their Treforest factory, near Swansea. Their excuse is a cut in Post Office spending on telecommunications, but the strikers believe the real reason is to break trade union militancy in Coventry which has won them high wages in the past.

Dundee, Timex
3 week strike at the firm's three plants is broken on the instructions of the AUEW officials. Two thirds of the labour force are women and the strike is in opposition to the Phase 3 pay laws and the threat of closure. Wage rates at Timex are £6 to £7 a week lower than other engineering factories in Dundee. Basic rates include £27 for toolmakers, £21 for labourers, and £19.11 for women production workers. In the past, management have exploited sex differences to take on one shop at a time and beat them. This is the first time the entire workforce, men and women, strike together. The claim for £10 across the board is met with a £2.50 offer plus 85p on the bonus rate for women. During the strike, women are the most militant. 'I didn't have a chance to make a recommendation to my members', said a woman steward. 'They were out of the door as soon as they heard the management offer'. There is great bitterness at the capitulation of the union to the phase 3 limits.

Dundee Bonar Long
All 500 workers walk out in support of three women laid off for refusing to accept £3 drop in earnings after being

transferred to different work. A strike takes place against the productivity agreement which allows the firm to move labour from job to job, without paying bonus rates while the workers are learning the new job.

Birmingham Lucas

2,000 production workers, 90% women, walk out and claim a lay-off when management announce a number of redundancies. A mass meeting votes to sit in against the sackings. 800 tool setters at another Lucas plant nearby strike in support. Management agree to take women shop stewards demands for greater job security and no further sackings back to the Lucas directors.

April

Lentheric, N. London

290 women strike because they are getting between £7 and £8 less than the lowest male rate. Their take home pay is about £15. 70 men come out in support. They win increase of £2.25.

British Domestic Appliance, Peterborough

1,300 workers, one third women, come out on strike over £10 a week increase and equal pay.

Chrysler Subsidiary Auto Machinery, Coventry

190 men and women strike for parity with workers at Chrysler Stoke plant, on the same site; they also demand a step towards equal pay which would give women 95% of the men's rate.

Carruthers, a subsidiary of Burmak Oil, East Kilbride, Nr. Glasgow

6 typists win increases of £4 - £6 after five week strike. One girl aged 21 was only getting £14 a week and they offered her another £1 with strings. The girls, members of TASS, quickly got their demands when engineering union members on the shop floor blacked deliveries in support.

NALGO, Islington

Men and women members of NALGO strike for 15 weeks

in pursuit of higher London allowance.

British Airways, Overseas Division, Heathrow

Men and women cabin crews vote to take strike action in a fortnight's time for a reduction in working hours from 12 to 10½ a day and additional pay for working anti-social hours.

Jonas Woodhead, Ossett, Yorks.

Part time women workers on the evening shift at this shock absorber plant, join up in the AUEW and elect stewards at a mass meeting. It is discovered that management is allowing men to work in the evening shift in defiance of national engineering overtime ban. Management back down after the meeting and recognise the union.

May

Renold Gear Division, Milnrow, Lancs.

100 clerical workers strike in dispute over equal pay.

London Transport

First woman bus driver

Thomas Danby College, Leeds

Trainee nursery nurses at this college are fighting a proposal to cut wages of future nursery nurses by £8 a week, from £20 to £12. Councillors have to run the gauntlet of silent pickets at Council meetings at the Town Hall.

Penguin Books, Harmondsworth

Claire Walsh, one of the pioneers of trade unionism in publishing, is re-instated by Penguin one week after she was vicitmised and sacked. 41 workers on strike took over the offices and switchboard, and 250 printers blacked the production of all hard back books. They got official support from ASTMS and won guarantee of no further redundancies. 'Penguins were amazed that their workers responded so violently'.

Nurses

Nurses begin nationwide campaign for substantial increases

in pay. In Edinburgh 250 nurses hand petition into the Scottish Office. In Leeds nurses call for public support - getting signatures outside Leeds United Club Ground and petitioning in the city centre.

British Leyland, Cowley

Women workers and car workers' wives outvote an attempt to set up a 'housewives association' by Mrs. Carole Miller. She and others have received widespread publicity when they picket British Leyland in opposition to the strike by transport drivers, claiming that TGWU convenor, Alan Thornett, and small minority are keeping their husbands on strike. The women with her are manipulated by both the press and British Leyland in an attempt to break the strike, though most men's wives support the strike action. Speakers say that it is British Leyland that is keeping the men out, not convenor Alan Thornett, and that the women should be putting pressure on the management, not on the unions.

Imperial Typewriters, Leicester

700 men and women, mainly Asian, come out on strike over long standing grievances: confusing bonus rates which mean their wage packets change from week to week; not being allowed to elect their own shop stewards; widespread racial discrimination, on the shop floor by management, the TGWU work convenor and some of the white stewards. District union secretary, George Bromley, JP, condemns the strike so the strikers march on the union's district office. three weeks later, they hold a protest demonstration outside the TGWU London headquarters.

Reg Weaver, the works convenor, and Bromley refuse even to call an official branch meeting so the strikers hold an unofficial meeting which both officials refuse to attend. All this time the 500 strong white workforce at the factory continue working.

On the pickets, the traditionally quiet and docile Asian women are the most militant. At the start of the strike, they taunt the Asian men who try to cross the picket lines by offering the men their wrist bracelets which are a traditional emblem of the women's inferior position in Asian society. The women earn £18 a week on average to the men's £25. The women are pushed around by the white foremen who play on racial differences to keep them ignorant of the complex wages scheme by which bonus rates are calculated and also never explain the details of union organisation to make it deliberately difficult for them to elect their own representatives to do something about the payments system.

The strike does not end until July when management finally reinstate all the strikers, including what they call the 25 'strike leaders' whom they had been trying to make a bargaining point in the negotiations. If they'd been successful, it would have set back the cause of union organisation among the Asian workers. Their return is accompanied by a one day strike by the white workers in the TGWU in protest: the bitter racial divisions still remain at this factory and, if anything, the union officials have made them much worse.

Nurses Pay

Marches in Teeside, Nottingham and Liverpool. In Liverpool there is a one hour lightning strike at the General Hospital by members of COHSE which is to set a precedent for similar actions up and down the country by COHSE members. The demand is also raised for an end to agency nurses - these are nurses who are trained on the NHS, contract out and are then re-employed from private agencies at higher wage rates than those paid from the NHS. This divides hospital nurses and makes it easier to keep the wages of NHS nurses down.

National Switch Factory, Keighley

A strike, which started among women assembly line workers, is subsequently joined by the men who also work at the factory. 400 women strike for 8 days when management welch on the national wages agreement for the engineering industry which would have given rises of £3.75 for women, £3.50 for skilled men, £3.10 for unskilled men. The men had worked to rule for over a month without getting anywhere until the women struck. 'This struggle has proved that women can fight for men. It's proved that men on the whole can't fight for themselves in a factory where more than half the labour force is women,' said one of the women strikers. 'When we first came out the men were amused and so were the management. Because we do repetitious work, they think we're cabbages.' After a day, the men joined the women strikers and the management moved to settle; the final offer accepted gives women £2.62 with a further £1.70 in the autumn towards equal pay; £3.25 for skilled men and £3.10 for the unskilled. 'We lost out in the end. But ... if there's another dispute over our equality money, then we can turn to the men for support and remind them that we came out for them when they weren't going to get any of the national agreement.'

June

Nurses Pay

In Newcastle more than 4,000 manual workers at C.A. Parsons Engeineering factory hold a one hour strike in support of the nurses. They march to a town centre demonstration led by 100 nurses in uniform.

In Nottingham a joint demonstration between nurses in COHSE and NUPE and miners takes place, led by the band of Calverton colliery.

In Carmarthen 200 nurses and trade unionists march.

In Portsmouth nurses at St. James Mental Hospital hold a one hour strike and, at a mass meeting, decide to ban all overtime work.

In Manchester, 1,000 nurses, radiographers and student doctors march. Dockers strike for one day in support of the nurses.

In Liverpool, 400 hospital workers march to the pier head.

In Doncaster, busmen strike for four hours in support. Workers at British Ropes and at Cementation promise strike action in support of nurses pay demands.

In Teeside Darlington NUPE sponsor two one day strikes by market workers and dustbin men in support.

In Leamington workers at Automotive Products stop work for an hour when local nurses picket the factory gates.

In Romford, Essex, 700 nurses march through the shopping centre. Several hospitals in the area hold two hour lightning strikes.

In Norwich, several hundred nurses and trade unionists on the march.

In the North East, the Nurses Advisory Committee consisting of 30 nurses representatives for the whole area, decide to ban the treatment of all private patients until their pay claim is met. In London, Ms. Brooksone of NUPE puts an end, until the nurses get a tangible increase in pay, to the luxurious treatment of private patients at the new Charing Cross Hospital paid for the NHS.

London Teachers

500 women and men members of the Rank and File Teachers group occupy the NUT headquarters after a lobby of the union action committee, demanding greater action for an increased London allowance. They hold an unofficial meeting which votes overwhelmingly in favour of unofficial strike action.

New English Library

Frieda Lockart, assistant editor at this large publishing house, is sacked for 'inefficiency' after she joined the NUJ and started campaigning for union recognition, better wages and conditions, and an end to management's paternalistic treatment of women. With two NUJ men she pickets NEL turning away postmen and dustmen. SOGAT workers, who distribute NEL's books and periodicals, threaten to black all their stuff: Frieda is unconditionally reinstated and wins an extra week's holiday into the bargain.

Nurses Pay

In Woking Trade Unions demonstrate in support of the nurses. There is a one hour stoppage by all ancillary workers at All Saints Hospital at Birmingham. In London, the Central Middlesex and Bolingbroke Hospitals put ban on private patients. In Sunderland 500 nurses, supported by 100 miners, march with union banners through the town. In Edinburgh there is a 500 strong demonstration of nurses and other hospital workers. In Manchester, dockers hold a further one day strike in support of the nurses pay demand.

Glasgow University

ASTMS members working on computers throughout Scotland on strike over regrading of jobs. 31 women operators picket Glasgow University, bringing much research work to a stop. At Strathclyde, women computer operators occupy the computer premises.

London Teachers

One day strikes in various London schools for a rise in the London allowance.

July

First national women's workshop to be organised by ASTMS.

Wingrove & Rogers, Old Swan, Liverpool

250 workers, mostly women, strike at this electrical engineering factory for five weeks over take home pay of £15 for a 40 hour week on average.

Easterbrook & Allcards, Sheffield

Women involved in strike of 600 workers at this small tools factory, demanding higher rises in pay under the cost of living threshold agreement.

London Hospitals

Technicians and Radiographers, many of them women, come out and join the nurses in a strike for 30% increase in basic pay.

Smiths Industries, Cricklewood

A 2 day sit-in takes place at this factory where they make car speedometers, when 177 women are laid off without pay. Management withdraws the lay off notices.

Nurses Pay

In Swansea a nurses flying picket brings out a 1,000 miners on a one day strike in support of the Swansea Nurses Action Committee. The nurses unfurl banners outside the colliery saying 'Strike a blow for the nurses' and hand out leaflets. Nurses' representatives address meetings of the miners at Morlais, Graig Merthyr and Bryn Lliw Collieries - saying that they have had ladlefuls of sympathy but what is needed is united industrial action in support of nurses to get their pay demands met.

Kenilworth components, Leicester

Asian women, paid £12 a week for working 48 hours come out on strike - other Asian workers, from Imperial Typewriters, help them to organise a strike lasting two days.

August
Courtline Aviation

40 men and women strike over sacking of station superintendent.

London Transport

Has first three women bus inspectors

Highcroft Hospital, Birmingham

First ever 24 hour strike takes place when nurses walk out for a whole day at this 700 bed psychiatric hospital.

September

Persona Razor Blades, Hillingdon, Glasgow

Two week strike for equal pay. Women on average paid £6 a week less than men. It ends in acceptance of managerial offer of a job evaluation committee of 2 union and 2 firm members.

Vauxhall, Luton, Beds.

Women office cleaners, members of the Transport Union, on strike for 3 weeks over pay of £9 for a 15 hour week. Victory of immediate 10p an hour increase and one week extra holiday.

Fords, Dagenham

Women machinists seize store of seat covers they have produced in defiance of management bid to pay them off because of a dispute.

Wingrove and Rogers, Old Swan, Liverpool

Strike now in its 15th week. 14 men are out in support and no lorries are entering the factory. Firm's supplies and products blacked by Merseyside dockers.

October

Salford Electrical Instruments, Heywood, Lancs.

40 women, members of AUEW, occupy the switchboard (they tried to occupy the whole factory) as part of an equal pay dispute. Male members of AUEW blackleg and management employs security guards in an attempt to intimidate them. The fight is for a bonus rate equal to that paid to men doing the same work.

M. Edney & D. Phillips

These reports were compiled from SOCIALIST WORKER and MORNING STAR.
For STRIKING PROGRESS 1972-73 see RED RAG, No. 5.

Documents

Working Mothers' Charter

BASIC PRINCIPLES

1 The right to work

Every woman, regardless of family commitments, should have the same right to work as every man.

2 Social services

Every woman with dependant children should have access to supportive services to allow her to work and no woman should be deprived of the right to work because of inadequacies in the social services.

3 Education and training

No woman should be deprived of the right to work because of lack of education or training. Every woman should be afforded the opportunity to complete or further her education, or to acquire new skills.

4 Discrimination

No employer should be allowed to discriminate against a woman because of her marital status or family commitments.

5 Vocational guidance

Every woman should be entitled to vocational guidance in order that she may realise her full potential.

6 Earnings

Every woman should be able to earn sufficient to enable her to be economically independent.

SPECIFIC PROVISIONS

Pregnant women

See Mothers in Action's *'Target' Maternity Leave Campaign*, page 353

Mothers and children

1   Adequate substitute care for babies and young children should be provided at all times necessary to enable the mother to work without undue worry.

2   Offices and clinics of welfare and social services departments to which mothers may require access should open one evening a week.

3   Paid leave of two weeks per annum should be available, on production of a doctor's certificate, to enable mothers to stay at home with their sick children if they so desire. Beyond this time, unpaid leave should be freely available. This leave should also be available to mothers who wish to stay with their children while they are in hospital.

4   Home helps and nursing assistance should be made available to the mother if she or the child is ill.

5   Unpaid leave taken because of family commitments should be treated as working time for the purpose of assessing sick pay, unemployment and pension rights.

6   A comprehensive scheme of play centres and other recreational facilities should be made available by the local authority and local education authority working, where appropriate, in conjunction with other voluntary and statutory bodies.

7   A reasonable amount (about two weeks per annum) of unpaid leave should be made available to a mother to enable her to spend additional time with her child during school holidays.

8   Employers should, as and when necessary, allow mothers flexibility in their working hours.

ACTION NECESSARY TO IMPLEMENT THE CHARTER

Legislation

1   To provide adequate facilities in rest rooms for pregnant women.

2   To forbid dismissal of pregnant women.

3   To give minimum maternity leave of twelve weeks.

4   To ensure restitution of mother in former position after maternity leave.

5   To allow time off to attend clinic, hospital, etc. during pregnancy.

6   To allow five days unpaid leave per annum to enable mothers to spend extra time with their children during school holidays.

7   To allow two weeks paid leave per annum and further unpaid leave where necessary when a child is ill on production of a doctor's certificate.

Legislation and finance

1   To set up sufficient day nurseries to cater for all mothers requiring this service.

2   To set up play centres and similar facilities to cater for the out of school needs of children of working mothers.

3   To recruit and train nursing auxiliaries to allow mothers to work during their children's illnesses.

Mothers in Action

'Target' - Maternity Leave Campaign

1. No woman should be dismissed from her employment because of her pregnancy or during maternity leave and her position should be held open during her absence on maternity leave.

We know that many women will still wish to give up work when they have a baby, but they should be able to make the genuine choice between staying at home and going out to work. At present, even if a woman intends to continue working after her child is born, she is, more often than not, expected to leave her job before the birth and reapply after the birth. This is absolute nonsense. Every woman should have the option of having a job held open for her during maternity leave.

2. Every woman should be entitled to a minimum of 12 weeks maternity leave with net wage to cover the ante and post natal periods.

We have been criticised for asking for this as we are told that the burden would be borne by the employer. In fact what would happen would be the woman would claim her maternity allowances and earnings related benefits and the employer would make this up to the normal net wage as if she were on sick leave. This system is used in Germany and Austria and raises no problems there.

3. Maternity leave to be considered as a period of employment for purposes of assessing pension, sick pay and unemployments benefits.

It is essential that the period of maternity leave should be counted as continuous employment so that the woman concerned is not penalised in any way.

4. Pregnant women should be entitled to time off, with pay, to attend a hospital or clinic.

It is vitally important that pregnant women should be seen by a doctor before the sixteenth week of pregnancy and that they should attend a maternity clinic regularly thereafter. At present, some women, particularly those who are single, are reluctant to ask for time off for this purpose and, indeed, many may lose money by doing so. It should be recognised by the employer that attendance at the clinic is essential for the health of the mother and expected baby alike and therefore time off for such visits should be allowed without question.

5. Sick leave should be granted during pregnancy on production of a medical certificate.

It sometimes happens·that a doctor will order a woman to take some time off or to work shorter hours during part of her pregnancy. This should be allowed on production of a medical certificate.

6. Nursing mothers in employment should be entitled to sufficient time off for this purpose.

In some countries, e.g. Germany and Italy, it is the practice to allow nursing mothers to work shorter hours than usual in order that they may continue to feed their babies.

Mothers in Action

354

TUC's Best Practise Maternity Leave Recommendations

1. Eligibility

The best agreements apply to all women employees, irrespective of marital status and some include part-time employees provided that they are eligible for paid sick leave.

2. Qualifying period of service

Normally twelve months' continuous service at the date of of application for maternity leave. The best agreements also make provision for some break in service (for example: a period of less than three months between the termination and resumption of employment is not regarded as a break in service).

3. Application for maternity leave

Normally application must be made not less than three months before the anticipated date of confinement. Some agreements require a declaration at the time of application that the woman intends to resume employment at the expiry of the leave.

4. Length of maternity leave

The 'best practice' is 18 weeks (but see paragraph 5 below). The period before and after the anticipated date of confinement varies but the best is 11 weeks before and seven weeks after. If the child does not live, the period after confinement is sometimes reduced to four weeks. Leave in excess of eighteen weeks may be granted in exceptional cases. Further absence due to, or attributable to, the pregnancy which occurs outside the period of eighteen weeks is usually treated as absence on sick leave within the provisions of the sick pay scheme.

5.   Scale of payment

The outstanding example is undoubtedly one nationalised industry which incorporates maternity leave into the normal sick pay scheme (thirteen weeks full pay less NI benefit and thirteen weeks half pay without NI deduction). Generally speaking, however, 'best practice' is four weeks full pay less NI benefit (irrespective of whether or not the woman herself contributes to National Insurance) plus fourteen weeks half pay without NI deduction — unless the combined total of half pay plus benefit is more than the normal full pay (in which case payment is that sufficient to bring NI benefit up to full pay).

6.   Relation to sick pay scheme

Pregnancy is not considered, medically, to be sickness but a number of schemes do incorporate maternity leave payments within the undertaking's sick pay scheme. 'Best practice' is that the period of maternity leave is not taken into account for the purpose of calculating sick pay entitlement.

7.   Resumption of work

Most agreements include certain restrictions designed to ensure that the woman will resume employment for a specified minimum period after maternity leave. 'Best practice' is considered to be the with-holding of payment for the last four weeks of maternity leave until the woman has been back at work for a minimum period of four weeks. One agreement provides that this payment will not be with-held if the child does not live. Another agreement which with-holds payment until the completion of three months' service, enables the woman, however, to resume initially on a part-time basis, provided that this is at least half the hours normally worked each week before the pregnancy. No agreement provides for appeal against the

with-holding of payment of the last weeks of maternity leave if work is not resumed. It is considered that, while it is reasonable to include some restrictions of this nature in the agreement, there should be provision for appeal and that each case should be considered jointly by the appropriate trade union and management.

8. Protection of health

Only one agreement examined included any protection for the health of the pregnant woman (relating to contact with german measles). Restrictions to protect the woman's health should be kept to the minimum and will vary according to the industry and the requirements of the particular job. Therefore unions can themselves best judge what protection is desirable for their women members. However, one issue which should be included in all agreements is that pregnant women should be granted leave, without loss of pay, to attend ante-natal clinics.

Women's Advisory Committee of the TUC

These recommendations have been taken up by such public employers as the Post Office and the UK Atomic Energy Authority. These 'Best Practice' maternity leave arrangements are guidelines for union negotiation.

Battered Women's Guide to the Law

First find a solicitor

It is not always easy to find a solicitor who is either or able or willing to handle these sorts of cases. Many of them have little experience in this area and they often prefer to avoid these cases which can be time consuming, not particularly lucrative and which often interfere with other work because of the speed with which action has to be taken.

First go to a Citizens Advice Bureau who will give you a list of local solicitors; if they are unhelpful, you can contact the Law Society for advice. Remember that if you have no income of your own (or a small one) you are entitled to free legal advice (watch out for a sign in the solicitors' window showing two people at a table) and legal aid. In emergencies you can get *emergency legal aid*, this means that the solicitor will help you fill in a legal aid form and an emergency application form. The two factors that the Law Society are looking for when they decide about emergency aid, are whether there is already extreme suffering or whether there is likely to be if nothing is done.

The solicitor should mark the application URGENT and telephone the legal aid office before sending it in. He should also be prepared to argue on your behalf if aid is not granted. It should be possible to get a decision from the office within 24 hours.

Now there are five different courses of action open

a) The Magistrates Court

The wife may take out a 'matrimonial summons for cruel-

ty'. This usually means that the husband is fined and bound over to keep the peace. Nothing more can be done to prevent violence recurring, if he does not comply with the order he will simply be fined again. Experience at Chiswick Women's Aid has shown that it is not really advisable to use the magistrates court particularly as the magistrates who are usually both male and middle class tend to be extremely patronising and unsympathetic towards battered women. They seem to feel in general that a woman who is beaten must have done something to deserve it, and that (particularly if she is working class) she should be prepared to put up with a bit of rough and tumble as a normal part of married life. They tend to regard the cases as private tiffs and are likely just to indulgently tell the couple to 'kiss and make up'.

b) The High Court

An inunction (a court order preventing harrassment) can be taken out against the husband without petitioning for divorce. This is not usually done. The husband is not presumed guilty but if he breaks the injunction he can be imprisoned for contempt of court.

c) Police Criminal Prosecution

The Police are reluctant to interfere in 'family matters' and in any case injuries must be severe and there must be evidence to prove that the husband was responsible.

d) Private Criminal Prosecution

This would mean the wife taking action against the husband herself and having him convicted of assault.

e) Divorce Registry or County Court

The wife may petition for divorce or for judicial separation, and at the same time, apply for an immediate injunction.

This has been found to be the most successful kind of action because it means that the woman is entitled to legal aid and she can be quickly reinstated in her home, financial arrangements can be made and a degree of legal protection against harrassment can be obtained.

Preparing the Case

The solicitor should contact a barrister and arrange a meeting with you within 24 hours of your contacting him. At this meeting a statement will be taken. You will need to give the names of possible witnesses, the name of a doctor or hospital who has treated you after an attack and a statement whould be written saying that you or your children would suffer unless you are separated from your husband and regain possession of your home.

The Barrister will now 'draft a summons for injunction', 'an affidavit' (signed statement) giving your evidence and a petition for divorce. The injunction can cover a number of things. The object is to prevent him from doing anything to hurt, frighten or worry you or your children. It can include getting him to leave your home so that you can live there, granting interim custody of the children and arranging money matters.

Going to Court

The case will go either to the family division of the High Court in London or to a local divorce county court. The injunction will be read out and handed to the judge, at the same time, the solicitor will promise to issue the divorce petition within 24 hours. If he is satisfied that the case is serious, the judge might grant everything in the injunction immediately (except vacation of the matrimonial home), even though the husband will not yet have had time to appear in court. A second hearing will be arranged for about a fortnight later and in the meantime the husband will be served with the injunction and the petition.

For the second hearing the solicitor will have to gather evidence against the husband, and he will have a chance to defend himself. On this occasion, the temporary injunction may be continued and possession of the matrimonial home should be arranged for the wife.

If the husband does not keep to the terms of the injunction, the solicitor should take out an application for a further hearing asking that the husband be sent to prison for

contempt of court. After this, it is simply a matter of waiting for the divorce proceedings to go through. The time this takes can vary a great deal, particularly if the husband is defending, but at least the wife should be economically secure and have a home with the knowledge of legal support should her husband mistreat her in the meantime.

There are no real remedies to this sort of violence in a society which extols strength as the greatest manly virtue and firmly believes that every woman is just waiting for some man to come along and beat her into submission. Heavier sanctions against violent husbands are unlikely to have any real preventive value while James Bond can bring people rushing to the box offices. However, the establishment of more women's aid centres will be the first step towards protecting women from the effects of an over-developed male ego.

Angela Phillips

This was first published in SPARE RIB 17 and is based on a report entitled BATTERED WOMEN AND THE LAW, from Chiswick Women's Aid.

NB Since this was written, an injunction kit for battered wives has been prepared. For details see page 358

Statement of Aims

No womens liberation without socialist revolution
No socialist revolution without womens liberation

Sexual exploitation and repression

We aim to end the idea of 'femininity' and 'masculinity' and therefore to end sexual repression and exploitation, e.g. an end to the use of women as passive sexual objects, as in advertising. We want to be able to live freely together, women with women, women with men, men with men.

Education

We aim at education geared to and controlled by the needs of the community and the individual in a socialist society.

- an education which does not define children as a separate species to be hived off from 'real' society.
- an education which treats everyone as people and does not foster sex and age roles
- an education which is based on a more flexible system, not centred in compulsory schools but which use community resources which now exist and which need to be developed
- an education which emphasises critical learning rather than 'being taught'
- an education which is open and readily available and accessible to all age levels

Fertility

We aim to control our own fertility. This should not be interpreted as an encouragement for individuals to please themselves regardless of the community, but it does mean that any decision about contraception, abortion and steril-

362

isation would be taken by the woman herself, *not* by doctors, social workers, psychiatrists etc. We also demand research into better and safer methods of birth control.

The family

We recognise the role of the nuclear family as a prop to the capitalist system

- using women to service the male labour force, physically, sexually, emotionally, and psychologically
- containing the militancy of the male labour force by compelling them to support women and children
- providing a reserve of cheap unorganised female labour
- preparing the future labour force
- functioning as a multiplicity of isolated consumption units which provide capitalism with an inexhaustible market and encouraging wasteful production and rapid obsolescence
- transmitting the dominant ideology (e.g. competitiveness, stereotype sex roles, possessiveness etc.)

The nuclear family is an oppressive institution. In theory it satisfies our emotional needs but in practice it stunts our emotional development. It restricts our intimate relationships to the family unit and divides us from each other. The nuclear family represses children by defining them as possession of their parents and subjects them to their arbitrary authority. Their socialisation is largely determined by two people about whom they have no choice - their parents - and gives them only limited exposure to other role models.

The nuclear family oppresses woman especially by giving her no option but to be a housewife regardless of whether or not she works outside the home. The survival of the family depends on her continuing unpaid labour, seven days a week. The housewife is in the classic colonised position — she is denied social, psychological, sexual and economic autonomy. She does not belong to herself.

We aim to create

better ways of living and working in which the nuclear family will be only one of many alternatives. We must break down obstacles to group living (conventional architecture, the law, planning, social prejudice).

community controlled child care facilities geared to the needs of those who use it. We want to end the idea that child care is women's work; men have as much right and as much responsibility as women for children.

community care of the sick and the old, for which men and women have equal responsibility.

facilities for communalisation of household functions (cleaning, cooking, shopping) thus ending the enforced privatisation of housework. This work is of course the equal responsibility of men and women.

In order that these responsibilities can be assumed by everyone, we must redefine 'work' — i.e. we must break down rigid job definitions.

Economic

From all according to their ability; to all according to their needs.

We aim to create a society where work is meaningful because we do it for ourselves in co-operation and not under someone else's orders or for someone else's profit.

We aim to work towards a society in which every individual enjoys as a right a fair standard of living not gained at the expense of other societies.

In working towards this we aim to take action in the following areas:

- we will encourage women to organise in unions and groups to fight for equal treatment and to fight against male chauvinism in the work situation and in the unions themselves.

- we will fight for an end to the trivialisation of the work women do and their exploitation as a reserve of cheap labour.

- we will fight against the definition and divisions of 'men's work' and 'women's work'.

- we will fight for equal pay for work of *equal value* for everyone, male and female, young and old.

- we will fight for equal job opportunities but we are not just fighting for an equal chance to be unequal.

- we will work for increasing ownership and control of the work situation by workers (i.e. organisation of work, hiring, firing, promotion), an end to rigid work discipline and an end to the industrial hierarchy.

We aim to make the production unit more responsive to the needs of the community.

But the struggle for economic rights does not end in the factory.

We aim to get

-   more control over *real* wages — i.e. what our money can buy. We aim to do this by such means as resisting price and rent increases, organising consumer co-operatives and consumer protection.
-   more control over our welfare provisions either by working with existing groups or setting up our own.
-   an end to sex discrimination in welfare benefits and we will fight attempts to erode welfare provisions.

We want to abolish the economic dependence of —
women on men
children on parents
the old on the young

Members of the North Eastern women's groups - York, Leeds, Hull & Durham. October 1972

This paper was presented at the National Women's Liberation Conference held in London in October 1972.

AWARE

AWARE is an advice, research and education project run by women for women

Since the emergence of the women's movement, it has become clear that there are large loopholes in the social services network. Often problems are not recognised, and assistance not readily obtainable. The women's movement has spotlighted the existence of battered women, given rise to support groups for women experiencing post-natal depression; it has examined the treatment (or ill treatment) of women by doctors and psychiatrists, and has pointed out inequalities like the cohabitation clause and in pension schemes.

Traditional advice centres (citizens advice bureaux, legal aid centres, family planning clinics) give traditional advice, ignoring new areas and perspectives that women are beginning to formulate about their needs and their positions in society. Since these agencies do not adequately service women, we need to answer our own questions, and trace our history and the roots of our problems so that we find the answers we need. We must do research and co-ordinate and index it with reference to those needs.

The history of AWARE

In early 1971 during the campaign for Willy Hamilton's Anti-Discrimination bill, the Women's Lobby received frequent enquiries from MP's and journalists requesting information about discrimination. The information was not readily available. *Women's Report* was started, in co-operation with the Fawcett Society, in an effort to collate and distribute information about women's activities. It soon became clear that a bi-monthly, small circulation magazine generated more enquiries and posed more questions than it could answer. The need for an information and research centre for women was clearly urgent and a public meeting was held to discuss the matter. The response was overwhelming and it came from women in many different fields, some already involved with women's activities and many others who came from a sense of personal frustration.

Since then a collective has been formed which meets every month. Already many different research projects are under way and as soon as sufficient information has been collected we will open our centre at the

SOUTH LONDON WOMEN'S CENTRE
14 Radnor Terrace   London SW 8

Initially the centre will be run on a volunteer rota basis but we hope to raise enough money to employ full time staff as soon as possible.

Archives collective

This group is responsible for collecting information which especially concerns women, from various sources e.g. magazines, newspapers and individuals. Information and research already gathered for *Women's Report*, articles for *Spare Rib* and the Penguin *Women's Rights: A Practical Guide* are also available to the group. The information is classified, collated and filed. We hope to provide an individual question/answer service by letter, telephone or personal visit. The service will be run by voluntary workers operating on a rota basis. At first it will be limited to a few hours per day, but subsequently we hope to employ full time workers. We also envisage producing information sheets concerning subjects about which we have most frequent enquiries.

Women's research index

We are compiling an index of work completed or in progress, in any subject area, at any level, by women, of interest to women, or with a feminist approach. Although published indices to university theses are available, we hope to cover non-academic areas also, so that women can share their knowledge and skills in more informal ways,

thus avoiding duplication of effort.

In this way women can gain a sense of their own history and achievements, by exploring their past and their talents. We hope the existence of the index will encourage further research by highlighting gaps, as well as making readily available to all, work already done. Also it will form a network for sharing skills and crafts, thereby opening up possibilities for self expression and self fulfilment for women.

Women and health collective

This group has two main aspects: research and self help. On the research side, a survey is under way to examine the attitudes of GP's to women patients and to document women's experience with the medical profession in general. Questionnaires form the basis of interviews for both and the main areas covered include vaginal and urinary infections, contraception, abortion, alleged psychosomatic disorders and childbirth. The results will be analysed and published with the intention of reaching a wide audience.

On the self help side, members of the group are becoming acquainted with self help techniques which initially involves self examination of the cervix. It is hoped to start up self help groups all over the country. An ultimate aim will be to establish in London a clinic staffed by feminist doctors and trained para-medics.

Members of the group are increasingly being asked to talk to community groups, women's groups and other organisations. We have been amassing a large amount of material on the NHS and the health care field in general and wish to spread this information and our views on various developments. Recently, two members have been invited to construct and teach a unit on women and medicine as part of a community medicine course at a medical school. We charge for such activities as this provides us with our sole source of income at present.

Alternatives to the nuclear family

This group arose out of discussions at the National Women's Conference in Bristol (July 1973). Many women expressed interest in trying to organise living situations outside the traditional structures of the nuclear family but had difficulty in finding like-minded people. Two women from AWARE agreed to set up a national directory to record the names of women who were living in 'alternative' situations or who would like to do so. The directory would be used to put people in touch with one another, to give advice on buying houses, setting up housing associations or simply giving women the chance to compare experiences. The project is still in its early stages but clearly, as more women - particularly single mothers - see the benefits of sharing facilities, the directory will become a valuable source of information.

Women in psychiatry

This group started independently of AWARE through a conference on psychiatry. Since then the group has received publicity through an article in the *Sunday Times*. The response was immediate and overwhelming. Over 300 letters were received providing fascinating though depressing evidence that discrimination and sexist attitudes are still widespread among doctors and psychiatrists.

The group has been answering letters and is in the process of compiling information sheets on the facilities available to these women. It hopes also to help the women contact others who are in similar situations.

Advertising project

The report produced by this group will not be as practical a guide as some of AWARE'S other material, but it is hoped that the findings will be of some interest and value in the fields of anti-discrimination and the image of women in the media. The study is divided into two sections:

1. A detailed analysis of selected advertisements from wo-

men's magazines. This section includes a description of the letters received from the advertisers, their agencies and the Advertising Standards Authority about AWARE's complaints of the selected advertisements.

2. A survey of all advertising in a) one month's weekend colour magazines and b) one month's selected women's magazines to discover the ratio of men to women depicted in different job and leisure pursuits. The aim in part is to compare the presentation of women in these two media, one of which is aimed almost exclusively at women while the other caters for a mixed audience. Most of the basic research has been completed already, and the group hopes to write up the data in the near future.

Mortgages collective

This group, as yet in its early stages, was formed with the intention of conducting a survey to find out whether building societies and other housing loan financiers discriminate against women in giving mortgages. A questionnaire has been drafted to this end, together with a letter to the Press, publicising the survey. It is hoped that the building societies etc. would be less likely to refuse information if the survey received wide publicity.

Women's art history collective

We are examining the role of women in art:

a) to explain and erase the prejudices which exist today concerning women's creativity;

b) to discover what characterises the values and framework of art which favours a small group of people and discriminates against women

c) to make up for the very real neglect of women artists of the past

One of the attitudes we share is a dissatisfaction with existing methods of teaching within the present structure of art edcuation. We are attempting a' method of collective teaching that logically develops out of our group work.

For further information contact AWARE at the South London Women's Centre, 14 Radnor Terrace, London SW8 Telephone 01-622-8494 or Julie Tant at 01 733 8630 or June Wilson at 01 445 0580

August 1974

AIMS

AIMS is a voluntary organisation which was established in 1960 with the object of bringing about improvements in the maternity services. Membership is open to anyone who is concerned for the welfare, physical, mental and social, of women and their babies during pregnancy, in labour and in the early post-natal period.

Early in its existence AIMS was recognised by what was then the Ministry of Health as representing the consumer; through meetings at the Ministry (now the Department of Health and Social Security) and through written comments on relevant DHSS reports we have since our foundation worked to put forward the views of our members at the highest possible level. To collect evidence in support of our cause we have conducted an essay competition, through the *Midwives' Chronicle*, entitled 'How to recruit and re-train more midwives'(1965) and a national survey on the kind of maternity services mothers would like to see (1971). Currently a local AIMS group is preparing another national survey, on mothers' experiences of 'daylight delivery'. As a result of such investigations as these, and using also the views expressed by members over the years, we have formulated a list of objectives:

1   No loneliness in labour

2   More midwives and more money for the maternity services

3   Research into pain relief and into the training of medical staff in the understanding of the psychological effects of childbearing

4   The treatment of women throughout pregnancy and confinement as human beings, not as objects to be processed.

To achieve these objectives, AIMS must continue to make its voice heard, in order to alert the medical and social services to the needs of *everyone* concerned in the events surrounding childbirth; to draw attention to deficiencies where they exist; to suggest improvements and ways in which they may be made; and to influence future developments, for the ultimate benefit of society as a whole. The executive committee (elected at the AGM) is therefore in regular contact with the general and specialist press and with related organisations (e.g. National Childbirth Trust, Patients' Association). As well as offering advice, information and comfort where these are wanted, AIMS issues to members a quarterly newsletter which discusses maternity matters generally as well as the activities of the Association.

What you can do

First, you can make your views as an individual known by joining AIMS, and through your subscription help us to continue our work: we are a voluntary organisation (not a charity) and so our income is derived entirely from subscriptions. Next, you can join or help to form a local group — there are local groups in Bury, Bedford and Farnham — to meet other like-minded people, to discuss matters of interest, to put forward collective ideas or to give practical help in a maternity hospital in your area by sitting with mothers in labour, fund-raising, etc. If problems arise locally, you can use the support of the national body to back your individual or concerted course of action. Do any of these things and you will be helping AIMS to achieve its most important objective, which is to become, one day, happily redundant.

H.Q. AIMS, West Hill Cottage, Exmouth Place, Hastings, Sussex TN 34 3JA Tel. 0424 420591

Annual Subscription 50p: Treasurer, Barbara Davies, 40, Mendip Crescent, Bedford.

May 1974

WACC

The beginning

Our campaign arose out of the women's liberation movement. All over the country, women were meeting and beginning to talk to each other about their experiences of abortion, contraception, about their sexual feelings, and relating it to their place in society. Some of us wanted to do something concrete about the facilities available, and so we began to meet in separate groups in order to discuss and organise.

In January 1972 the London Abortion Action Group called a meeting and many women from other cities went to it. It was at that meeting that The Women's Abortion And Contraception Campaign (WACC) was formed and we set out our demands.

Class and sex

The right to choose when, and if, to have a child is a fundamental women's right and is basic to the liberation of women. If we cannot decide when we are to give birth then we cannot decide anything about our lives.

The medical profession is male-dominated: medical schools deliberately restrict their intake of women, and of the working class. How do men know how women feel about pregnancy, abortion, about bearing a child they do not want? There is no question that the right to control our own fertility is important, but women who consider themselves to be socialists must realise the special importance of this right. Manipulating the family unit, even to the extent of manipulating its size, is to the advantage of the class in power. It is in the interests of big business and their representatives to be able to control reproduction, just as it is in their interests to control production. We must fight for more control over our lives in every sphere, every victory for us is a defeat for them.

Beware the complacent attitude that abortions are easily available nowadays, and that any woman who wants one can easily obtain it! Getting an abortion still depends on where you live and how much money you have. For instance in 1972 in Newcastle there were eleven NHS abortions for every hundred live births, whereas in Birmingham there were 3.2 abortions for every 100 live births. The number of abortions performed has risen, it's true, but the number of *NHS* abortions has declined. More women are turning to the private sector — in 1969, 62% of all abortions were NHS, whereas in 1972, 36% of all abortions were NHS.

There has been much talk about free contraception on the NHS, but we still have not got that. Contraceptives are available on prescription — but the prescriptions have to be paid for. Doctors — who have dragged their feet for the past 50 years on birth control — are still reluctant sometimes, they don't want to prescribe condoms, and they have the power to decide on quantities.

We know that for women to able to have the right to choose they must also have the necessary housing, money, social support, to enable them to bring up the children they want. We do not need to be told that the WACC campaign does not fulfill all the needs that women have, but that is not an argument against WACC, it is an argument for more campaigns, and for the Women's Liberation Movement to be the co-ordinating body of all those campaigns, making up a whole feminist platform. There are women who want the right to choose, but perhaps are not convinced that nursery centres are the right thing for children, or they may not believe that an equal pay campaign is a must. A separate campaign with specific demands can win support, and we will learn from this involvement in action. If we keep hedging everything round with 'ifs' and 'buts', we finish up doing nothing.

The demands

The policy statement which we drew up when we formed

WACC demanded the right to choose and the following:

1 Free, safe and reliable contraception available to every woman on the National Health Service.

2 Abortion – a woman's right to choose; any woman who is unwilling to continue her pregnancy should have the undisputed right to a free and safe abortion.

3 No forced sterilisation; pressure should not be put on any woman to accept sterilisation as a condition for abortion.

Some of us had been very unhappy with the slogan 'Abortion on demand' which was commonly heard in the women's movement. There were those who felt it was highly emotive, and unnecessarily provoked an antagonistic response. But more important, we felt that it did not reflect our need to control our own fertility, but simply suggested that what we all needed was *not* to have children. Abortion on demand is not a revolutionary slogan, just because it is phrased in apparently militant language. We must not be taken in by revolutionary phrase-mongering. The right to chose reflects the needs of women, is easily understood and supported by women, and potentially much more of a threat to the State than abortion on demand will ever be.

The groups

There are a number of groups and the addresses of these can be supplied by the group which is currently doing the newsletter. They fluctuate largely from city to city, and from time to time. Sometimes groups fold up for a while, but someone picks up the pieces and has another go. There are groups which always exist, although their level of activity may vary from time to time. In other words, the groups are typical of any campaigning force!

The groups are autonomous, in the same way that the groups in women's liberation are, except that we have an agreed, recognised set of demands around which we work and ask for support. The groups decide their own activities, and their own direction of work - whether it be political campaigning, self examination, or pregnancy testing or a combination of all of them.

377

WACC and the anti-abortionists

One of the most consistent activities that we have carried out has been the counter demonstrations against the anti-abortionists. The Society for the Protection of the Unborn Child (SPUC) and the 'Life' groups have had rallies and marches in all the major cities. Sometimes with very small, but always very vocal support, we have taken our slogans 'Back Street Abortion Kills Women' and 'Women must Decide their Fate, not the Church and not the State' and made our presence felt. These demonstrations would have been impossible without the help and support of the women's liberation movement (and more recently, some help has been coming from left groups too).

It is very important that we should be seen opposing the anti-abortionists. Think of all the women who have had an abortion, and of the great difference it must make to see groups of women (and men) who believe they are entitled to make a choice. Sometimes some of us come back a bit disheartened because the anti-abortionists seem so powerful but we have women's real experience on our side.

The main arguments of the right-to-lifers are centred around the question of when life begins and their literature talks only of the needs of the foetus (which is always male - until we challenge them, and then they rather awkwardly try to remember to say 'she' sometimes). We can and must combat their arguments by talking about viability, and about when it is possible for the foetus to have a separate life from the woman. Until that time, it is the woman who must be able to decide whether or not to become a mother. The rights of the foetus must not be put before the rights of the woman.

Increasingly, SPUC has been turning its attention to parliament where it has powerful support, and it has had letter writing campaigns and deputations to MP's. They would like to get the 1967 Abortion Act repealed, which would mean that the previous more repressive Acts would come back into force. If not repealed, then they would

like to see the Act reformed to make abortion more difficult. They are on record against IUD's, as abortifacients,
and would like to ban their use.

WACC and the over-populationists

The over-population groups are potentially just as reactionary and just as anti-woman as the right to life groups.
Their arguments are based on the point of view that our
economic and social problems are caused by the indiscriminate breeding of women and men. In a leaflet produced
for Population Day in May 1973, they say that over-population is responsible for the shortage of land for building
houses, for our school classes being overcrowded, and for
rises in prices, among other things.

These people are very fond of quoting massive lists of
figures and statistics about world population and food resources. We must quote them some figures of our own
which are more relevant to an economic system in which
maximum profit is the driving force, and not people's needs.
In the first six months of 1973, the profits of Marks and
Spencers rose by £35 million, of Tesco by £10 million and
of Boots by £27 million. The price of a plot of land for
a house rose from £840 in 1969 to £1,770 in 1972. Where
is the population increase to equal that?

There are a lot of dangerous proposals which have aris-
en out of the discussion on over-population, which are not
only anti-human but anti-woman. For instance, there is
Professor Ehrlich's suggestion of putting contraceptive
chemicals in our drinking water or his less publicised one
of finding a way of ensuring that all first born children
are male, so that parents stop 'trying to have a son'!
Then there is Dr. Shockley's proposal that everyone with
an IQ of less than 100 should be sterilised, and the London
Councillor who thought that people applying for Council
houses should be sterilised. The final solution to the woman
question is the suggestion of the Professor at Sussex University who thinks we should try and find a pill which
would produce male children only so there will be very
few women to bear children ....

While these groups are often on record for better abortion facilities and better job and educational opportunities for women, don't be fooled! They are very silent on abortion, almost as silent as the anti-abortionists are on contraception. They have a very judging attitude about the use of contraceptives, and label people 'careless' or 'irresponsible' if they don't achieve a 100% success with less than 100% effective methods. They must understand that we are not going to exchange having children we don't want for *not* having children we do want. They should be campaigning for women's rights, not for government control of population.

Betty Underwood
1974

An abridged version of a paper presented at the Women and Socialism Conference at Oxford in March 1974.

Women & Psychiatry

Who are we?

An informal group of women concerned with society's attitudes to women suffering mental stress. Our group includes psychologists, therapists, psychiatric social workers and nurses, journalists and teachers, women who care about this issue without being professionally concerned and women who have been patients. We are trying to understand how social attitudes about women's role and identity produce not only current psychiatric theory and practice but also psychiatric disorder. The current upsurge of interest in women's roles and conflicts in society has given us additional insights, convincing us we have a vital contribution to make to understanding these questions.

What are we doing?

1   Research into
        a) the causes of mental stress in women
        b) attitudes to and treatment of mental stress
    With this object we are currently building up a file of relevant material.

2   Education. This will involve both acting as a resource for professional conferences (such as the MIND conference) and setting up our own discussion groups, seminars and conferences.

3   Forward thinking about the provision of treatment networks and centres which take due account of women's social and psychological problems without focussing on one at the expense of the other. These activities are not, of course, discrete but feed back into each other.

How did we start?

Our group originated when one or two of us decided to organise a conference on women and psychiatry. The large number of women who came suggested this was a crucial issue. Afterwards this Workshop, based in London, was formed. An article in the Sunday Times mentioned us and, as a result, we have received about four hundred letters from interested women. Many of these letters confirm our impression that women's psychological problems are inadequately understood. We have compiled a detailed reply sharing our perspective about women's experiences and the factors causing pschological stress in women. We have compiled a list of resources that may be helpful to women under stress and a reading list. If you would like a copy of this list, please send us 10p and we'll send you one.

What can you do?

There is enormous scope for any of you with definite interests to pursue them with the workshop. And, if you live outside London, we can help you set up similar groups and we can work together.

Further inquiries:
Women and Psychiatry Workshop,
c/o Vicky Randall, Room 708, Polytechnic of Central London, Elsley Court, 20-22 Great Titchfield Street, London W.1.

Guide
to Groups

WOMEN'S CENTRES

Acton Women's Centre
c/o The Priory Youth Centre,
Petersfield Road,   tel. 01 994 4244
Acton, London W.4   01 997 3275

Open Monday and Tuesday afternoons 2 - 4 p.m. (toddlers club). Thursdays 7.30 to 9.30 pm (Information Service on housing, squatting, help etc.) Also a nursery education campaign in connection with Working Women's
Charter Campaign (WWCC).

Brent Women's Centre,
138 Minet Avenue,
London NW10   tel. 01 965 3324

Brighton Women's Centre
79 Buckingham Road,
Brighton Sussex   tel. 0273 27612

Open day and evening and used by several women's groups
including women's liberation and Working Association of
Mothers. There is an information service, library, play
group, health collective, women's studies and WWCC group.
A pregnancy testing service is planned.

Bristol Women's Centre
Basement,
11 Waverley Road,
Bristol 6   tel. 0272 38120

Open 10 - 12 a.m. and 2 - 4 pm weekdays; 10 - 12 a.m.
on Saturdays; 8 - 10 p.m. some evenings. The centre is
a meeting place with an information service, bookshop
and library. There is a free pregnancy testing service on
Saturday mornings and Thursday evenings. Also local groups
in South Bristol, Westbury Park and Clifton. The Children's
House happens every Thursday - contact Jill Robin 40611.
The Gay Women's Group meets every Wednesday at the centr
at 8 pm. The Wages for Housework group - if interested
contact Suzie Fleming 422116. The Women's Abortion and
Contraception Campaign also based at the centre. (See

Documents) Sistershow Theatre Workshop - see *Women &
the Arts)*

Brixton Women's Centre
207 Railton Road,
London SE24   tel. 01 733 8663

Not directly involved in the women's movement, but is
used by both women and men. An integral part of the
community together with the Gay Centre (78 Railton Rd,
tel. 01 274 7921), People's News Service, Food Co-op,
Black Women's Group (see below) and the Women's Place.
Squatting group meets Tuesdays at 8 pm, new squatters
at 6.30 pm Brixton Claimants Union meets on Mondays
at 8 pm. Thursday there is legal advice and Friday the
women involved in the Centre get together. The Centre is
also open every afternoon between 2 and 5.pm.

Black Women's Group
65 Barnwell Road,
London SW2

Meet every Wednesday from 8. pm and together with
some nurses are conducting a campaign against the banning
of agency workers.

The Women's Place
80 Railton Road
London SE24   tel 01 274 8498

Includes in its activities a self help play group - weekdays 10 -
12 a.m.; a Working Women's Charter group - Wednesdays
6 - 8 pm (contact Ann 01 701 5601); a general meeting -
Wednesdays at 8 pm (discussions, films, work on campaigns
etc.); a self help group - time not decided.

Cardiff

No centre as such but 108 Community Bookshop is used
which the Women's Action group help to run. There is
a general meeting every Monday at 7.30 pm at The
Friends Meeting House, 43 Charles St, Cardiff which is a
business/discussion meeting where new members can find
out about the group. There is also a health group which

meets every three weeks, a women's socialist study group and a consciousness raising group. Some of the women are also involved in running Women's Studies courses under the auspices of the WEA and Adult Education in Cardiff, Caerphilly and Newport. For further details contact 108 Community Bookshop, 108 Salisbury Road, Cardiff   tel. 0222 28908

Kingsgate Women's Centre,
1 Kingsgate Place,
London NW6   tel. 01 624 1952

Offers information on London groups, pregnancy testing and advice, help with medical problems and referrals. The Women & Ireland collective, concerned to make people aware of women's problems in Ireland, occasionally meets at the centre. There is also a WACC group. The centre is open Tuesdays 2 - 5 pm, Wednesdays and Thursdays 2 -5 and 7 - 10 pm, Sundays during the day.

Lancaster Women's Centre
33 Primrose Street,
Lancaster   tel. 0524 64785

Advises on social security etc. and gives support to battered wives though as yet they have no accommodation. There are business meetings every Monday at 8 pm. Other groups include WWCC, consciousness raising, older women and a lesbian group. Some members are also interested in self defence.

London Women's Liberation Workshop
38 Earlham Street,
London WC2   tel 01 836 6081

Information and co-ordination centre with bookshop. Open Tuesday to Friday 10.30 am to 8 pm and Saturdays 11 am to 4 pm.

Manchester Women's Centre
218 Upper Brooke Street,
Manchester 13   tel. 061 273 2287

Runs an information service 7.30 to 9 pm Monday to Friday. No longer do pregnancy testing as there is now a local branch of the British Pregnancy Advisory Service. (BPAS) Groups using the centre include Women and Health, Women and Education and WWCC.

Nottingham Women's Centre
26 Newcastle Chambers,
Angel Row,
Nottingham   tel 0602 863894

There is a weekly meeting at 8 pm on Thursdays. Several campaigns are being run from the centre; Anti-Discrimination Campaign - contact Margaret Purdy 863894; WACC contact Rose Knight at the Women's Centre; WWCC -contact Gill Haynes 604074; battered women's campaign - contact The People's Centre 411227.

Scottish Women's Liberation Workshop
31 Royal Terrace,
Edinburgh   tel. 031 556 5655

Monthly general meetings on the first Monday of every month at 8 pm to discuss running of the workshop, reports of sub groups, to meet new members and time permitting, discussions on a topic agreed at a previous meeting. Other weekly groups; Monday - Campaign group (initiates campaigns, calls on support from general meeting); Tuesday - new members group (old members have a rota for meeting new members in a more informal atmosphere than the general meeting); Wednesday - Sexuality group; Thursday - Working Women's Charter.

South London Women's Centre
14 Radnor Terrace,
London SW8   tel. 01 622 8495

There is an AWARE general meeting once a month, a health collective meeting once a month and a lesbian meeting every Monday. The centre is also used by the feminist artists' group (see *Women & the Arts)*

Essex Road Women's Centre,
108 Essex Road,
London N. 1   Tel. 01 226 9936

NB. Many women's groups are, at the time of going to press, in the process of setting up Women's Centres in their towns. To find out about your local women's group, write or telephone your nearest women's centre, or contact the London Women's Liberation Workshop who keep an up to date list of women's groups throughout the country or write to SPARE RIB (9 Newburgh Street, London W.1) who put women in different parts of the country in touch with each other. Check SPARE RIB's Classified Advertisement section for new and established groups.

WOMEN'S AID HOUSES

It has been found, through experience, that it is inadvisable to publicise the addresses of refuges for battered women. For this reason we are listing here only the telephone numbers of the contacts for the houses or an organisation through which they can be contacted.
All the houses need help - in terms of womenpower, money, and usually household equipment.

Acton	01 567 4708
Brighton	0273 61664 (Citizens Advice Bureau); 0273 27612 (Women's Centre)
Birmingham	021 772 5017
Chiswick	01 995 4430
Edinburgh	031 443 9832
Glasgow	041 429 5398 (Mary Redfern)
Hackney	Citizens' Advice Bureau
Haringey	Citizen's Advice Bureau
Hull	0482 23218
Islington	01 607 2461 (Islington Community Law Centre)
Lambeth	01 674 3692

Leeds	Citizen's Advice Bureau
Lewisham	01 692 0231
Manchester	061 881 4106 (Not really suitable for children)
Norwich	Citizen's Advice Bureau
Teeside	0642 783 513 (Social Services Department)
Tower Hamlets	Citizen's Advice Bureau

There are also many other houses being opened all over the country. For details contact the local Citizen's Advice Bureau or Jo Sutton (01995 2082) who is co-ordinating information on women's aid houses.

Injunction Kit for Battered Wives

Shows women how to apply in the divorce courts for a non-molestation order and expulsion of their husbands from the matrimonial home. Notes for lay advisers and women's aid homes are also included.

Available at 25p plus postage from:

Ruth Holt, Paddington Neighborhood Law Centre, 465 Harrow Road, London W.10.

Getting Unmarried

A comprehensive pamphlet of self help accounts. 5p plus postage from:

Swansea Women's Liberation, 53 Bryn Road, Swansea.

SUPPORT TO SINGLE PARENTS

The Child Poverty Action Group
1 Macklin Street, London WC2

Campaigns on issues such as improved family allowances for all children, payable to the mother and has carried out research into the cohabitation rule and the treatment of single mothers on supplementary benefit, amongst other areas. CPAG's Citizen's Rights Office at the same address gives advice and assistance on social security, national insurance and tenancy problems.

The National Council for One-Parent Families
255 Kentish Town Road,
London NW5 2LX   tel. 01 267 1361

Exists to help all one parent families through practical
advice, professional counselling, and direct financial aid.
The Council also fights for the rights of one parent families to a special cash allowance, better community services, a fair share of housing and for a reform of the
present system of family courts.

Gingerbread
9 Poland Street,
London W1V 3DG

A self help association which pressures for a better deal
for lone parents and their children. Gives information and
advice, by letter on legal, money and other matters. 160
groups throughout the country.

Mothers in Action
9 Poland Street,
London W1V 3DG

Have produced a publications list comprising survival kit,
fact sheet, study pamphlets (unsupported mothers, adoption)
and TARGET pamphlets (recommendations on pregnancy,
day care, housing). Available with order form from the
above address (see documents section)'

SUPPORT TO PRISONERS' WIVES

Prisoners' Wives Union
14 Richmond Avenue,
London N.1.

Is pressing for family visiting centres in prisons to maintain
relationships between prisoners and their families. The Union
has a house at the above address - near to Pentonville
Prison - for the use of visiting wives and their children,
with a play centre, open 10 am to 5 pm five days a
week. For more information contact 01 278 3981 or 01
883 2001

Prisoners' Families and Friends Association
29a Hornsey Rise,
London N.19   tel. 01 263 2288

A pressure group for prisoners' families and friends demanding that all prisoners be allocated to prisons near their homes and should get automatic arole after serving one third of their sentence, that the present system of categorisation be reviewed and that a maximum ceiling of 7 years be fixed on all sentences. The Association also helps with housing and social security.

WOMEN'S RIGHTS

National Council for Civil Liberties
186 Kings Cross Road,
London WC1 NDE   tel. 01 278 4575

Are campaigning around the anti-discrimination bill and hope to organise advocacy courses to help women use industrial tribunals and courts to bring cases under the new law. They are publishing a leaflet on the legal rights of battered wives.

Sex Discrimination Act Campaign
c/o Pat Howe,
148 Bushey Mill Lane,
Watford, Herts

The Campaign's aims are:

1. to have parliament recognise that any legislation that treats women differently from men solely on the grounds of sex e.g.taxation, pensions, social security, welfare benefits and industrial legislation militates against the psychological, economic, political and social development of women.
2. to secure the passage through parliament of legislation declaring discrimination on the grounds of sex to be illegal and providing for the equal treatment of women with men under the law through the gradual repeal/amendment of existing discriminatory legislation.

National Union of Students Women's Campaign
Sue Slipman,
NUS, 3 Endsleigh Street,
London WC1H 0DU   tel. 01 387 1277

Is pressing the NUS to highlight the married woman's grant campaign; demanding nursery facilities within all colleges; asking for an end to restrictive quotas; attacking the use of sexist material in education at teacher training level; supporting the demand for free contraception and abortion on demand; pressing the Students Union to refuse to allow firms denying opportunities for women to recruit on campuses.

Campaign for Independence
Leonora Wilson,
21 Castle Street,
High Wycombe,
Bucks.   tel. 01 671 2779
See page 269

Working Women's Charter Campaign
National WWCC Newsletter,
31 Panton Street,
Cambridge,
London WWCC
Flat 4,
20 Queens Gardens,
London W.4

There are many groups all over the country. Contact London address for details of local groups.

Equal Pay and Opportunities Campaign
20 Canonbury Square,
London N1   tel. 01 226 5261

Is a pressure group of men and women campaigning for women's rights in employment and within the trade union movement. Also provides information and practical help to women in the area of grievances under the equal pay and sex discrimination legislation.

Power of Women Collective
64 Larch Road,
London NW2   tel. 01 452 1338
Groups also at 79 Richmond Road, Montpelier, Bristol (tel. 0272 422116); Joan Hall, 11 Chedworth St., Cambridge (tel. 0223 52867); Jenny Lister, 32 Ambassador Bracknell, Reading, (tel. 0344 28169

A Wages for Housework group who publish, among other things, a journal of the same name (available from London address) and will be setting up a stall in Church St. Market, London NW1 to raise money and to provide publicity.

The Nursery Staff Action Group
St. Peters Toddler Club,
St. Peters Church,
Eaton Square,
London SW1

CHILDREN'S RIGHTS

Independent Child at Risk (ICARE)
39 Stoke Road,
Linslade,
Leighton Buzzard,
Beds.   tel. LB 4156
'Our aim is to make clear that the attitude towards the child at risk and the policies involved in 'helping' that child are always adult-biased and we want it changed. Children under threat should be judged on one maxim

only: a child belongs only where it loves and is loved'.

Parent to Parent Information on Adoption Services
26 Belsize Grove,
London NW3   tel. 01 722 5328
Assist in the placement of older, mixed race or medically handicapped children. The group hopes that a better network of information will help many more people to adopt children who would otherwise grow up in care.

Children's Rights Workshop
c/o 73 Balfour Street,
London SE 17   tel. 01 703 7217
Are 'looking into the different areas and levels of children's reality (at home, in the street, in institutions, at schools etc.) and report on all that is being done by and for children'. See also Childrens Books Section.

CHILDREN

Children's Community Centre
123 Dartmouth Park Hill,
London N19   tel. 01 272 9383
An experimental community nursery for 18 children aged from 2 to five years, open five days a week from 8.30 am to 6 pm. There are no fees; parents pay for food and give their time. The centre is also used for films, meetings, workshops and a weekly food co-operative. Intake has to be confined to those living in the immediate area but the collective welcomes visitors who are thinking of setting up similar centres.

CHILDREN'S BOOKS GROUPS

Children's Rights Workshop Book Project
73 Balfour Street,
London SE 17   tel. 01 703 7217
Have produced a list of children's picture books which are

either 'non sexist, non racist, socially realistic, avoids class bias' etc. The project aims to campaign against bad children's books and to develop a more grass roots distribution of good children's literature.

CISSY: Campaign to impede sex stereotyping in the young

Sheila Ebbutt,
(Information officer)
35a Eaton Rise,
London W5   tel. 01 997 0846
or
Helen Pettit (press Officer)
24 Cressida Road,
London N19   tel. 01 272 0784

Is a feminist group which wants to get rid of the steretyped (traditional) sex roles offered as models in most children's books. The group has made surveys of sexism in reading primers, elementary science books, sex education books, under fives picture books and career novels.

The Education Collective Kids Books Group

c/o Ann Heyno,
Flat 3,
36 Lady Margaret Road,
London NW5   tel. 01 267 4966

'The kids' books group is a group of 12 writers and illustrators who are attempting to produce a series of supplementary readers for remedial kids aged 6 - 16. It is hoped the books will be non sexist, non racist and free from class bias.' The group meets twice a month for mutual support and criticism.

Children's Books Study Group

c/o Jill Pinkerton,
42 Kynaston St.,
London N 16

A closed collective of men and women who have been meeting regularly for a year to examine the contents of children's picture books with regard to sexism, class bias or racism. Hopes eventually to publish findings.

Merseyside Children's Reading Scheme Group
c/o Jenny Flintoft,
25 Byron Road,
Lydiate,
Liverpool   tel. 051 526 2176
                                   (evenings)

A group of women have been writing a non sexist children's reading scheme for the past two and a half years and have now written 12 books. They are also in the process of writing a novel for seven year olds and looking for illustrators and publishers.

Leeds Women's Literature Collective: Children's Books
c/o Anne Geraghty,
22 Stanmore Road,
Leeds 4.

A small group of women who produce a twice yearly newsletter containing reviews of non sexist, non racist socially real children's books with occasional articles and letters. Subscription 50p for four issues.

Librarians for Social Change Children's Group
c/o John Vincent,
7 Dellcott Close,
Welwyn Garden City,
Herts.

Puts interested people in touch with each other; gives information of and attends meetings/conferences/seminars in connection with children's books.

WOMEN AND EDUCATION

The Women's Education Collective
c/o Glenys Lobban
41 Durham Road,
London N.2.   tel. 01 883 3145

Is a group of London based teachers and others interested

in education who meet once a month to discuss all aspects of sexism in schools. Under its umbrella several
groups have emerged; one fighting sexism in the teachers
union; one compiling a book of personal experiences of
sexism in schools; one planning to make a film on sexism
for use in schools and the Women's Education Collective
Kids' Books group.

Feminist Teaching Resources
c/o Sarita Cordell,
139 Hemingford Road,
London N1

tel. 01 359 2831

A small group formed as a result of the Institute of
Education conference on sex role stereotyping which has
collected and held an exhibition of feminist teaching resources, including films, slides and books.

The Homosexual Teachers Group
See Lesbian Groups and Organisations

Librarians for Social Change
Anne Colwell (Feminist Co-ordinator)
35 Hardy Road,
London SW19

Produce a journal several times a year containing articles
on information sources, children's literature, libraries, action
groups etc. Subscription 60p for 3 issues from John Noyce,
Flat 2, 83 Montpelier Road, Brighton, Sussex.

Women and Sociology
Jalna Hanmer,
LSE, Houghton St.,
London WC2
also: Helen Lewis Jones, 2 Bank Mansions, 140
Herne Hill, London SE24 and Margaret Jarvie,
Moray House College of Education, Holyrood
House, Edinburgh 8.

A number of caucus groups have been set up within the
British Sociological Association, concerned with women's
studies and the treatment of sex roles in sociology studies.

Manchester Women & Education Group
See Newsletters Section

WOMEN'S STUDIES

It is thought that the following courses will be run again in 1975.

WOMEN'S HISTORY

Contact Sally Alexander, 91 Alderney Street, London SW1

HISTORY OF WOMEN'S ART

Holloway Institute, Montem School, Hornsey Rd., London N.7

From patchwork to painting and a look at images of women in advertisements, cartoons etc.

WOMEN IN SOCIETY

Dept. of Extra Mural Studies, The University, Birmingham.

a 20 week course

WOMEN'S STUDIES COURSE

The Women's Liberation Group,
c/o LSE Students Union,
Houghton St., London WC 2

Will either be run by the women's group or in association with the sociology unit.

RETURN TO WORK

N.M. Page, Extra Mural Dept., The University,
Manchester M13 9PL   tel. 061 273 3333
                                              ext. 524

A course for women who have interrupted their careers and now wish to extend their capabilities in the light of changed circumstances.

WOMEN'S STUDIES

For details of courses at London University contact Margherita Rendel, London University Inst. of Education, 55 Gordon Square, London WC1H 0NT

WOMEN'S STUDIES GUIDE

c/o Oonagh Hartnett,
Dept. of Applied Psychology, University of Wales,
Inst. of Science and Technology, Llwyn-y-Grant,
Llwyn-y-Grant Rd., Penlan, Cardiff CF3 7UX

Margarita Rendel and Oonagh Hartnett are compiling a guide to women's studies throughout the UK.

NUS

The National Union of Students have also produced a booklet on women's studies. Available from Student Union Offices or 3 Ensleigh St., London, WC1

WOMEN AND HEALTH

Women and Community Health

Archway Women's Group,
Joan Scott, 3 Churchgarth,
St. Johns Road, London N.19   tel. 01 263 2809

A group set up to question how women's health can be introduced into the consciousness of community health councils and has one member elected to the local council.

'Having Your Baby'

Swansea Women and Health,
53 Bryn Road, Swansea

A comprehensive self help pamphlet, full of pictures and with a useful glossary of medical terms. 5p plus postage.

National Childbirth Trust

9 Queensborough Terrace,
London W.2 3TB   tel. 01 229 9319

Through its teachers, ante-natal classes and film shows, parents are prepared for childbirth. Support and non-medical advice is given in the weeks following birth and breast feeding is encouraged where this is desired.
Every major town has a local teacher/group., which hold classes, film shows etc.

Association for the Improvements in the Maternity Services (AIMS)
Anne Taylor, (Secretary),
West Hill Cottage, Exmouth Place,
Hastings, Sussex
See Documents Section. Annual Subscription and newsletter 50p available from Barbara Davis, (Treasurer), 40, Mendip Crescent, Bedford.

Pressure Group for Home Confinements
c/o Margaret Whyte,
17 Laburnam Avenue,
Durham
A pressure group to ensure that women have a choice of home confinements and to see that these aren't phased out.

Mastectomy Association
c/o Betty Westgate,
1 Colworth Road, Croydon CR)
Croydon CRO 7AD   tel. 01 654 8643
A nationwide organisation planned on a personal basis so that women who have had a mastectomy can talk with and reassure other women who have recently had a breast removed. Also information regarding breast prosthesis, swimwear etc.

Women's National Cancer Control Campaign
9 King Street,
London WC2 8HN   tel. 01 836 9901
Co-operates with local health authorities by ledning fully equipped mobile units for servical smear screening programmes throughout the country. Also have available pamphlets on self examination of the breast.

Self help
Nancy McKeith,
c/o Feminist Books,
P.O. Box HP 5
Leeds LS6 1LN

Nancy McKeith trained in a self help clinic in America and now helps to set up new groups, sells speculums etc. Is compiling a self help pamphlet and welcomes contributions.

Rape

A Woman's Rape Crisis Centre is in the process of being set up to offer medical advice and emotional support to rape victims. For more details contact Judy Gilley at 01 458 1348.

CONTRACEPTION AND ABORTION

The British Pregnancy Advisory Service,

Branches at: Birmingham 021 643 1461, Brighton 0273 509726, Coventry 0203 51663, Leeds 0532 443861, Liverpool 051 227 3721, Manchester 061 236 7777

A non profit making organisation which offers contraceptive advice, sterilisation, vasectomy and free pregnancy testing services. Runs three nursing homes for abortions — Leamington Spa, Liverpool and Brighton and the cost of abortion is £66 unless the pregnancy is over 17 weeks, in which case the cost is £115.

Marie Stopes Memorial Clinic
108 Whitfield Street,
London W1P 6BE   tel. 01 388 0662

A private charity which provides the following services; 'All methods of birth control, help with marital and sexual problems, and with menopause problems, pregnancy testing, advice and referrals for termination of unplanned pregnancies, male and female sterilisation'. The fee for consultation is £15 which covers the cost of a pregnancy test if necessary (also the fee for birth control advice for one year). The standard nursing home fee is £35 providing the pregnancy is no more than 12 weeks.

Brook Advisory Centres
Caroline Woodroffe (General Secretary),
233 Tottenham Court Rd.,
London W1P 9AE   Tel. 01 580 2991

A registered charity with 19 centres offering advice about
birth control, help with sexual problems and relationships,
pregnancy testing and referral. Consultation, contraceptive
supplies and pregnancy tests are free at the centres in
Birmingham, Edinburgh and London. Abortions are referred to the NHS where possible, otherwise to sympathetic
doctors, the cost being between £50 and £60. There are
centres in Birmingham. Bristol, Cambridge, Coventry, Edinburgh, London and Liverpool and addresses are in the
local telephone directory or write to the above address.

The Family Planning Association
Head Office: Margaret Pyke House,
27/35 Mortimer St., London W1A 4QW
Central enquiries: Tel. 01 636 7866

Over 800 clinics throughout the country which offer help
with birth control and medical advice including examination,
consultation, prescription and regular medical supervision;
investigation of fertility problems; sexual problems; cervical
smear tests; pregnancy tests; sale of contraceptives; home
visiting schemes for those who cannot attend clinics or
car ferrying service and vasectomy sessions (in some
clinics). In most clinics consultation, advice and contraceptive supplies on prescription are free. For local addresses
see Telephone Directories or phone as above.

The London Pregnancy Advisory Service
40 Margaret Street,
London W.1   tel. 01 409 0281

Free pregnancy testing service and abortion referrals. Up
to 16 week pregnancy £67.50p including counselling fee.

Release
1 Elgin Avenue,
London W9   tel. 01 289 1123

Pregnancy counselling and referral to sympathetic doctors (within the NHS where possible). Abortion up to 16 weeks of pregnancy costs approximately £80 incl. Release may also help with legal problems.

NB. All the above mentioned organisations stress that fees may be reduced in cases of financial hardship.

ABORTION & CONTRACEPTION ACTION GROUPS

The National Committee against SPUC
Jackie Titton, 37 Kinross Close,
Kenton, Middx.

Formed as a result of the anti-SPUC (Society for the Protection of the Unborn Child) rallies and the Oxford Conference and has produced printed postcards for sending to the Department of Health and Social Security in support of the present abortion law. Also two anti-SPUC posters (10p for 10 plus 3½p postage) and sheets of stickers (10 sheets for 20p plus 5p postage).

Abortion Law Reform Association
c/o NCCL, 186 Kings Cross Rd.,
London WC1 9DE   tel. 01 278 4575

'Aims to obtain and publish information 'on the legal, social and medical aspects of abortion, to encourage research into these aspects and to secure such changes in relevant British Law as may be considered necessary. The Association was formed in 1936 to campaign for a change in the law on abortion which was still based on a Statute of 1861. As a result of ALRA 'efforts, a bill to liberalise and clarify the law was passed finally in 1967.'

Women's Abortion and Contraception Campaign (WACC)

Active groups, or individual contacts for groups, within WACC

BIRMINGHAM	Angela Lloyd, 27 Prospect Rd. B'ham 13
BOLTON	Elaine Glover, 3 Lightburn Ave.
BRIGHTON	Kate Packham 20 Milnthorpe Rd. Hove
BRISTOL	11 Waverley Rd. Bristol 6
CAMBRIDGE	c/o Pregnancy Advisory Group, 40 Eden St.
CHELTENHAM	Horse & Groom, 30 St.George's Place
CHIPPENHAM	Kate Teller, 61 Long Close
EDINBURGH	31 Royal Terrace, Edinburgh 7
EXETER	Cheryl Price, 57 East St. Crediton, Devon

GLASGOW	Kathleen Engleman, 156 Wilton St.G2
LUTON	Liz Durkin Partisan Books, 34 Dallow Road,
MANCHESTER	218 Upper Brooke St. Mcr. 13
MERSEYSIDE	c/o Seel St. Liverpool 1.
MIDDLESEX	Sue Spilling, 54 Pinner Rd., Harrow
NOTTINGHAM	Rose Knight, 3 Dunlop Ave.Lenton
SHEFFIELD	Rose Star, 7 Coupe Rd. S.3
SOUTHEND	Jane Kearsley, 67 Burnham Rd. Leighton on Sea, Essex
YORK	Angela Levine, 2 Spring Lane, Heslington.

WOMEN AND PSYCHIATRY, CO-COUNSELLING and GROWTH

Women and Psychiatry Workshop
c/o Vicky Randall,
Polytechnic of Central London, Room 708,
Elsley Court, 20/22 Gt. Titchfield Street,
London W.1.
See Documents section

Depressives Anonymous
London area: Anne Gaines, 243 Dartmouth Road,
London SE 26   Tel. 01 699 1655
Midlands Area: Mr. K.G. Middleton, 5 Newport
Drive, Alcester, Warks. Alcester 2741
Hants,Wilts, Dorset: Jean Stevenson, 19 Merley
Ways, Wimborne Minster, Dorset Tel. 020 1253957

An organisation of men and women recently formed to
provide help for those undergoing a period of depression
who need to talk about their problems to someone who
is willing to listen and who has experienced similar feelings.

Lesbians and Psychiatry Collective
c/o 4 Manor Park Road,
Glossop, Derbyshire.
Are writing a booklet about lesbians and their experiences
of medical and other professional organisations. It should

be available in spring 1975 and will be distributed amongst the professions.

MIND
22 Harley St.,
London W.1.   tel. 01 637 0741

Sponsors all aspects of mental health. Services include counselling, with psychiatric social workers and referral where necessary to appropriate organisations and advice on patients rights. MIND organised the 'Women and Psychiatry' conference held in London in Autumn 1974 and will continue to work in this field.

Co-counselling classes
Flat 7, Callcott Court,
Callcott Road, London NW6   tel. 01 624 9131

Classes to teach the technique of co-counselling. The course is about 40 hours and the charge about £10.

Bio-energetic Movement and Encounter
Community, 15 Highbury Grange,
London N5   tel. 01 359 1372

Various groups including a Women's Movement Group: working through many of the feelings associated with shame, jealousy, fear, pain, pleasure, spite, sexuality and the need for sincere friendship with other women. A 4 week course costing £5.40 and a group for bi-sexuals: on-going groups for gay women and men between 21 and 35 who are coming out.

Women against Ageism
Margaret Morgan,
40 Cork Road,
Lancaster

Its general aim 'is to examine the images of the 'older woman' in our society; to discover her vital interests and to tackle these factors in society and in ourselves that prevent us from seeing the process of ageing in women in positive terms of growth and development'. No age limit either way as long as there is strong interest in the questions affecting middle aged and older women.

LESBIAN GROUPS AND ORGANISATIONS

Campaign for Homosexual Equality (CHE)
28 Kennedy Street,
Manchester M2 4BC   Tel. 061 228 1985

Gradual recognition of specific women's problems led to the setting up of the women's campaign committee which aims to contact and befriend gay women and encourage separate women's groups within CHE. Also to inculcate feminist principles in male CHE members and CHE policy, and to provide befrienders for FRIEND, CHE's befriending and counselling service.

Sappho
BCM/Petrel
London WC1 6XX

A monthly magazine published by homosexual women for all women - 40p including postage.
There is a meeting the first Monday in every month in the Upstairs Room, Euston Tavern, Judd St/Euston Road, London NW1 at 7.30 pm.

Lesbian Collective
c/o 4 Manor Park Road,
Glossop, Derbyshire

'We want to find out what it means, to ourselves, to be lesbian in work and social situations and from our understanding of our position, fight against discrimination against lesbians .... we feel that it is very important for the group to offer support and sisterhood to its members in their individual struggles, as isolation is the worst form of our self oppression'. The collective is working on two projects; the lesbian survival kit - a guide for women coming out in society as lesbians, covers the N.E. of England to be published in Spring 75. The Lesbians and Psychiatry Collective - see 'Women and Psychiatry' section

Teachers in the collective have set up a homosexual teachers group to try to stop discrimination against homosexuals and get a ruling from local authorities on their attitudes to homosexual teachers.

Icebreakers
Tel. 01 274 9590

Homosexual men and women can ring icebreakers every evening between 7.30 and 10.30 to talk over their problems with other gay people. More men than women use the service and more women enquirers and 'icebreakers' would be welcome.

WOMEN AND THE ARTS

Women & Music Collective
38 Earlham St.,
London WC 2   tel. 01 836 6081

Meetings for discussions on the history and role of women in music and holds workshops for jam sessions etc. on Fridays at members' homes.

Northern Women's Rock Band,
c/o Angie, Manchester Women's Centre,
218 Upper Brooke Street,
Manchester 13   tel. 061 273 2287

Six women playing music (political, against sexism) by women for women. Only at weekends. Any profits go to women's organisations in financial need.

Disco Collective
Holds a women's disco every Saturday night at the Crown and Woolpack, St. John St., London EC1 (Angel Tube Stn.) 8 pm. Always phone 01 837 0164 on Friddays to confirm.

Feminist Artists Group
South London Women's Centre,
14 Radnor Terrace,   tel. 01 622 8495
London SW8   (Kate Walker) 01 733 6929

A loose association of women working together and

moving towards setting up a co-operatively owned gallery.

Women's Workshop of the Artists' Union
c/o ICA,
Nash House,
The Mall,
London W1

A group of women who exhibit together and are attached
to but have an independent life to the Artists Union.
Members meet every two weeks in each others' homes
to see each others work. For details write with s.a.e.

Free Art Alliance Centre
c/o WLW,
38 Earlham St.,
London WC2

For women wishing to explore/express themselves creat-
ively. Formerly of King Henry's Road, NW3, the group
have been forced to look for new premises.

Writers Workshop,
c/o Astra Blaug   Tel. 01 346 1900

A group of women who meet in North London and have
been active for over a year writing political poetry etc.
and have produced a booklet of their work. Open to all
women.

Sistershow Theatre Workshop
c/o Jackie Thrupp,
49 Berkeley Road,
Bristol 6   Tel. Bristol 32843

Put together and perform plays and sketches for and about
women. They meet on Wednesdays at 8 pm at Durdham
Park School (off Blackboy Hill) Bristol.

The Women's Theatre Group
Tel. 01 794 2445
or   01 624 5343

The work of the group is 'directed towards exploration
of the female situation from a feminist viewpoint. It aims
also at increasing understanding of the political and social

context in which women operate'. The group is planning a tour of schools, colleges and youth clubs with a show for teenagers about the sexual contradictions and problems confronting adolescent girls.

WOMEN'S FILMS

Bolton Women's Group Video Tape

HOW IT IS, 25 minutes long and made by the group with Further Education audiences in mind. It is intended to raise issues of sexism and stereotyping and includes a discussion of the aims of the Women's Movement. For use on a Sony CV-2100 ACE video recorder or a Shibadin EIAJ/1 610/620 machine. Available from Bolton Women's Group, c/o 3 Lightburn Avenue, Bolton, Lancs.

The London Women's Film Group,
c/o WLW,
38 Earlham St.,
London WC2

Make and distribute films for women and like to send a speaker with the films to encourage discussion after the show. The following films are available from the group or The Other Cinema, who also distribute their films.

BETTESHANGER, KENT 1972	10 mins.
WOMEN OF THE RHONDDA	20 mins
FAKENHAM OCCUPATION	10 mins
MISS/MRS	6 mins
SERVE AND OBEY	3 mins
WOMEN AGAINST THE BILL	20 mins
PUT YOURSELF IN MY PLACE	25 mins

The Other Cinema,
12/13 Little Newport St.,
London WC2   tel. 01 734 8508

Films include:

BLOW FOR BLOW	90 mins £20 rental
THE WOMEN'S FILM	40 mins £5
COME TOGETHER	22 mins £5

Free film list available from the above address.

WOMEN AND THE MEDIA

Women in Media
c/o Sandra Brown,
Flat 10, 59 Drayton Gdns.,
London SW10

'Is for women who work at every level in journalism,
television, publishing, radio, cinema, theatre and publicity
who believe in women's liberation and want to work for
an improved situation for all women'.
Sub groups: Advertising, Broadcasting, Education and Anti-
Discrimination Action Group. The main group meets monthly at the ICA in The Mall.

See Red Women's Collective

Aim to put forward a positive image of women by making posters and providing facilities and showing printing
methods to other women so they can do the same. The
collective also collects past, present and future images
which indicate the position of women in our society.
Contact Pru (01 267 2309); Susie (01 720 4746); Julia (01
720 4746); Christine (01 272 3252) Michael Ann (01 607
4728)

Feminist Press Collective,
c/o 4 Compton Terrace,
London N.1 and
139 Hemingford Rd.,
London N.1.

A group of women who are working together in order
to set up a women's printing press co-operative, with the
aim of printing and publishing feminist material. Some
members of the collective are studying printing.

Women's Press Group,
c/o Lilian Mohin,
89 Ladbroke Grove,
London W.11

A group of women working towards setting up a woman's
press which will print and publish work by, for and

about women.

Women's Writers Group,
c/o Judith Kazantzis,
7a Clarendon Road,
London W.11

Published Women's Liberation Review Nos. 1 and 2 and
an anthology of recent work. Continues to meet regularly.

PUBLICATIONS

Down Tools   Occasional journal
Colchester Women's Group, 39 Charles St., Colchester.

Enough   Occasional journal
Bristol Women's Centre, 11 Waverley Rd., Bristol 6

Power of Women Journal
64 Larch Road, London NW2

Red Rag   Quarterly journal
9 Stratford Villas, London NW1

Sappho   Bi-monthly lesbian journal
BCM/Petrel, London WC1

Shrew   Occasional
c/o WLW, 38 Earlham St., London WC2

Socialist Woman   Quarterly
97 Caledonian Rd., London N.1

Spare Rib   Monthly magazine
9 Newburgh St., London W1

Women's Report   Bi-monthly
75 Albert Palace Mansions, Lurline Gdns., London SW11

Women Speaking   Quarterly
The Wick, Roundwood Avenue, Brentwood, Essex

Women's Voice   bi-monthly
61 Tylney Croft, Harlow, Essex

Case-Con Radical Social Workers Journal
c/o 23 Haverstock St., London N1

Women Now   Occasional
c/o Jane Williams, 36 Beardall St., Hucknall, Nottingham,
NG15 7RP

SUPPLIERS

Feminist Literature Distribution Network

Feminist Books,
P.O. Box HP 5,
Leeds LS6 1LN

A national network for the distribution of literature produced by the women's movement. All the above periodicals
as well as other books, pamphlets, posters, cards and newsletters are available. The network always needs volunteers
to ensure that these publications reach their local book-
shops, women's centres and bookstalls and conferences in
their area. Catalogues and mail order forms available on
application. Bulk discount rates on application.

Retail/Mail Order Suppliers

WOMEN'S BOOKS 11 Waverley Road, Bristol 6
SCOTTISH WOMEN'S WORKSHOP, 31 Royal Terrace,
Edinburgh
WOMEN'S LIBERATION WORKSHOP, 38 Earlham St.,
London WC2
SISTERHOOD BOOKS, 22 Windmill St., London W1
108 COMMUNITY BOOKSHOP 108 Salisbury Rd., Cathays,
Cardiff

NEWSLETTERS

BRISTOL NEWSLETTER AND WACC, 11 Waverley Road,
Bristol 6
GLASGOW WOMEN IN ACTION NEWSLETTER, 87 Gib-
son St., Glasgow
LONDON NEWSLETTER, WLW, 38 Earlham Str., London,
WC2
MANCHESTER WOMEN'S NEWSLETTER, 218 Upper
Brooke St., Manchester 13

MOTHERS IN ACTION NEWSLETTER, Munro House, 9 Poland St., London W1
NEWS FROM WOMEN'S LIBERATION, 2b Batoum Gdns., London W6
SCOTTISH WOMEN'S NEWSLETTER, 31 Royal Terrace, Edinburgh 7
WOMEN AND EDUCATION NEWSLETTER,107 Egerton Road, Fallowfield, Manchester 14
BIRMINGHAM WOMEN'S LIBERATION NEWSLETTER, 55 Grove Avenue, Moseley, Birmingham.

Compiled by **Jan Savage   December 1974**